Unknown ananymous

Rochester New Hampshire City Council Minutes BK A 1891 1893

Unknown ananymous

Rochester New Hampshire City Council Minutes BK A 1891 1893

ISBN/EAN: 9783743454668

Manufactured in Europe, USA, Canada, Australia, Japa

Cover: Foto ©Andreas Hilbeck / pixelio.de

Manufactured and distributed by brebook publishing software (www.brebook.com)

Unknown ananymous

Rochester New Hampshire City Council Minutes BK A 1891 1893

Adoption of Charter – 19–21
Appropriation 1892 88–89
Appropriation 1892 – 92–93
Appropriation to March – 178
Abbott J. W. protest of 256
Appropriation '93 267
Appointments 1893 270
Assessors bill for trams 348

Bonding of water debt 119-121
Bruno Joseph communication 23
" " Bid to complete
Sewer 235
Badges for Fire Dept 315
Bennett C. A. claim 319
Bond Stand 362-355
Bruno on communication 371

City Charter 1–11 | 51
Call for first city election 2
City Clerk election of 51 | 1
City Solicitor election of 51
B City Ordinances adopted 1
B Civil Engineer 101
B. Com on Sewerage Elections 111 | 1
B. Com on. Police 118
Cold Spring Park Land 144
Chandler W. to Sitter 211
Committee on Elections 241
Civil Engineer Salary 251
City Clerk Election of 1893 260
Com on Legal affairs 305
Court Square resolution to Improve 326
Collector to issue notices 321 | 1
Carson Jas A. petition 357
Common resolution. 364
Clark Smith claim of 381 | 1

Fireman & Co. Permit to build 11
Fire Dept By Laws 1
Fire Horse resolution to purchase 94
Fire alarm resolution 311
Flag Pole Hanson St 335
Factory Court - Petition to widen 367, 346 337
Fire escape Hoyer Block 372, 342
- Fire escapes 351 344
Fire Public Library 345
Falker & Evans Street 382 379 364

Guide Posts
Gates Main St Crossing

Horses purchase of 101
Hose wagon purchase of 108
Hose purchase of 109
Hale to state communication 161
Hale Statue at Concord 168- 169
Hubbard E. T. Claim of 187 174
Hall J. G. Claim of 207 176
Hale John P. remarks on 181
Highway Pine St to Pebbetts Ave 213-185
Hose Reel resolution 187
Hall Sophia D thanks to 227
Hose Wagon purchase 24[illegible]
Hale H. Estate sewer 326
Hurd Paul property sale of 331
Hose Wagon resolution 332
Hanson D. Statement 337
Sturgeon C C Claim of 342-338
Hobbs J. F. Claim of 340
Hayes Ham St. Petition to confirm 348-351 34[illegible]
Howe Sarah A. Claim 35[illegible]
Hanson D Communication 366
Hearse Com to investigate 369
Hooks & Ladder House repaired 378
Hale St Sewer 397-394 391
Hanson D Communication 397 392

Inaugural Address of
Mayor Whitehouse 26 – 56
Inspectors appointment 227
Inspectors pay of 248
Inauguration '93 26[illegible]

J
K
L
M
N
O
Q
R
S
T
U
V
W

Lease of Rooms Grange Block 80

Liquor Saloons resolution 30[illegible]

Library Public 323

" " Ordinance for 3115 329

Lonvif J. Claim of 365

Land near Cold Spring Park 375

Lease of land near H. L. Stowe 385

Linden St. Petition for 400

Market St. Bridge estimate
cost of consulting 12[illegible]
Market St Bridge proposals 146
" accepted 166
Mayor's Veto Dodge proposal 198
Morrill J. B. claim paid 250
Market St Widening of 366-356 368 345-341
Market St to be surveyed 35[illegible]
Mason Mrs Land damage 360, 353

Organization of First City Government 23–[illegible]
Ordinances to be printed 35,

Petition of Physicians in regard to Drug Stores 77
Peoples Share Co Exempt 191
Printing resolution for '13 302
Petition of Physicians to open Drug Stores 323
Printing City reports
Petition H D Whitehouse Stone Co 340 347 333
Police (Vacations) 380–375

Resolution to prepare plans for Sewerage 10[illegible]
River St petition to widen 113
Rock. Fair association purchase
of land 139
River St widening of 177
Rock Enterprise association
Exempt 192
Resolution to extend Water Works 3[illegible]
Railroad crossing resolution 341
" " Petition 355
Resolution to purchase land at
the reservoir 357
River Street plan of 359

School Board Election of 57
Standing Committee 1892 78
Smith Brook Closing of 86
Schedule of prices for license 8
Storage of books Com on 113
St Light at Willow Brook 114
Sewerage resolution for 130-131
Sewer, Protest against emptying
at Walker Bridge 136
Sewer below Lonie Dam 115
Sewer resolution referred 149
Sewer Pipe bids 151
Sewerage bids opened 188
Sewer Bruno's bid accepted 191
Street Lamps old. 223 217-211
Sewerage outlet 219
Sewer Work Suspended 236
Sleds & Harness purchased 238
Sewer Bills to be paid 209
Sub-Registrar to be paid 256
School Board Election of -93 261
Standing Com 1893 268
Sewerage Resolution to complete 330
Signs (overhead) 349
Signal Station (Summer St) 382

Treasurer Election of
Trask & F. petition of
Tiger Engine Co. report on petition
Trask & F. petition allowed
Tiger Engine Co. report on
Trustees Library election of
Town Clock to be repaired
Town Hall Sale of 390

V

V

Water Commissioners ap. audited 143
Water Rates Schedule 153
Water Board Rules & Regulations 157
Willey Geo. W. bill of 325
W. C. T. U. appropriation for 327
Wentworth F. P. bill referred 328
Wentworth St. ~~St.~~ Sidewalk 334
Willey Geo. W. claim of 335
Whitehouse Ex Mayor Portrait 336
Water Pipe Concord St & Stinson St 341
Wakefield St Line of 377
Water Works Surplus invested 382

An act to establish the city of Rochester

Be it enacted by the Senate and House of Representatives in General Court convened:

Sec. 1. The inhabitants of the town of Rochester, in the county of Strafford shall continue to be a body corporate and politic under the name of the City of Rochester.

Sec. 2. The said city of Rochester is hereby divided into six wards which shall be constituted as follows, namely: Ward No. 1 shall include all that part of said Rochester bounded northwesterly by the town lines of Farmington and Milton, northeasterly by the Salmon Falls river, southeasterly by the town line of Somersworth, and southwesterly by a line commencing on the Farmington town line at the road leading past the dwelling-house of J. C. Kimball, thence running southeasterly by said road past the dwelling house of Leonard W. Smith to the Portsmouth, Great Falls & Conway branch of the Boston & Maine Railroad, thence by said railroad southeasterly to its first intersection with the Wakefield road thence southeasterly in a direct course to the Portland & Rochester Railroad in a direct course to the intersection of the old and new roads from Rochester Village to East Rochester near the dwelling house of Maynard Russell thence by the center of said old road past the dwelling-house of Frank P. Wentworth to the Chamberlain road, thence by the Chamberlain road (but excluding all inhabitants residing upon it) to the road from Rochester Village to Great Falls thence by said road southeasterly to the easterly corner of the homestead farm of George D. Pike, thence southwesterly by said Pikes land to a point on a line with the Chamberlain road aforesaid, thence southeasterly on a line with said Chamberlain road to said branch of said Boston & Maine Railroad, thence by said railroad to the town line of Somersworth. <u>Ward No 2</u> shall include all that part of said Rochester bounded northwesterly by a line commencing on the Cocheco river at a passway on the northwesterly side of land of Viola A. Hodgdon in Rochester Village, thence by said passway northeasterly to the junction of Spring and Sheridan streets, thence by Spring street to Charles street at its junction with Knight street, thence by Knight street to Main street, thence by Main street to Winter street, thence by Winter street to Adams street, thence by Adams street to said old road leading from Rochester Village to East Rochester, thence by said old road to the Chamberlain road aforesaid; northeasterly by the southwesterly bound of Ward No 1, including all the inhabitants residing upon said Chamberlain road;

southeasterly by the town line of Somersworth; and southwesterly by a line commencing on the town line of Somersworth, at the road leading from near the dwelling-house of John S. Young in said Rochester to Great Falls, thence running by said road to the old Dover road, thence by said old Dover road past the dwelling house of James H. Hussey and the homestead of the late Louis McDuffee northwesterly to the Worcester, Nashua & Rochester Railroad, but excluding all inhabitants residing upon either of said roads, thence westerly by said railroad to Cocheco river thence northwesterly by said river to the passway aforesaid.

<u>Ward No 3</u> shall include all that part of said Rochester bounded northwesterly by a line commencing on the town line of Farmington at the Dry Hill road, near the dwelling-house now or formerly of William Howard, thence running easterly in a direct course to the Meaderborough road on the northwesterly side of the dwelling house of Charles V. Foss, thence easterly in a direct course to the junction of the French Hussey road so called with the lane leading to the dwelling house of Walter S. Hussey, thence by said road southeasterly to the road leading past the French Catholic cemetery to the brickyard thence to the Hurd brook and by said brook to the Cocheco river and to the southwesterly bounds of Ward No 2; northeasterly by said southwesterly bounds of Ward No 2;

and including all inhabitants residing upon the two roads herein described as forming in part said southwesterly bounds of Ward No 2; southeasterly by the line between said Rochester, Somersworth, and the city of Dover; and southwesterly by the town line of Barrington.

Ward No 4 shall include all that part of said Rochester bounded northwesterly by the town line of Farmington, northeasterly by a line commencing at the junction of the Hurd brook aforesaid with the Cocheco River, thence running northerly by said river to Bridge street, thence by Bridge street northeasterly to Market street; thence westerly by Market, Elm and Walnut streets and the road leading to Meaderborough Corner to the road leading past the late residences of Benjamin Page and John S. Calef, thence by said last named road, and on a line with it northwesterly, to the Farmington town line; southeasterly by the northwesterly bounds of Ward No 3; and southwesterly by the town lines of Barrington & Strafford.

Ward No 5 shall include all that part of said Rochester bounded northwesterly by the town line of Farmington, northeasterly by the southwesterly bounds of Ward No 1; southeasterly by a line commencing on the Portland & Rochester Railroad at its intersection with the southwesterly bounds of ward No 1, thence running southwesterly by said railroad to Autumn street, thence by Autumn street and Dodge's private way to Market street, thence by Market street [illegible]

Bridge street to the bounds of ward No 4; and southwesterly by the northeasterly bounds of Ward No 4.

Ward No 6 shall include all that part of said Rochester not embraced in the other wards as herein constituted

Sec 3. The administration of all the fiscal, prudential, and municipal affairs of said city, and the government thereof shall be vested in one principal officer to be called the mayor, and one board consisting of eighteen members to be called the council, the members whereof shall be called councilmen, and the mayor and council shall sit and act together and compose one body, and in their joint capacity shall be denominated the city council.

Sec 4. Said city shall also constitute one school district and all school property owned or possessed by the two school districts in said town, or either of them, shall be vested in said city; and the administration of all fiscal and prudential affairs of the school district newly constituted shall be vested in the city council, excepting such as the administration of shall hereafter be vested in a school board.

Sec 5. The mayor and council created by this act shall have all the powers, and do and perform in reference to each other or otherwise, all the duties which mayors, boards of aldermen and common councils of cities are by law authorized or required to do and perform, either separately or otherwise and all provisions of statutes pertaining to the duties of boards of aldermen and common councils of cities, separately or otherwise, shall be construed to apply to the board of council created by this act, unless a different intention appears.

Sec. 6. Each ward shall elect one representative to the General Court until such time as their constitutional rights shall entitle any to a greater number.

Sec. 7. Each ward at every state biennial election shall choose by ballot and plurality vote, one supervisor of check-lists; and the city council shall also on the Wednesday next following each state biennial election, by ballot and major vote, choose one supervisor of check-lists, who shall hold office for the term of two years. The persons thus chosen shall constitute a board of supervisors of check-lists of all the wards of the city, and the member chosen by the city council shall be chairman of the board. All vacancies occurring in the board shall be filled by the city council by ballot and major vote.

Sec. 8. Said supervisors having been first duly sworn to the faithful discharge of the duties of their office and a certificate thereof recorded by the city clerk, shall, previous to every election, prepare, revise and post up, in the manner required by law, an alphabetical list of the legal voters in each ward. In preparing said list they shall record in full the first or christian name of each voter, but may use initial letters to designate the middle name of any voter.

Sec. 9. Said board shall be in session at such places as they shall designate for the purpose of revising and correcting the lists of voters, four days for state and three days for other elections, within the ten days next preceding the day of election, the first day of such sessions to be at least six days before the day of election, another to be within the week next preceding, and the last to be the day next preceding the day of election, from nine o'clock in the forenoon till noon and from two till five o'clock in the afternoon of each of said days; and no name shall be added to said lists after the last meeting, except such as may have been left off through mistake and not then unless the supervisor in attendance in any ward where such omission occurs clearly knew before the list was made out that the name thus omitted legally belonged upon it. In the preparation of said lists said board shall have all the power granted, and perform all the duties prescribed, in sections five, six, and seven of chapter thirty of the General Laws.

Sec. 10. Said supervisors shall deliver to the clerk of each ward an attested copy of the list of voters in his ward prepared and corrected as aforesaid before the hour of meeting, and said clerks shall use such lists, and no others, at the elections in said wards; and the clerk of each ward shall, within one hour after the adjournment of such meeting, pass said lists and also all ballots cast thereat, to each sealed, inscribed, attested, and directed, into the hands of the supervisor in attendance who shall within twenty four hours thereafter pass them, sealed and unchanged, to the city clerk to be preserved as required by law.

Sec. 11. The chairman of said board, with the advice and consent of the other members, shall at every election select one of their number to serve in each ward, whose duty shall be to decide such contested cases as may arise by reason of the missions specified in section [illegible] of this act.

Sec. 12. The meeting of the inhabitants of said city for the choice of such other city, ward and town officers as are elected by the people shall be held annually on the first Tuesday of December, and their election shall be by ballot, and the terms of their respective offices shall commence on the first Wednesday of January next following such election.

Sec. 13. At each annual election a moderator and town clerk shall be chosen by and from the qualified voters of each ward, who shall hold their respective offices for the term of one year, and at the first annual election after the adoption of this act three selectmen shall be chosen by and from the qualified voters of each ward to serve, one for the term of one year, one for the term of two years, and one for the term of three years, and at each annual election thereafter one selectman shall be chosen by and from the legal voters of each ward to serve for the term of three years.

All vacancies in any of said offices in any ward shall be filled by the city council.

Sec. 14. The mayor shall be chosen annually, and shall have a negative upon all the actions of the council to which his veto power would extend had the city government herein constituted provided for a board of aldermen. He shall also preside in the meetings of the city council, but shall have no vote except in case of an equal division. Whenever the mayor shall be absent or disabled by sickness or otherwise, or whenever the office of mayor shall become vacant by death, resignation, or otherwise, the council may choose one of their number to be chairman, who shall have all the powers and perform all the duties of the mayor during his absence or disability, and in case of a vacancy until a mayor shall be elected and qualified to fill. The mayor shall receive an annual salary of two hundred dollars, to be paid him at stated periods out of the city treasury, and said salary shall be in full for services of every kind rendered by him in the discharge of all duties pertaining to his office.

Sec. 15. At the first annual election after the adoption of this act three councilmen shall be chosen by and from the qualified voters of each ward to serve one for one year, one for two years, and one for three years, and at each annual election thereafter one councilman shall be chosen by and from the qualified voters of each ward to serve for the term of three years.

Sec. 16. In balloting for city, school, and ward officers, the ballots for so many of said officers as are then to be voted for or so many of them as the voter determines to vote for shall be given in on one ticket or list with the respective offices designated against the name of each person voted for, and, at the first annual election under this act, with the length of the term of service of each of the selectmen and councilmen indicated upon the ballots.

Sec. 17. The mayor and council shall annually, on the first Wednesday of January, meet for the purpose of taking the oaths of their respective offices, and when so met they shall elect a city clerk, who shall also be clerk of the city council.

Sec. 18. The city council first elected under this act shall in the month of January, and as soon after their first meeting as convenient, elect three persons, legal voters of said city, to constitute a board of health, to serve one for one year, one for two years, and one for three years; and thereafter they shall annually in the month of January and after the first Wednesday therein, elect one such person to serve on said board, for the term of three years. Selections shall be so made that at least one member of said board shall be a physician.

Sec. 19. The city council first elected under this act shall in the month of January, and as soon after their first meeting as convenient, elect three persons, legal voters of said city, to constitute a board of assessors, one to serve for the term of one year, one for the term of two years, and one for the term of three years; and thereafter they shall annually, in said month and after the first Wednesday therein, elect one such person to serve as a member of said board for the term of three years.

Sec. 20. The general management and control of the public schools in said city, and of the buildings and property pertaining thereto, shall be vested in a school board consisting of nine members, each to serve for the term of three years from the second Wednesday of January next after their respective elections under this act, and who shall have the powers, perform the duties, and be subject to the liabilities pertaining to school boards of towns, except wherein a different intention herein appears; but all bills, notes, and demands, made or contracted for school purposes, shall be paid from the city treasury.

Sec. 21. The members serving upon the town school board, and also those serving upon the board of education of school district No. 8 in said town at the time of the first annual election under this act shall, together, constitute the school board herein provided for, and shall continue [illegible] thereof until the second Wednesday

[illegible]

tive terms of office would expire should this act not be adopted. And for the further continuance of said school board, one member thereof shall be elected by the city council annually between the first and second Wednesdays of January, and members thereof shall be elected by wards as follows: At the first annual election after the adoption of this act and at every third annual election thereafter, wards one and two shall each elect one member; and at the second annual election after said adoption, and at every third annual election thereafter, wards three and four shall each elect one member; and at the third annual election after said adoption, and at every third annual election thereafter, wards five and six shall each elect one member, and a residence within either of the wards electing shall not be necessary to eligibility for the office.

Sec. 22. Said school board may elect one person to visit, and under their direction, to have the general supervision of the schools. He shall make an annual report at such time as the board shall determine, shall report his proceedings and the condition and progress of the schools as often and in such manner as they may require, and perform such other duties as the board may direct, and as are not repugnant to the laws of the state, and shall receive such compensation as the school board shall determine.

Sec. 23. The city council shall elect a collector of taxes, city treasurer, city solicitor, city physician, street commissioner, a chief engineer and assistant engineers of the fire department, and elect or appoint all other officers necessary for the good government of the city, not otherwise provided for, in such manner and for such terms as the city council shall by ordinance determine.

Sec. 24. All vacancies occurring in any city or school office, except that of mayor and councilmen, shall be seasonably filled for the unexpired term by the city council, unless herein otherwise directed, and shall be filled by election unless an office originally filled by appointment.

Sec. 25. The choice of all officers herein required to be elected by the city council shall be by ballot and major vote, the length of the term of service of each member of the boards of health and assessors first elected being indicated upon the ballots; and all city officers whose terms of office are herein specified and all whose terms may be specified by ordinance, shall hold their respective offices during such specified terms and until their respective successors are elected, or appointed, and qualified; but all such officers, excepting those elected by the qualified voters of the city or of wards, and the members of the school board, shall be removable at the pleasure of the city council.

Sec. 26. The police court of the town of Rochester as

[illegible] and established as the police court of the city of Rochester, and shall hereafter be denominated the police court of the city of Rochester. And all precepts civil and criminal, which by law are made returnable to, or which may be instituted and pending before said police court of the town of Rochester, when this act shall take effect shall be heard and determined before said court under the name of the police court of the city of Rochester, and all money payable by said police court of the town of Rochester to said town shall be paid to the city of Rochester.

Sec. 27. The justice and clerk of said court shall once in three months, render to the city treasurer an account under oath, of all fees and costs by them received or receivable, and shall at the same time pay over to said treasurer all fees and costs received.

Sec. 28. All the powers conferred upon said town by chapter 242 of the laws of New Hampshire, approved August 12, 1881, authorizing and empowering it to construct and maintain water works for the purpose of supplying Rochester Village with fresh water, shall vest in said city of Rochester; and said city is hereby also authorized and empowered to extend said water works, or construct others so as to in like manner furnish the Villages of East Rochester and Gonic therein with an adequate supply of fresh water; and for this latter purpose said city shall be subject to all the duties and have all the rights and powers contained in said chapter in reference to supplying Rochester Village therewith.

Sec. 29. Said city is authorized to acquire by purchase the stock, property, rights, and franchise of the Rochester Aqueduct and Water Company, provided it can do so at a fair and reasonable price, and to make it a portion of the system of water works provided for in the preceding section of this act.

Sec. 30. Said city is authorized to levy taxes to defray the expenses of said waterworks, and to borrow money, not exceeding in the whole the sum of two hundred thousand dollars, and to issue the notes, bonds or other obligations of the city therefor, payable at such time or times, and on such interest, as the city council, at a legal meeting, shall determine, and such bonds and notes or other obligations shall be legal and binding on said city.

Sec. 31. The question of the adoption of this act shall be submitted to the legal voters of said town at a meeting thereof legally called. The vote shall be taken by ballot and the polls shall be opened for that purpose at nine o'clock in the forenoon, and after the election and qualification of the moderator of said meeting, they shall continue open not less than five hours, and the affirmative votes of a majority of the voters present and voting thereon shall be required for its adoption. If at any meeting so held this act shall fail [illegible] of three months [illegible] such previous meeting be again thus submitted for adoption, but not after the period of two years from the passage hereof.

Sec. 32 If this act shall be adopted in the month of November and subsequent to the Tuesday next following the first Monday thereof, then the first meeting under it for the election of ward, city, and school officers, excepting supervisors of check-lists, shall be held on the first Tuesday of the second succeeding December, but if said adoption shall occur at any other period of the year, then said first meeting shall be held on the first Tuesday of the D[illegible] succeeding such adoption.

Sec. 33 After the adoption of this act the selectmen of said town shall seasonably appoint four persons, legal voters in said town, two from each of the two leading political parties of the town, who, after being duly sworn to the faithful performance of their duties, shall, together with the supervisors of check lists then in office in said town, constitute a board of supervisors of check-lists as provided for in this act, and shall elect one of their members chairman. Said board shall, for the purpose of the first election under this act, seasonably prepare, revise and post up, in the manner required by law and according to the provisions of this act, an alphabetical list of the legal voters in each ward, and shall have and continue to have the powers and perform the duties of said supervisors, until others are elected and qualified in their stead. Said selectmen shall also seasonably appoint a moderator, clerk [illegible] three selectmen in and for each ward [illegible] the legal voters thereof who shall after being duly sworn to the faithful performance of their duties have the powers and perform the duties of their respective offices at the first annual election under this act, and until others are elected and qualified in their stead.

Sec. 34 After said adoption the selectmen of said town, for the purpose of said first annual election, shall seasonably call a meeting of the legal voters of each ward for the choice of all ward, city, and school officers, then to be chosen at some convenient place to be designated in their warrant, within the respective wards, and said meeting shall be called in the same manner as town meetings are called by selectmen.

Sec. 35 The returns of votes provided by law to be made to the city clerk shall, at said first annual election, be made to said selectmen, who shall forthwith perform all the duties in relation thereto which are [illegible] assigned to the mayor and council and city clerk respectively; and if no mayor shall have been chosen at said first annual election, then said selectmen shall forthwith, in manner aforesaid, call another meeting of the voters of each ward, and in relation to the returns thereof shall perform all the duties assigned them in this section, and the same proceedings [illegible] until a mayor is elected. They shall also select and provide a suitable place for the first meeting of the city council, and shall seasonably notify the members thereof of the place selected.

Sec. 31. So much of this act as authorizes the submission of the question of its adoption to the legal voters of said town shall take effect upon its passage, but it shall not take further effect unless adopted by said voters as herein provided. When so adopted it shall take effect as to the election of ward, city, and school officers under it; and for other purposes when said ward and city officers enter upon their respective duties.

Frank G. Clarke
Speaker of the House of Representatives
John McLane
President of the Senate

Approved March 31, 1891

Hiram A. Tuttle
Governor.

Approved by Legislature
3-31-1891

1st T. meeting
4-23-1891

982 votes — Charter to be adopted
687 yes
295 NO

1-6-1892 –

Mayor elected 12-1-1891
+ 3 council from each of the 6 wards

State of New Hampshire

To the inhabitants of the Town of Rochester qualified to vote in town affairs.

You are hereby notified to meet at the Town Hall in said town on Thursday the twenty third day of April 1891, at nine of the clock in the forenoon to act upon the following subjects:

Article 1st To choose a moderator to preside in said meeting.

Article 2nd To bring in your ballots on the question of the adoption of the Act of the Legislature providing for the town of Rochester to become the city of Rochester, passed at the January session 1891. Section 31 of said Act reads:—"The question of the adoption of this act shall be submitted to the legal voters of said town at a meeting thereof legally called. The vote shall be taken by ballot and the polls shall be opened for that purpose at nine o'clock in the forenoon, and after the election and qualification of the moderator of said meeting, they shall continue open not less than five hours, and the affirmative votes of a majority of the voters present and voting thereon shall be required for its adoption."

Given under our hands and seal this eighth day of April 1891.

Augustine S. Parshley
John W. Tebbetts
Edmund A. Evans

Selectmen of Rochester

Rochester N.H. April 22 1891

We hereby certify that on the eighth day of April 1891 we posted an attested copy of the within warrant on the door of the town hall the place of meeting herein specified, and like copies in the Post office in Rochester Village and the Post office at East Rochester Village both public places in said town

Augustus S. Parshley } Selectmen of
J. Thos. W. Tibbetts } Town of Rochester

At a special meeting of the inhabitants of the Town of Rochester on Thursday the twenty third day of April 1891 at the town Hall in said town at nine o'clock in the forenoon

The meeting was called to order and the Warrant read by Frank L. Decatur Chairman of the board of supervisors and balloting proceeded

For Moderator

On motion of Elmer J. Smart seconded by William Jenness that J. Frank Springfield cast one vote for Charles W. Brown for moderator then polls to close, and the motion prevailed.

Whole number given in for moderator was one and Charles W. Brown having had that one was by Frank L. Decatur chairman of the board of supervisors declared elected and in open meeting took the oath of office by law prescribed.

Voted on motion of Charles S. Whitehouse and seconded that the polls be kept open until four o'clock.

Voted on motion of A. S. Parshley and seconded that check list be used.

Vote on City Charter.

Whole number of tickets given in was 2821 upon which for City Charter had

Yes votes were 647

No votes were 2295

And the "Yes" votes being a majority of all the tickets given in the city charter was declared to be adopted

All the business having been transacted the Moderator adjourned meeting without day.

A true record

Attest

Fred L. Chesley
Town Clerk

A true copy of town record

Attest

Chas. W. Brown
City Clerk

In accordance with section 34 of the city charter, the selectmen of the town called a meeting of each ward for the election of ward city and school officers, of which the following is a copy.

"To the inhabitants of ward —— in the city of Rochester qualified to vote in town affairs in said ward. You are hereby notified to meet at the —— —— in said ward in the city of Rochester on Tuesday the first day of December 1891, at nine of the clock in the forenoon to act upon the following subjects

To bring in your votes for mayor of said city

To choose by ballot the following ward officers for the term designated.

Moderator for the term of one year
Town clerk for said ward for one year
One selectman for one year
One selectman for two years.
One selectman for three years.
One councilman for one year.
One councilman for two years.
One councilman for three years.

Given under our hands and seal this thirteenth day of November 1891.

Augustine S. Parshley } Selectmen
John W. Tebbetts }
Edward [illegible] } [illegible]

City of Rochester

Wednesday January 6th 1892

Pursuant to the election of December 1st 1891 to elect mayor and three councilmen from each of the six wards, and that they appear on Wednesday the sixth day of January 1892 at ten o'clock in the forenoon at McDuffee Hall for the purpose of taking the oath of office as by law prescribed. Meeting called to order by Selectman Augustine S. Parshley, the mayor and council being present. The following were returned as having been elected councilmen from the several wards.

Ward one Charles W. Allen
John W. Tebbetts
Albert S. Richards
Ward two Edwin A. [illegible]
Charles H. Willand
Simon S. [illegible]
Ward three George A. Bickford
William Flagg
Joseph Warren
Ward four Cyrille Pagnett
George A. Bickford
Edward Josselyn
Ward five [illegible]
Dudley B. Waldron
J. Thorn Dodge
Ward six John D. Philbrick

Ward Six continued. Charles S. Parker
Charles E. Woodward

The roll was called and all were present except Flagg of ward three. On motion of John W. Tibbetts and seconded by Charles S. Parker voted that the meeting be adjourned until one o'clock P.M.

Attest Fred L. Chesley
Council Clerk

A true copy
Attest Charles W. Brown
City Clerk.

City of Rochester January 6th 1892

Adjourned meeting called to order by Augustine S. Parshley, the canvas of the votes of last December being read as follows.

To Hon. Charles S. Whitehouse

Rochester N.H.

A canvas of the votes cast for Mayor in the city of Rochester in the several wards on the first day of December 1891 is as follows:—

	Wards						Total Votes
	1	2	3	4	5	6	
Charles S. Whitehouse	154	160	73	137	173	249	972
Samuel D. Felker	106	61	124	155	164	127	76[illegible]
Martin Burnham	11	2	4	3	3	8	31
A. W. Hayes	1						
Edwin M. Stendley							1
Totals	274	223	220	315	340	397	1769

and Charles S. Whitehouse having a plurality of the votes cast, we declare him elected Mayor and order that you appear on Wednesday the sixth day of January 1892 at ten o'clock in the forenoon at McDuffee Hall for the purpose of taking the oath of office by law prescribed

A. S. Parshley
John W. Tibbetts
Edward E. Evans
} Selectmen of Rochester

The mayor elect Hon. Charles S. Whitehouse then took the oath of office as by law prescribed. The mayor called the council to order and ordered the clerk to call the roll of the council all were present except councilmen Flagg and Allen. The mayor administered the oath of office as by law prescribed. The council then elected Fred L. Chesley city clerk pro tem. The mayor then called upon Rev. Edward Martin Chapman who offered the inaugural prayer after which the mayor delivered his inaugural address.

An invitation was extended to the people to attend the reception in the evening at McDuffee Hall. On motion the meeting then adjourned until Saturday at two o'clock P.M. January 9th 1892

Attest
Fred L. Chesley
City Clerk pro tem

A true copy attest Chas. W. Brown

Inaugural Address
of Hon. Charles S. Whitehouse
First Mayor in the City of Rochester

Gentlemen of the City Council.
In accepting the positions of Mayor and Councilmen to which the people by their votes have elected us and having taken upon ourselves a solemn oath to perform to the best of our ability the duties and obligations pertaining to these honorable places we at this hour begin the history of the City of Rochester.
The occasion is one that marks, like the decades in a human life, an event big with possibilities for material progress and greater happiness to this community. What more fitting occasion or greater incentive can there be for the invocation of divine power and grace and wisdom than when the people through their duly chosen representatives, seek a better way to those methods of government which means greater prosperity and enlarge happiness and enjoyment. At such an hour it is the part of wisdom to ask the guidance and approval of that Supreme Being who was the stay and support of the [illegible] who made [illegible] Liberty and Freedom our birthright, and [illegible] like them, who began all their public acts with asking the blessing of God, you will please give devout attention to a prayer by the Rev. Mr. Chapman. The gentlemen of the Council will please rise.
Prayer by Rev. C. H. Chapman pastor of the First Congregational Church.

The first and last Town Meetings of Rochester.
I hope it may not be thought inappropriate at this time, standing as we do on the threshold of a new order of municipal government, to refer in a brief way to the time and circumstances when the first settlers organized the town with their first town meeting. The town was granted by the crown to certain proprietors principally inhabitants of Dover, and incorporated May 10 1722, and comprised 60,000 acres; from which original grant however, 25,000 acres were afterwards set off to make a part or all of the towns of Farmington and Milton. This grant at that date was undoubtedly a speculative venture for there was no settlement made in the town until December 28th 1728 when Capt Timothy Roberts moved in with his family. He was soon followed by Eleazer Ham, Benjamin Frost, Joseph Richards, Benjamin Tebbetts, and some others. These men came from Dover and settled in the lower part of the town near Dover line in the first division of lots laid out. These lots extended across the town from the Salmon Falls river over the top of Haven's Hill past the foot of Gonic Hill by the way of Pickering's crossing to Barrington line. The road following this line was one of the earliest, perhaps the first,

road built in town, as the bridge over the Isinglass river near Pickerings Crossing built in 1702 was probably the first bridge built. The bridge at Gonic and the one where the stone bridge in this village is, were both built in 1704, and Capt. Timothy Roberts, the first settler and first selectman of the town, and Edward Rollins were the builders of the latter, and John Leighton and James Place of the former. The Benjamin Tebbetts mentioned above was the direct ancestor of our townsman Mr Edward L. Tebbetts, and his farm was the one near Gonic Hill, which was in the Tebbetts name and family till within a few years. Eleazer Ham and Captain Roberts took up farms on opposite sides of the Main road beyond the top of Haven's Hill and lived there for some years. Eleazer Ham, or a son of the same name afterwards located at Gonic on what is now the John Sullivan McDuffee farm who is a direct descendant of Eleazer Ham. I have been unable to find at this time where Benjamin Frost and Joseph Richards first settled, but probably very near the others. John Bickford who was one of the first selectmen elected in town, is undoubtedly the direct ancestor of our citizen George H. Bickford who sits with us to day as one of the representatives of Ward 3, and whose farm has been in that name and family ever since. The same is probably true of the farm and ancestry of Joseph Jenness who I think is a descendant of John Jenness [illegible]

and who has himself served the town honorably and well as a representative in the Legislature.

There is no record of any town organization until nine years after Capt. Timothy Roberts first settled here, though he and his associates may have had something of the kind. At any rate there is in the early records of the town a copy of an Act passed by the Province of New Hampshire, over which Jonathan Belcher was the Royal Governor and Richard Waldron was secretary, dated April 1st 1737. This act is undoubtedly the starting point in our political history as a town, and is in part as follows:-

"Whereas the inhabitants of ye town of Rochester in this Province have petitioned the Court setting forth that there being about sixty families were without a settled ministry and in such low circumstances that they were unable to support the same. That they were not invested with sufficient authority to choose town officers and do other acts necessary to the civil order of the town.

Wherefore they prayed that a committee might be appointed by the Court to call a meeting of ye inhabitants of said Town, that they might make choice of proper persons for Town officers and do other things proper for said meeting and that a tax might be laid on ye non-resident Proprietors of ye land in ye said Town towards ye support of ye Gospel Ministry there"

It would seem from the above that up to this

town officers for it is an established fact, that in the organization of all the early towns of New Hampshire the first thing was to settle a Minister that being invariably specified in all the Royal Charters. The Court taking into consideration the prayer of the petitioners, duly appointed Paul Wentworth and Capt Thomas Millett, at that time two of the selectmen of Dover, and Stephen Berry of Rochester the Committee, and authorized them to call the inhabitants together to choose town officers, and as the act reads, "the officers so chosen shall have the same power and legal authority, which town officers have in any other Town, and all matters which shall be legally transacted shall be held good and valid."

Paul Wentworth and Stephen Berry of the committee on the 9th. day of April issued the call for the inhabitants to meet together the 26th day of April 1737 and on the latter day the first town meeting was held. In the quaint and simple language of that time it is recorded.

"1 Timothy Roberts. Chosen Moderator"
Joseph Main .. Chosen Town Clerk"
"2... Timothy Roberts }
Stephen Berry } .. Chosen Selectmen"
John Bickford.. }

There is no record of how many votes were cast and it is a singular fact, that no record of the numbers of votes cast for any candidate at any [illegible]

day of March 1784, nearly 47 years afterwards, when occurs the following entry.

"John [illegible] Chosen Moderator"
Josiah Ham Chosen Town Clerk and
"it was unanimously voted that the Honorable Meshech Weare is chosen President for the State of New Hampshire agreeably to the New Constitution, to the number of two Hundred and nine votes." This was 47 years after the first Town Meeting in 1737.

Thus on the 26th day of April 1737 Timothy Roberts, Stephen Berry and John Bickford were chosen the first board of Selectmen of Rochester, and nearly one hundred and fifty four years afterwards, on the 10th. day of March 1891 the people chose the last board in the persons of Augustine S. Parshley, Chas W. Tibbetts and Edward E. Evans.

I have been thus particular in drawing your attention to the first town meeting, as it marks like a granite monument the beginning of our Town history, as the election on the first day of last December marks in a like manner the beginning of our City history.

What a theme for reflection do the years between these two periods present. Who can depict the struggles, privation and anxieties of these early settlers, when scarcity of provisions failure of crops, the isolation of neighbors, the fear of wild beasts and dread of a [illegible] their lives day

of vigilance and nights of watchfulness. And yet the strong men and women of that early time, grappled with their lot with brave hearts and heroic fortitude. Not even the brutal Indian murder of Joseph Heard, John Wentworth, Joseph Richards and Gershom Downs in June 1746, nor the slaying of the wife of Jonathan Hodgdon of a Sunday morning in May 1748, nor the constant apprehension of other and more fearful occurrences, could frighten them from their determination to make homes for themselves in this fair township. They multiplied and increased and to day many of their descendants, some of whom are in this hall, are among our citizens.
In the long stretch of years between these two events, from clergymen like the Reverends Amos Main, and Samuel Hill, and Avery Hall, and Joseph Haven with a pastorate of fifty years, and Isaac Willey and Thomas W. Upham, the poet, scholar and college professor with a long list of a later day, moulded the religious sentiment of the people and engrafted into their hearts a reverence for piety and virtue. Later the war of the Revolution aroused their patriotic zeal, and the deaths of twenty one men from this town attested their devotion to the cause of Liberty. The deeds of Captain John Brewster, Capt. David Place and Col. John McDuffee, and the patriotic righteousness of John Pl.......

Drown, James Knowles in that war, are a proud legacy to their descendants living in our midst and the stalwart virtues of those hardy settlers of Rochester, handed down from father to son finds a fitting and impressive illustration in the names of the fifty four on the soldiers monument, who gave their lives in the war of the Rebellion. In these years skilled physicians like Jackson, Howe, Dow, Bray and Farrington illustrated that unselfish devotion to the sick and suffering which has ever been the characteristic of a noble proffession.
The Plummers, Hansons, Sibleys, Uphams, Dames, Smiths, Tebbetts, Marshes, Palmers, Barkers, McDuffees, Hayes, Whitehouse and scores of others in their lives have added prosperity to the town, through their financial, mercantile and manufacturing professions. The Bar and the Bench have been represented by Woodman, Kimball, Tebbetts, Barker, Upham, and others.
In the legislative halls of the state the town has held a reputation the equal of others, and in Congress Nathaniel Upham, David Barker, Dr. James Farrington and Jacob H. Ela were once honored members. Nor can we forget that the spot where that apostle of human rights, Vice President Henry Wilson was born was once a part of our honored town. And who is there, who does not feel a thrill of pride, at

the champion of human liberty, and the soundness of a pure soul and a pure manhood, John P. Hale. That here almost within the sound of my voice he was born. In these streets he played as a boy. In our schools he took his first lessons. In our midst he passed his early manhood, and throughout the State and Nation is spread his reputation.

What changes in the material aspect of things has this period of a century and a half witnessed. Then an unbroken forest covered the land whereon are fruitful farms, thriving villages, busy workshops and factories, schools and churches. Then on that eventful April morning barely a score of hardy settlers assembled to found a town and settle a Minister of God. Last December nearly a hundred score of citizens assembled to create a city. Then the smoke from sixty dwellings ascended in the air, where now nearly two thousand hearth stones greet as many families. Then one hundred and fifty pounds lawful money, less than four hundred dollars, comprised the tax list, where this last year it amounted to about seventy thousand dollars. Then less than three hundred souls made the entire population where now eight thousand find a home. Through all these one hundred and fifty years, the people of this town have each year assembled and chosen from their number three men to administer their town affairs, and as you scan the roll list of those selectmen and ponder on the duties they have performed, and the results that have followed, one can but be impressed with the sturdy integrity and honesty of purpose which has characterized their acts. No matter how hot and violent may have been their political passions from time to time, when once they were clothed with the mantle of public duty, they performed that duty with faithfulness to the town and credit to themselves. Whatever may be the future of our new city, however well or poorly the new officials may carry out the trust confided to them, the past, at least is secure, and it is but simple justice, that all the people on this the last day of our organization as a town, should give honor and credit to the men who in the past have served as Selectmen so faithfully, loyally and well.

The Present

Taking up the duties that will devolve upon us for the ensuing year, it is proper gentlemen of the Council, that I should call your attention in a general way, to some of the matters that you will have to deal with. I shall follow no stereotyped method, but only speak of matters and follow such suggestions, as appear judicious to one who has had little practical experience in town affairs and none in city.

Before doing so, however, I wish to make a personal explanation not only to you audience attracted here by the novelty of the occasion. The framing of our City Charter has been mainly credited to your Mayor. When the subject was first discussed he conferred with Mr Henry Kimball of the board of education and that gentleman assumed the labor of framing the Charter. While your Mayor only offered some suggestions regarding its general features, and what he thought was best adapted to this community, to Mr Kimball is due the credit and honor of all the details. Only Mr. Kimball's great modesty and at his urgent request has your mayor kept silent so long. He cannot remain silent any longer. First in importance that you will have to consider is

The City Finances.

The indebtedness of the town March 1st 1891, when the Selectmen made up the accounts, consisted of Notes outstanding amounting to $51,592.13

Less uncollected taxes and sundry items 26,764.?? leaving the net indebtedness at that date 24,828.?? The chairman of the board tells me that this indebtedness may be reduced some when this years accounts are made up. This debt is the result of building the stone bridge and various other improvements to which the town from year to year has ordered; and represents the ordinary indebtedness of the town as it has existed for several years, varying in amount from year to year. These notes are all running to our own citizens and bear interest at four or five per cent.

The town at the last annual meeting voted to build a set of Water Works or purchase the existing plant and extend the same to East Rochester and Gonic and voted a sum not exceeding ($200,000) for the same, and at the same time chose a board of five commissioners to carry the same into effect. The purchase of the works then existing was made and the property transferred to the town June 1st 1891, the income to begin July 1st. By this purchase there has been created a new debt of $111,000

for the "plant" and for the extension to East Rochester and Gonic, there has been raised on notes of the town and paid over to the treasurer of the water board, the additional sum of 59,500

making a total of $170,500.

This sum has been obtained by the Selectmen on temporary loans at the following rates. ($100,000) at 4% and the balance ($70,500) at [illegible] to 5 1/2 %. Undoubtedly there will be a further outlay to be expended on the works, before they may be considered complete. The problem that will confront you will be to provide for this debt, which may reach ($200,000) by the time you can arrange for it. [illegible] which is common [illegible] will readily suggest itself to you, and that is by bonding the debt at as low a rate and on as long a term of years as in your judgment you may think judicious, and capitalists may be inclined to accept. With our present valuation of over three and a quarter million dollars and increasing at the rate of over [illegible] annually, these bonds ought to be readily disposed of and on advantageous rates of interest.

A sinking fund will have to be provided, in order to redeem a portion of the bonds yearly, and this fund with the interest on the bonds will have to be provided for from the water rates and the annual tax levy. In this way the payment for the works may be extended through a series of years and not [illegible] on the people. I ask your careful consideration of this subject and would suggest that you discuss the matter freely with the citizens, in order that you may be sustained by their approval in whatever financial action may be.

Schools

There is no surer standard of the character and intelligence of a community than its schools. No other subject in municipal affairs fill so large a space in the public mind, or one in which the people are more sensitive or guard with more jealous devotion than the education of their children. Indeed it is no simple figure of speech to say that in them hangs the destiny of the State and nation, and the prosperity of a republican form of government. Ignorance is the usual confederate of idleness and crime. No more [illegible] duty exists in a town or city government, than devolves upon the School Board, and it is to them and the conscientious discharge of the delicate and at times perplexing duties that come before them, must we look with confidence to sustain the high standard of excellence which the city now enjoys. The present board of education are fully alive to the great responsibility [illegible] upon them and are [illegible] the requirements of their position with earnestness and good judgement. They are heartily in sympathy with the needs of our increasing population and I am confident they will receive your cordial cooperation. Our present school system comprises 21 public and 2 parochial buildings, and maintains 1 High, 7 Grammar, 4 Intermediate, 8 Primary, 12 mixed, and 4 Parochial Schools, with a total enrollment of [illegible] 1120 pupils in the Public Schools, and 160 in the parochial and 40 teachers.

The Wakefield street school house is manifestly unsuited to the requirements of the present day, and should be replaced with a new and larger building. The brick house on Main street can be made to serve a good purpose for some years to come by making [illegible] repairs and alterations. The increase of school children in the [illegible] district will make [illegible] another school room in that village in the near future. These and such other changes and improvements as may require your official action will be suggested by the School board from time to time and which I am confident will receive your careful consideration, feeling assured you recognize the importance of this part of our administration.

The Water Works.

Within the past year the town consummated one of the most important actions that it has had to deal with for many years. The purchase of the franchise and plant of the Rochester Aqueduct Company. It is but justice to the water board who were chosen at the last annual meeting to say that the preliminary negotiations and final completion of the purchase through arbitration Committee was carried through with rare skill, excellent judgement and financial benefit to the city. Pending a detailed report by the water board which will be presented to you at a later date, I simply refer to this subject in a general way.

By the terms of the purchase the city acquired the property as it existed on the first day of June 1896. Immediately after the property was transferred to the city the water board through its energetic chairman began a well matured plan of improvements and extensions. The wells [illegible]

use having been severely criticised the board with commendable promptness made connection with Round Pond. This source of supply is ample for many years and the quality of the water unsurpassed. In extending the works to East Rochester there has been laid 20,045 feet of pipe, to Genesee 5527 feet and in this Village about 1100 feet, in all 26,274 feet. The entire system now comprises about twenty miles of pipe. There have been set 72 additional hydrants for fire purposes making now 151 in all. The number of taps in use by consumers July 1st was 577. January 1st the number had been increased to 645. The stand pipe at Adams Corner 40 feet in diameter and 27 1/2 feet high with an estimated capacity of 300,000 gallons has been completed quite recently. This while affording a valuable reserve in case of fire also serves to keep the pressure at a standard guage. The books of registry and diagrams prepared are admirable in detail as a whole. There is no greater boon to a people in their every day life than a liberal supply of pure water. It enters into every relation of life and as a sanitary measure its benefits are incalculable. Its use should be encouraged with a liberal policy and at rates that will promote its usefulness.

Streets and Highways

While the sidewalks in the central part of the city are not open to much censure, I think few will dispute the fact that many of the streets are in a deplorable condition a great part of the year. In referring to streets and highways you will understand me as making a distinction, the former being the avenues of travel in the compact parts of the city, and the latter those leading out into the farming sections. The condition of some of the streets, notably Railroad Avenue, Hansons, Portland, Wakefield, Union and Liberty streets for much of the time are no credit to an enterprising community. Like the great truths of the Declaration of Independence this is "a self evident fact" to any one who has had occasion to travel them after a two days rain in spring time and early fall they are a quagmire and in summer full of holes and ruts. At certain seasons of the year when a sharp frost follows a heavy rain one cannot ride faster than a walk without injury to himself, his horse or vehicle, until by incessant pounding the frozen mud wheel track is worn down, or a kind Providence sends rain or snow to remedy the faults of an indifferent community, or a negligent road surveyor. While the streets are in this questionable condition, the highways are better and more satis-

The matter of transportation is the question of this age as it has been of all ages, whether it has to do with the freightage of a barrel of flour from Minneapolis, the cartage of a load of bricks to the railroad station, or the moving of a wagon load of potatoes from the farm to the provision store. The great volume of internal trade in every town and city is the common highway trade. In fact it exceeds the carrying trade of railroads far in addition to the fact, that the carrying trade of railroads, is in the first instance carted in one form or another over the common highways of the country, there is the enormous quantity of produce of all kinds wheeled over the common roads for the requirements of local trade which have no connection with railroads whatever. If any class of citizens more than another, in which all should have [illegible] a direct interest in this matter of good highways, it is the farmer and the surprising thing to me is, that they have endured the infliction of bad roads so long as they have. An intelligent observer has asserted, that farmers and teamsters are supporting a third more draft animals to do the work required just for the satisfaction of pulling their loads over elevations that could easily be cut down, and dragging through low places that could easily be filled up. Every one knows that the strength of a chain is its weakest link much [illegible] on as roads drawn over or through the worst places. At the present time we have thirty five highway districts, with thirty-five highway surveyors, and I may add thirty five different individual methods of repairing.

The present methods pursued are very nearly the same as fifty years ago, and the time of year when the average surveyor considers it the right time "to work on the road" is in some cases when he has nothing else to do.

An examination of the Town Accounts for the past six years shows an expenditure of $64.024.11, an average of $10,620 yearly for surveyors bills alone. And this sum does not include the items of "Miscellaneous Highway Bills" which for the same years amounted to $28.698.07 a total of over $93,000 in six years. I do not cite these figures to criticise the surveyors or cast any reflection on their integrity, as a class they are among our best citizens. It is the fault of the system and the absence of a responsible head. I am firmly of the opinion the methods of working the streets and highways can be improved, and though the city may spend no less money on them in the future than in the past, the people can have more to show for it.

This matter of good streets and highways I consider of great importance to the future prosperity of the city and have dwelt longer upon it than I other [illegible]

the radical change from the old methods of repairing and improving highways and streets which the city is about to adopt. At the proper time, gentlemen, it will be your duty to elect a Street Commissioner or Road Master to take entire charge of this part of the public service and in your selection, I doubt not you will give the matter careful thought, seeking the best man for the place, giving him your cordial support and sustaining him with your counsel and then put the responsibility of good or bad roads and streets on his shoulders and let him stand or fall on the merits of his work.

The Police Department

Probably no branch of a town or city organization is attended with more perplexities than the police management. The nature of the duties required of a policeman are of a kind the sober minded, law abiding citizen sees but little of and knows less. He expects riots to be quelled, but gives little thought of the risks encountered in quelling them. He expects policemen to be present wherever trouble occurs, forgetting that he cannot be in two different places at one and the same time. On the other hand the citizen has a right to expect the police force shall be made up of men of upright character, temperate, discreet, [illegible]

In the choice of men to fill the responsible positions of Marshal and Patrolmen I have full faith you will make a selection, unbiased by any consideration but the protection of the citizen in his person and property and the prompt suppression of wrong doing.

Fire Department.

This branch of the service is reported me to be in good and effective condition, and whenever called upon has responded promptly, and performed its duties with good judgement. The few fires that have occurred in the past year and the excellent manner they have been handled, entailing but small losses, speaks well for the department its engineers and members.

The department consists of one Chief Engineer, four Assistants and one hundred and seventy two members four hand engines, three in good condition and ready for use, three hose reels, one hook and ladder truck, with the requisite number of ladders and one forty foot and one sixty foot extension ladder and about thirty six hundred feet of two and one half inch hose, in good condition and twelve hundred feet of poor, with the usual supply of tools and fixtures. A report in detail will be presented you by the Chief Engineer in due time.

In view of the extension of the Aqueduct pipes to [illegible] and East P[illegible] limits of the compact parts of the city, and the liberal placing of hydrants, it is a question whether the time is not near at hand, when it will be policy to reorganize the department disbanding some or all of the Engine Companies, and creating in their place Hook and Ladder and Hose companies. These hand engines are of but little benefit outside the villages where the old reservoirs are located, and the three villages are already well provided with hydrants, or can readily be made so. Such a change would reduce the expenses of the department very materially. The trouble of promptly indicating a fire, by the present method of ringing the church bells is apparent. At certain hours of the day and evening it is difficult to determine whether they are ringing an alarm of fire or calling the people to church service. Every one will recognize the importance of the first ten minutes of a fire. The advisability of establishing an electric fire alarm system is something for you to think about. I commend the consideration of these two subjects to your attention.

A System of Sewerage

Among the important matters, and I may not be far out of the way if I say the most important, which will demand by a system of sewerage for the three villages. With the introduction of an abundant supply of water and owned by the city, there is no reason why this great sanitary measure should be ignored any longer, and many reasons why it should be considered now. For several years it has been fully discussed by our most thoughtful and discerning citizens. Our physicians have urged it and our boards of health have added their testimony to the necessity and urgency of this measure. In the more thickly settled parts of the city it is imperatively demanded by every consideration of public health and policy. How can it be otherwise than that the porous soil of these plains, after an occupancy of more than one hundred and fifty years, can but be saturated with the excrements of human beings and beasts, and the drainage of privies, sinks and cesspools? It has been abundantly proven that the germs of certain diseases may be readily transmitted for a considerable distance through porous soils and in this way introduced into wells or other water supply. The mephitic effluvia arising from these foul receptacles of invisible vapors, carrying with them the germs of diphtheria and fever, are an ever present danger to health. If the pollen of flowers, plants and trees can be carried miles in the air and germinate, is it probable that the germs of disease, [illegible] more minute, and which emanate from decaying and refuse matter of the human system, [illegible] not deposit themselves with those in their immediate vicinity? In the year 1890 there were twenty six burials in Rochester from diphtheria alone, one in every two weeks. Physicians I believe class diphtheria among the diseases caused by filth. It does not follow however, that an unsanitary condition always exists in the house where the case occurs. In the majority of cases we know the contrary is the fact. But may not the disease germs have floated in the air from some neighboring cesspool or privy and been taken into the system of the victim in this way. I know this sewerage will be expensive but can the city afford to let it remain undone any longer. Public health and public policy both forbids. Progress and prosperity of the city; loss of strength, vigor and health of its citizens; depreciation of values that invariably being over an unhealthy locality, and the unspeaking grief of a parent who has lost a child by unhealthy surroundings, all forbid. Give it serious thought councilmen.

New Appraisement

An equitable levying of taxes, so that the burden of government and society shall bear equally upon all in proportion to their property, is the foundation of every common has been made in the town for many years. It is folly to suppose that the selectmen in the limited time allowed them to take the annual inventory can do more than go over the property in a hurried and imperfect way.

The season of the year is generally unfavorable for a careful examination of much of the landed property, and some of it is probably not examined at all. In a matter of such importance as fixing a fair and equitable basis on which depends the money to defray the varied expenses of the city, the most capable and discreet men should be selected for Assessors that circumstances will permit, and then ample time be given them to examine in detail every kind of property that is taxable by law. It is not enough that they should affix a lump value, often suggested by the owner himself: but they should see and know of their own knowledge whereof they assume to fix a value. There are many pieces of property in the city that the valuation has been increased but slightly, if at all, for several years. It has simply been continued from year to year at the same old rate, and there are pieces that would find a purchaser in a week's time at two or three times its assessed value. This subject concerns every person in the city, whether their tax is large or small. It is a fair question for discussion whether a l[illegible]

high rate, or the opposite is the better policy for a community. In the one instance the state and county tax may be lessened, and in the other, people who may be inclined to make the city their home may be deterred by the high rate. Again the market value, which is the proper basis for all valuations, undergoes more or less change every few years, according to location and surroundings. Particularly is this the case with wood and timber land and village property.

By the city charter this matter will be committed to a board of Appraisers, in the choice of whom you will exercise that careful consideration which the importance of the subject requires.

City Building

The project of a new City building, to take the place of the present venerable and dilapidated structure, known as the "Old Town Hall" is being discussed by some of our citizens, and very likely the discussion will increase in the near future. While such a building is needed for the accommodation of the City government, and the convenience of the public, and would gratify the public spirit of the people, there are so many other and more important things required, that you may deem it wisdom to let this project wait for a more convenient occasion, preserving the present unique structure political wrangles of other days

— Early Town Records

The proper care and preservation of the records of a town or City is of vital importance, as every one must readily admit. The Town's Records of recent date are unquestionably properly cared for, but many records and papers of value pertaining to its early history are in a very unsafe place and condition at this time. Many without doubt have been destroyed or carried away. Some of them, nobody knows how many, or what, are supposed to have been destroyed some twenty years ago, by a fire which occurred in the building occupied by the town clerk at that time. Those that escaped the fire were stored in various places from time to time, until finally they were carted to the police lock up, where they have quietly rested for a number of years, disturbed only by the prying curiosity of rats and mice and the scrutiny of the gentry who are occasionally accommodated with board and lodgings by the authorities. Fortunately two very valuable volumes, literally worth their weight in gold to any, have been spared the pillage of rats and tramps and fire. One of these is the original Proprietor's Records, embracing the names of the proprietors and the number of their lot, and a full report of all their doings to the year 1784. The other is the records of the town from the first town meeting April 26th 1737. to March 25 1772. There are in them descriptions of roads laid out, bridges built, and reservations of mill privileges and water rights for public uses, which may some day be of use to the City should litigation arise. There are the names and ages of many families whose descendants are living here to day, and many a quaint memoranda that would delight the heart of an antiquarian or the seeker for genealogical lore. Every sentiment of pride in and reverence for our past history, should stimulate us to preserve these priceless books and papers; once lost or destroyed they can never be replaced. I hope it will be one of your first acts, to see that they are removed from their present unsafe and agreeable surroundings, and in due time carefully transcribed.

— Street Grade —

The importance of a uniform Street grade is a matter that will claim your attention and none too soon for the general appearance of the three villages. Building operations are already being considered by many citizens, and it is very essential that the grade should be permanently fixed. It will save annoyance and uncertainty to people meditating part parts of the city and perhaps save litigation and damages to the city in the future. The first Mayor of Dover, I have been told urged the matter at the inaugural of that city in 1856. It was not done till some considerable time afterwards. much to the peoples regret.

Another subject may be worthy of consideration at this time, and that is, the advisability by city ordinance of limiting the erection of wooden buildings in the compact part of this village particularly. There are pieces here now existing, that if fire occurs in them in the night must entail serious loss. Some of the public buildings are not properly arranged for the exit of audiences in case of a panic from fire or any other cause. As there is ample statute law governing such cases you should see that it is enforced.

– Railroad Crossings. –

There is one other subject gentlemen to which I am impelled by every consideration of public duty to call your attention to and at the same time ask that you give it prompt and [illegible] action. And that is the dangerous railroad crossings at Railroad Avenue and Portland street and the main street at Waldron's factory. That no person has been killed outright at [illegible]

places in years past is a [illegible]. That there have been innumerable narrow escapes from injury or death, one has only to consult the files of our local newspapers to be convinced. The close proximity of dwellings and freight buildings to the tracks, shutting off the view and the constant shifting back and forth of trains makes Railroad Avenue and Main Street crossings veritable death traps, into which at any moment some person may be caught and mangled or killed. More than once the people at their annual town meeting have asked for suitable protection in the shape of gates. It has not been attended to. I know not what remedy the city has against this daily menace to the lives of its citizens but I hope you will take measures to find out, and apply the remedy, before some valuable life is destroyed and some home made desolate.

Finally, gentlemen, with unwavering trust in your integrity, discretion, and honesty of purpose we enter on our duties. That there will be many things to annoy and perplex, is to be expected. That circumstances, which you may not be able to control, will sometimes prevent the consummation of all you may think is for the public good, is the fate of all administrations. That the impatience of some, the selfishness of others, and the fault finding of the chronic grumbler will at times vex and endured with philosophical resignation. Partisan politics will undoubtedly creep into your deliberations, but this is by no means an unmitigated evil, so long as you hold to the resolution to act for the good of all the people, and the reputation of the City as a city. The people as a whole are seldom wrong; they may censure at times, but in the end seldom fail to do justice to their public servants. Let us hope that they, seeing our honest intent to do the best we know how, will at the end of our several terms of office say, "He served his City honestly and well."

Chas S. Whitehouse

Dec 30 1891.
[illegible] N.H.

A true copy
Attest
Chas W. Brown
City Clerk.

City of Rochester
January 9th 1892

Adjourned meeting of January 6th called to order by the mayor. The roll of council being called, all were present except councilman Hagg. The records of last meeting read and approved. Councilman Allen took the oath of office as by law prescribed. Voted to proceed to the election of city clerk. The mayor appointed councilmen Waldron and Bickford of ward 2 as tellers.

Whole No of votes cast	17
Charles W. Howe had	7
Charles W. Brown had	10

and Charles W. Brown was declared elected. Proceeded to the election of ......ber of the School Board.

Whole No of votes cast	17
Mrs Lorrinna J. Wentworth had	1
Elias F. Smith had	4
John L. Copp had	5
Edward H. Meader had	7

and there was no choice

Barker and seconded by councilman Warren voted that a committee of three be appointed by the mayor to frame city ordinances, and councilmen Barker Dodge and Willand were appointed. On motion of councilman [illegible] and seconded by councilman Dodge voted to proceed to elect the City Solicitor

Whole number of votes cast	17	Election of
Geo A Cochrane had	1	City Solicitor
Elmer J Smart	2	
George E Cochrane.	14	

and George E Cochrane was declared elected. On motion of councilman Josselyn and seconded by councilman Woodward voted that the mayor appoint a committee of three to select a suitable room for holding future meetings of the council. The mayor appointed councilmen Josselyn Tibbetts and Warren. On motion of councilman Dodge voted to proceed to the election of City treasurer

Whole number of ballots cast	17	Election of
Dana Howell had	1	City Treasurer
John L Copp had.	5	
George D Howell had	11	

and George D Howell was declared elected. On motion of councilman Tibbetts voted that this meeting be adjourned until Saturday January 16th at two o'clock. Attest

City of Rochester
January 16 - 1892

Adjourned meeting of the council called to order by the mayor. Roll of the council called and councilman Bickford of ward three was absent. Record of meeting of January 9th read and approved. The mayor called for report of committee on rooms. Councilman Josselyn reported they had selected the police court rooms as a temporary place for holding meetings of the council. On motion of councilman Barker and seconded by councilman Varney voted that the matter of rooms be recommitted to the same committee for further consideration to report at the next meeting of the council. Councilman Flagg of ward three appeared and took oath of office as prescribed by law. On motion of councilman Warren voted that so much of the city ordinances as relates to the salary of officers be read. On motion of councilman Woodward and seconded by councilman Josselyn voted that the salary of each officer be considered separately. Preamble of city ordinances read and approved. Salary of mayor reported two hundred dollars adopted. On motion of councilman Barker and seconded by councilman Warren voted that further action on the ordinances be

On motion of councilman Tibbetts and seconded by councilman Woodward voted to proceed to the election of overseer of the poor. Councilmen Duncan and Pigeott appointed tellers by the mayor.

Whole number of ballots 17 Election of
Frank L Decatur had 4 Overseer of
A. S. Pushley had 4 the Poor
J. S. Daniels had 9.

and J. S. Daniels declared elected.

On motion of councilman Dodge and seconded by councilman Willand voted to proceed to the election of Tax collector.

Whole number of ballots cast 17 Election of
Frank L Decatur had 17. Collector

and declared elected.

On motion of councilman Josselyn and seconded by councilman Woodward voted to proceed to the election of city physician.

Whole number of ballots cast 17.
Charles Blagg had 1 Election of
F. L. Whitney had 1 City
J. S. Daniels had 4. Physician
C. P. Hubbard had 11

and C. P. Hubbard was declared elected.

On motion of councilman Vassey and seconded by councilman [illegible] voted to proceed to the election of Sanitary officer

Whole number ballots cast 17

and George F. Willey was declared elected.

On motion of councilman Dodge and seconded by councilman Willand voted to proceed to the election of street commissioner.

Whole number of ballots 17
Ed Twombly had 2 Election of
Geo McDuffee had 1 Street
John D Pushley had 3 Commissioner
Silas Hussey had 1
Daniel Hussey 2nd had 10

and Daniel Hussey 2nd was declared elected. On motion of councilman Josselyn voted to proceed to the election of City Marshal.

Whole number of ballots cast 17 Balloting
Louis McD Hussey had 2 for
C. L. Kimball had 1 City Marshal
F. J. Smith had 2
Nahum L Berry had 5
Joseph S Norris had 7

and there was no choice

Second Ballot

Whole number of votes cast 17
C. L. Kimball had 1
Louis McD. Hussey had 1
Frank Greenfield had 2
Nahum L. Berry had 6
Joseph S. Norris had 7

and there was no choice

Whole number of votes cast 17.
S. G. Smith had 1
Louis McD Hussey had 2
C. L. Kimball had 1.
Nahum L. Berry had 4
Joseph S Norris had 7
and there was no choice.
Fourth Ballot.
Whole number of votes cast 17.
Louis McD Hussey had 3
Joseph S Norris had 7
Nahum L. Berry had 7
and there was no choice.
Fifth Ballot
Whole Number of ballots cast 17.
Frank Greenfield had 1
Joseph S Norris had 1
Nahum L Berry had 6.
Louis McD Hussey had 9.
and Louis McD Hussey was declared elected.
Treasurer bond presented and referred to councilman Varney, Clagg & [illegible] on motion of councilman [illegible] and seconded by councilman Josselyn voted to proceed to the election of Asst city Marshall. Election Asst Marshall
Whole number of votes cast 17.
Albert S. Wilkinson had 1
Joseph S Norris had 7
Edgar H. Gate had 9.

The committee to whom was referred the treasurer bond reported favorably, and on motion voted that the bond be accepted and placed on file.
On motion of councilman Josselyn voted to proceed to the election of night watch.
A petition was presented from the French citizens signed by D. Boisclair and others for the election of Peter Sylvain.
Whole number of ballots 17
Moses Sterrett had 8
Ferdinand Sylvain had 4
Peter Sylvain had 5.
and there was no choice
Second Ballot.
Whole number of votes cast 17
Moses Sterrett had 8
Ferdinand Sylvain had 9
and Ferdinand Sylvain was declared elected.
On motion of councilman [illegible] voted to proceed to the election of policeman for East Rochester.
Whole number of votes cast 17
Thomas Gotts had 1
George W. Pankins " 16
and George W Pankins was declared elected.
On motion of councilman Wassier voted to proceed to the election of police officer for Gonic
Whole number of ballots 17

Carlos C. Pearl had 1 Election of

C. C. Pearl had 15 Chief of

and C. C. Pearl was declared elected. Police

On motion of councilman Josselyn voted to proceed to the election of chief engineer of the Fire Department;

Whole number of ballots 17 Election of

W. C. Sanborn had 17 Chief

and declared elected, Engineer

Councilman Willard presented the resignation of Fred P. Webber, third Selectman in ward two. Resignation accepted. On motion of councilman Duncan voted to proceed to fill the vacancy caused by the resignation of Fred P. Webber,

Election of

Whole number of votes 17 Selectman

C. D. Elliott had 7 Ward two

Lewis A. Gardine had 10

and Lewis A. Gardine was declared elected. On motion of councilman Tibbetts voted that the committee on ordinances be empowered to have the ordinances printed as they are prepared for the information of the council. On motion of councilman Dodge voted to take a recess of thirty minutes to talk over the matter of Assessors. George D. Towle, treasurer, appeared and took the oath of office as prescribed by law.

Council called to order and on motion of councilman [illegible]

to ballot for assessor for three years. Election of

Whole number of ballots 17 Assessors

Nahum Grafton had 17

and was declared elected

On motion proceeded to ballot for Assessor for two years.

Whole number of ballots 17

Ezra Gray had 17

and was declared elected

Proceeded to ballot for assessor for one year

Whole number of ballots 17

Hiram Parker had 17.

and was declared elected.

On motion of councilman Dodge voted to adjourn to Police court room to Saturday January 25 at 7 1/2 o'clock p.m.

A true record

Attest

Chas. M. Brown

City Clerk

City of Rochester
January 23 1892

Adjourned meeting of the council called to order by the mayor.
Roll of council called and the following councilmen responded to their names.
Tibbetts and Richards of ward one
Duncan Willand and Horn of ward two
Flagg of ward three
Paquette Bickford and Josselyn of ward four
Varney and Dodge of ward five
Philbrick Parker and Woodward of ward six.
Record of meeting of January 16th read and approved. The mayor read a communication from Eyra Pray declining to accept the office of Assessor. On motion of councilman Tibbetts and seconded by councilman Dodge voted that the matter of election of Assessor be deferred until the next meeting. Committee on rooms stated they were not prepared to make a report. Councilman Parker of the committee on ordinances reported they had procured the printing of the ordinances as previously instructed. On motion of councilman Duncan voted that the consideration of the ordinances be deferred until the next meeting. Councilman Marion of ward three appeared at this time and took his seat in the council. [illegible]

Declination of Eyra Pray

Charles W. Brown as town clerk in ward six read. On motion of councilman Parker voted to proceed to the election of town clerk in ward six. Councilman Philbrick and Flagg appointed tellers.

Whole number of votes 10
A. T. Kimball had 4
J. Harry Paquette had 7.

and J. Harry Paquette was declared elected. On motion of Councilman Tibbetts voted that the complaint of a Mr Colby on Main street hill in regard to the location of a certain well said to be on the old town line be left to the mayor to investigate
Moved by councilman Tibbetts and seconded by councilman Flagg that when we adjourn we adjourn to two o'clock Tuesday p.m. January 26.
The mayor was in doubt of the viva voce vote and ordered the yeas and nays called which resulted nine nay and six yea so the motion did not prevail. On motion of councilman Parker voted that when we adjourn we adjourn to next Monday night January 25th at 2 o'clock p.m.
On motion of councilman Richards voted to adjourn to the time specified.

A true record
Attest
Charles W. Brown
City Clerk

City of Rochester
January 25th 1892

Adjourned meeting of the council called to order by the mayor. Roll of council called and the following councilmen responded to their names.
Ward one Tebbetts and Richards.
Ward two Duncan and Willand
Ward three Flagg.
Ward four Pageott and Josselyn
Ward five Varney Waldron and Dodge.
Ward six Philbrick Parker & Woodward.
Record of previous meeting read and approved.
Councilmen Warren of Ward three and Rochford of Ward four sworn in and took their seats in the council. The mayor stated the object of the meeting to be the consideration of the ordinances as reported by the committee. The council then proceeded to the consideration of the ordinances, taking them up section by section. After acting upon the first seven chapters of the ordinances, on motion of councilman Tebbetts voted to adjourn to Wednesday January 27th at seven o'clock p.m.

A true record
Attest: Chas W. Brown
City Clerk.

City of Rochester
January 27th 1892

Adjourned meeting of the council called to order by the mayor.
Roll of council called and the following responded to their names.
Ward 2 Duncan
Ward 4 Pageott and Josselyn
Ward 5 Varney and Dodge.
Ward 6 Philbrick Parker and Woodward.
No quorum being present, voted to adjourn to Friday evening January 29th at 7 o'clock p.m. and instructed the clerk to notify absent members Adjourned

A true record
Attest
Chas W. Brown
City Clerk

City of Rochester.

January 24th 1898

Adjourned meeting of the city council called to order by the mayor.
Roll of council called and the following councilmen responded to their names.
Ward two Duncan and Willard
Ward three Flagg.
Ward four Pagett Bickford and Josselyn.
Ward five Varney Waldron and Dodge
Ward six Philbrick Barker and Woodward.
Record of last two meetings read and approved.
Bond of the city marshal presented and referred to councilmen Willard Woodward and Bickford of ward four. Councilman Horn of Ward two came in and took his seat in the council. The committee to whom was referred the marshals bond reported favorably. Voted that the Bond be accepted and placed on file.
The council took up the several sections that were passed for "future consideration" at the meeting of January 25th. Before taking up chapter eight relating to the fire department, the chief engineer was called upon to report the condition of the department and to offer such suggestions as he thought advisable.
On motion voted that the [illegible] of [illegible] as suggested by the chief engineer.
Bond of Assistant [illegible]

referred to councilmen Horn Josselyn and Philbrick
Bond of collector presented and referred to councilmen Dodge Flagg Duncan. Committee to whom was referred the bond of C. H. Cate asst. marshal approved the same and ordered to be placed on file. Committee to whom was referred the bond of the collector, Frank J. Drown, approved the same and it was ordered to be placed on file.
After considering the ordinances as far as Chapter 23, on motion voted to adjourn to Saturday evening January 30th at seven o'clock p.m.
Adjourned A true record

Attest

Chas. W. [illegible]

City Clerk.

City of Rochester

January 31st 1898.

Adjourned meeting of the city council called to order by the mayor. Roll of council called and the following councilmen responded to their names. Ward two Duncan Willard and Horn

Ward 3 Flagg

Ward 4 Pagett and Josselyn

Ward 5 Varney and Dodge

Ward 6 Philbrick Barker Woodward

Record of last meeting read and approved.

that the report of the chief engineer as read at the last meeting, be accepted and placed on file. Councilman Richards of Ward One came in at this time and took his seat in the council. After considering the remaining chapters of the ordinances, and the rules and orders of the city council, with the exception of chapter twenty three relating to the salaries of officers, a recess was declared for twenty minutes. After recess chapter 23 read by the mayor, and on motion voted to adopt the chapter as read.

On motion of councilman Barker voted that a committee to consist of the mayor, clerk, city solicitor, and committee on ordinances be appointed a committee to compare copies of the ordinances for final enactment, and that they meet at two o'clock p.m. Monday February first in the mayor's office. On motion of councilman Dodge voted to proceed to elect a Superintendent of Water Works. The mayor appointed as tellers councilmen Richards and Willard.

Whole number of votes 12. Election of
H. M. Kelley had 1. Supt of
Leander P. Pickering had 11. Water Works.

and Leander P. Pickering was declared elected. Councilman Josselyn of the committee on accounts reported that all the rooms necessary for the council and city offices can be procured in McDuffee block [illegible] was accepted. On motion of councilman Barker voted that a committee shall be appointed of which the mayor shall be a member to constitute a committee of supplies.

Appointment of Committee on Supplies.

On motion of councilman Philbrick voted that the same committee prepare the rooms for future occupancy. The mayor appointed as that committee the mayor, councilmen Varney and Philbrick. On motion of councilman Barker voted that when we adjourn we adjourn to Saturday February 6th at seven o'clock p.m. On motion of councilman Richards voted to adjourn to the time specified. Adjourned.

A true record
Attest
Chas W. Brown
City Clerk

City of Rochester
February 6 1892

Council met according to adjournment. The mayor in the chair. After calling the council to order the roll of councilmen was called which was responded to as follows.
Allen of ward one
Willard of Ward two
Stagg & Warren of Ward three
Fogerty Beckfors and Josselyn of ward four
Varney Waldron and Dodge of ward five,
Shelburne Barker and Woodward of ward Six.
The clerk read the record of the last meeting of the council which was approved.
The mayor called for a report from councilman Barker of the committee on ordinances.
Councilman Barker then reported the action of the committee. Councilman Horn of ward two and Tebbetts and Richards of ward one now came in and took seats in the council. On motion of councilman Barker voted that [illegible] of Sec [illegible] chapter [illegible] as relates to price of licenses be as originally reported by the committee. On motion of councilman Barker voted that section [illegible] chapter [illegible] be adopted as amended. Also that section 3 chapter [illegible] be adopted as amended. On motion voted a recess of ten minutes. After the council was called to order the city solicitor [illegible] called [illegible]

situation as existing between the water works and the council, came forward and read from the general laws extracts of acts passed by the legislature in relation to the water works. Moved by councilman Barker and seconded by councilman Josselyn that we enact the ordinances as presented with their amendments with the exception of chapter 20. The mayor was in doubt as to viva voce vote, and ordered the yeas and nays, 10 voting in the affirmative and six in the negative, the motion prevailed. — Ordinances [illegible] of Ordinances

Moved by councilman Richards that the ordinances be printed in the Rochester Courier. The yeas and nays were again called for by the mayor nine voting in the affirmative and seven in the negative the motion was carried. — Ordinances ordered to be printed in the Rochester Courier

On motion of councilman Warren voted that the printing of the ordinances be deferred until adopted in full. On motion of councilman Josselyn voted to proceed to the election of the assistant engineers. The mayor appointed as tellers, councilmen Waldron and Allen.

Election of Asst Engineers

Ballot for first asst engineer

Whole No. of votes	16
John Thompson had	3
John W. Thompson had	13

and John W. Thompson was declared elected.

Ballot for second asst engineer

Whole No. of votes	16
Geo A Webster had	5

as there was no choice the mayor cast his vote for Charles Sleyt and he was elected.

Ballot for third assistant.

Whole number of votes 16.
W. H. Adams 1.
William H. Adams 15.

and William H. Adams was declared elected.

Ballot for fourth assistant.

Whole number of votes 16.
James Lucy had 8.
Geo. W. McDuffee had 8.

and it being a tie vote, the mayor cast his vote for James Lucy, and he was elected.

On motion of councilman Parker voted that the clerk be instructed to cast one vote for George S. Weller sanitary officer, as a member of the Board of Health for the term of three years and the clerk deposited the vote as directed. On motion of same councilman voted to instruct the clerk to cast one vote for John S Daniels, overseer of the poor, as a member of the Board of Health for two years and the vote was so deposited. On motion of same councilman voted to instruct the clerk to cast one vote for L. C. Hubbard city Physician, as a member of the board of health for one year and the clerk voted accordingly. On motion of councilman Josselyn voted that when we adjourn we adjourn to Saturday Feb. 20 at seven o'clock p.m. On motion of councilman Bickford of ward 4 voted to adjourn to the time above...

City of Rochester

February 13 1892

Adjourned meeting of the council met according to adjournment with the mayor in the chair. Roll of council [illegible] called by the clerk, and the following responded as their names were called.

Tibbetts of ward one
Willand of ward two.
Bickford and Warren of ward three.
Pageott and Josselyn of ward four
Varney and Dodge of ward five
Philbrick and Woodward of ward six.

Record of last meeting read and approved.

The city solicitor was called upon and expressed his opinion that the council had the right to appoint a committee to manage the water works. On motion of councilman Dodge voted that chapter 20 relating to water works be enacted. Chapter relating to the city seal was adopted and enacted.

On motion of councilman Dodge voted to grant permission to Feineman Bros to put another story to the small one story building in the rear of McDuffee Block. Voted to grant the committee on same an extention of time. — *Permission to Feineman B to build*

The mayor presented a petition signed by twelve physicians, asking that the council change the hours which they had adopted for keeping open [illegible] [illegible] so that they may — *Petition of physicians to change hours of closing*

be kept open from 8 to 10 a.m. and from 4 to 6 p.m.
On motion of councilman Philbrick voted to postpone the consideration of the matter one week.
On motion of councilman Dodge voted that the appointment of surveyors of wood and lumber &c. be postponed for one week. The mayor presented a list of appointments for special police which were not confirmed. The mayor announced as the standing committees for the ensuing year.

Standing Committees

On Finance and Appropriations,
The Mayor Councilmen Dodge & Tebbetts

On Shade Trees Parks & Commons.
The mayor Councilmen Willand & Woodward.

On Public Instruction.
The Mayor Councilmen Waldron & Richards

On Claims and Accounts.
Councilmen Barker Duncan & Dodge

On Public Buildings and Street Lights
Councilmen Philbrick Blagg & Stevens

On Roads Bridges and Drains.
Councilmen Nason Bickford of ward 4 & Abbott

On Water Works
Councilmen Varney Abbott and Warren

On Fire Department.
Councilmen Josselyn Bickford of ward 3 & Barker

On Printing.
Councilmen Woodward Waldron & Pigeott

On Adams and Cemetery Fund.
Councilmen Richards Bickford of ward 4 & Philbrick

On Elections and Returns
Councilmen Josselyn Blagg and Duncan

On Bills in their Second Reading and Enrolled Ordinances & Resolutions
Councilmen Barker [illegible] & Pigeott.

Recess of ten minutes declared by the mayor.
After calling the council to order voted on motion of councilman Tebbetts to proceed to ballot for assessor in place of Ezra Tray who declined to accept. The mayor appointed as tellers councilmen Tebbetts and Bickford of ward 3.

Ballot for Assessor

Whole number of votes	10
S. F. Shorey 2nd	5
John D. Pershley	5

there being a tie the mayor cast his vote for John D. Pershley, and he was elected.
Resignation of Isaac D. Percy as selectman in ward five was read and on motion of councilman Dodge voted to proceed to fill the vacancy.

Election Selectman Ward 5

Whole number of ballots	10
R. Salinger [illegible]	5
Luther Sampson [illegible]	5

as there was a tie the mayor cast his vote for Luther B. Sampson and he was elected.
The mayor again presented the appointment of the Special Police, taking them up separately.

Appointment of Special Police

The following were confirmed by the council
George F. Mitley. Leslie H. Demey. Frank [illegible]
Fred B. Wentworth. Fred H. Seavey. Francis
[illegible]

Marshall S. Moses Stincon Louis Lock[illegible]
[illegible] James B. Young Charles A. Osgood
Frank E. Edgerly Cyrill V[illegible] Adrienne Jacques
Warren W. Daggett John W. Horn [illegible]
Lewis Thomas W. Hollis on motion of
councilman Josselyn voted that when we
adjourn we adjourn to Wednesday evening
February 17 at seven o'clock. On motion of

councilman Woodward voted to adjourn to
the time specified

A true record

Attest.

Chas. W. Brown

City Clerk

City of Rochester

February 17 1892.

Council met as per adjournment. The mayor in the chair. Roll of council called by the clerk and the following councilmen were present
Willand and Horn of ward two.
Bickford Flagg & Warren of ward three
Bickford and Josselyn of ward four
Varney Waldron and Dodge of ward five
Philbrick Barker and Woodward of ward six
Record of last meeting read and approved.
The mayor read a communication from the state officials in relation to public libraries which was referred to the committee on Public Instruction. Communication from Piper Longman & Co. of Gonic in relation to the Engine House at that place. Referred to the committee on claims and accounts. — *Communication of Piper Lon[illegible] of Gonic*
The code of By-Laws for the fire department and approved by the committee on fire department were presented by councilman Josselyn and on motion of councilman Dodge were approved by the council. — *Code of By-Laws for Fire Department*
On motion of councilman Dodge voted that the vote of the last meeting to postpone the election of surveyors of wood &c. for one week be reconsidered, and that we take up the matter at the present time.
On motion of councilman Dodge voted

that [illegible] S. Glidden be confirmed as sealer of weights and measures. The following were nominated and confirmed as surveyors of wood and lumber. Laskin P. Moulton John W. Dame Pardon R. Francis Lemas [illegible] George K. Ames, Nahum S. Woodman John H. Meserve: George O. Richards: Charles H. Whipple: George W. McDuffee Sewell J. Cilley: Sidney B. Hayes: Joseph O. Hayes

Appointment of Surveyors Wood

Fence Viewers Ezra Standley: John P. Dickey.

Fish and Game Wardens. Fred H. Crocker. Cornelius Daley and Fred. B. Wentworth:

Measurers of Stone Silas Hussey: Clarence Howard and Theophilus D. Pickering.

Weighers of Hay, Straw and Coal

J. F. Dodge: Albert Wallace Nahum Seaton and John W. Tibbetts.

Field Drivers O. W. Ramsey: M. S. Bradley: M. B. Plummer: George F. Babb: and Silas and Silas J. Wentworth:

Pound Keeper John F. Quinlan.

On motion of councilman Barker voted that the committee on rooms keep the rooms now occupied by the council properly warmed and ventilated until such time as other rooms are procured and made ready for occupancy. On motion of councilman Dodge voted to adjourn to Saturday night February 20 at seven o'clock.

[illegible]

City of Rochester
February 20 189[illegible]

Adjourned meeting of the city council met tonight according to adjournment with the mayor in the chair.

Roll of council called and the following councilmen answered to their names.
Allen Tibbetts and Richards of Ward one
Willand of Ward two.
Bickford and Warren of Ward three
Pageott Bickford and Josselyn of ward four.
Varney Waldron and Dodge of ward five
Barker and Woodward of ward six.

Records of last meeting read and approved. Councilmen Horn of ward two and Shuttleworth of Ward six came in and took seats in the council. Committee on rooms made their report. and on motion of councilman Varney voted that the report be accepted. Councilman Flagg now entered and was seated with the council. Moved by councilman Barker that the committee on rooms be authorized to take a lease of the rooms in Grange Block, as recommended by the committee. The mayor called councilman Richards to the chair and took the floor and advocated the leasing of the rooms in McDuffee Block. The motion of councilman Barker prevailed.

Lease of Rooms in Grange Bl

[illegible]

opening of drug stores on Sunday that was laid on the table for one week was now taken up and considered. On motion of councilman Tibbetts that the ordinances be changed to conform to the request of the petitioners was lost. The mayor nominated as special police for the west part of the town, Willis O Higgins, and also by request Albert C Rollins was nominated as special police both of the above named were confirmed.

Appointment of Higgins & Rollins

Councilman Josselyn presented a request from the fire department as to the amount of money needed for the department. Referred to the committee on fire [illegible]. John D. Pershley having declined to act as Assessor, after a recess of twenty minutes, on motion of councilman Woodward voted to proceed to ballot for Assessor for two years.

Declination of J D Pershley

The mayor appointed as tellers Councilmen Bickford of ward three and Pagents of ward six.

Election of Assessor

Whole number of votes 17
Charles M Hilliard has 1
D. J. Wentworth has 8
Sidney B Hayes has 8

and Sidney B Hayes was declared elected. Moved by councilman Josselyn that when we adjourn we adjourn to May 1st. The motion did not prevail. On motion of councilman [illegible] voted that when we adjourn we adjourn to Saturday [illegible] o'clock p.m. On motion of councilman Richards voted to adjourn to the time specified.

A true record
Attest
Chas B. [illegible]
City Clerk.

City of Rochester.
February 27. 1892.

Adjourned meeting of the city council met according to adjournment the mayor in the chair. Roll of council called and all responded to their names except Richards of ward one and Flagg of ward three.

Record of last meeting read and approved.

Moved by councilman Dodge that the matter of furnishing the council room with suitable furniture be left with the mayor and committee on supplies. Councilman Wentworth moved an amendment that the cost shall not exceed three hundred dollars. The amendment was adopted and the motion of councilman Dodge was carried as amended. A communication from Sidney B Hayes was read by the mayor declining to serve on the board of Assessors. On motion of councilman Dodge voted that the mayor [illegible] candidate for assessor to be voted for at the next meeting. The committee on finance presented a report of the appropriations necessary for the various departments for the ensuing year. Recess of fifteen minutes declared after the council was called to order the report of the finance committee on appropriations was referred to the committee on bills in their second reading. Communication from Frank A Smith claiming damages on account of defective highway. was read and referred to committee on claims and accounts.

Claim of Frank A Smith for damages

On motion of councilman Parker voted that the committee on claims and accounts with the mayor be a committee to prepare a schedule of prices for licenses &c. The mayor appointed as the committee to nominate a person to be voted for as assessor councilmen Dodge Willard & Tebbetts. On motion of councilman Wilson voted that when we adjourn we adjourn to Monday February 29th at 7 o'clock,

Committee to prepare schedule of prices for licenses.

On motion of councilman Bickford of ward four voted to adjourn to the time specified

Adjourned

Attest:

Chas W. Brown

City Clerk.

City of Rochester

February 29 1892

Adjourned meeting of the city council met according to adjournment.

Roll of councilmen called and all were present except Tebbetts and Richards of ward one and Willard of ward two. Record of last meeting read and approved. Communication of James Corson claiming a balance for building [illegible] the new highway to East Rochester referred [illegible] to committee on claims and accounts.

Petition from the W. C. T. U. asking for an appropriation for the reading room was read.

Bill of Geo. P. Twombly for labor on highway was presented, and on motion of councilman Parker voted to refer to committee on highways to investigate and itemize.

Report of committee on bills in their second reading to whom was referred the appropriation report of the finance committee was read as follows. "In regard to the resolutions before the council for the various appropriations for the year 1892 the committee on bills in their second reading report, that as the first financial year of the city begins on the first day of March 1892 and expires on the last day of December 1892 that a tax assessed for the months of January and February 1892

Charles L. Parker } Committee
Lyselle Pagest } on bills in their
Simon L. Horn } Second reading

Moved by councilman Duncan that the report of the committee on bills in their second reading be adopted and the motion prevailed. **Report Accepted**

On motion of councilman Duncan voted that the appropriation bill be now taken up and considered item by item. After acting upon two items of the bill the mayor called councilman Warner to the chair, took the floor and advocated the importance of appropriating the sum as reported by the finance committee. Councilman Parker thought the appropriations too much and should be cut down one sixth. The bill as finally passed by the council reads as follows. Appropriations for 1892 **Appropriation for 1892**

For Town Poor and Soldiers aid		100.
" County Poor and Soldiers aid		2,500.
" Police Dept. including Salaries		3,000.
Street Lights 75 lights at 78 each		6,000
" Fire Department Salaries etc		5,800
2500 ft new Hose	2000	
100 membership badges	80	2,700
Rubber coats and hats	120	
Building Stable	500	
Highways and Bridges including Horses		12,700
Side Walks and Crossings		4,000
School Department		18,500
[illegible]		
Salaries		3,300
Interest on water works and other notes		12,500
State and county tax		28,602.28
Miscellaneous expenses		5,000
East Rochester Free Library		200
Sampson Post Memorial day		150.

and on motion of councilman Duncan voted that two hundred dollars be appropriated for W.C.T.U. reading room. 200

Making the total appropriations 101,602.28

From this amount there is reasonable expectation that the city will receive back from the state estimated.

From the Literary Fund	1,500
Savings Bank Tax	12,300
Railroad Tax	2,000
" Insurance Tax	150
" County for support of poor	2,500
" Water Works Income	5,000
A total of	23,450
Leaving the amount to be raised by taxation	78,152.28

On motion of councilman Shillaber voted that the report of the finance committee on appropriations be accepted and adopted as amended. The mayor in the chair.

On motion of councilman Dodge voted that when we adjourn we adjourn to one week from next Tuesday March 8 at seven

Warren voted that the chief engineer with the committee on Fire Department be authorized to purchase the 2500 feet of Hose Rubber coats and Badges and also to reorganize the fire department. On motion voted to adjourn to the time specified

Authorized to purchase Hose

A true record

Attest Chas W. Brown
City Clerk

City of Rochester
March 8 1892

Adjourned meeting of the city council met according to adjournment with the mayor in the chair. Roll of council called and the following responded to their names.
Ward one Abbotts and Richards
Ward two Duncan
Ward three Warren
Ward four Pegeott and Josselyn
Ward five Varney Waldron and Dodge
Ward six Philbrick Barker and Woodward.
Record of the last meeting read. Willand of Ward two came in during the reading of the record and was seated in the council.
Councilman Duncan moved that the record of the last meeting be changed substituting [illegible] was adopted [illegible]

"that the report of the committee on bills in their second reading be adopted," the motion did not prevail. Councilman Dodge of the committee to nominate an assessor asked for more time which was granted. Communication of Charles E. Hodgdon claiming damage for injuries received on account of defective highway was read and referred to committee on claims and accounts.

Claim of C.E. Hodgdon

Report of the city Marshal was read and ordered to be placed on file. Moved by councilman Barker that the action of the council in passing the appropriation bill at the last meeting be reconsidered. Doubt being expressed as to the result of the viva voce vote, councilman Barker called for the yeas and nays, which resulted as following. Yeas Willand Warren Pegeott Josselyn Varney Barker and Woodward. 7 Nays Abbotts Richards Duncan Waldron Dodge and Philbrick 6. It requiring a majority vote of the whole council to reconsider, the motion of councilman Barker did not prevail. On motion of councilman Dodge voted that when the fire companies are disbanded they be paid in full for their services.

Firemen to be paid in full

On motion of councilman Dodge voted that we adjourn to Saturday March 12th at 7 o'clock p.m. Adjourned. A true record

Attest
Chas W. Brown

City of Rochester
March 12 1892

Adjourned meeting of the city council met according to adjournment with the mayor in the chair. Roll of council called and all responded with the exception of Tibbetts and Richards of ward one. Record of last meeting read and approved. Communication of George H Rowe claiming damage to horse on account of defective highway was read. On motion of councilman Barker voted that hereafter all claims for damage be referred to a special committee of which the city solicitor shall be one.

On motion of councilman Jocelyn voted that a janitor be appointed to take charge of the rooms occupied by the city government together with the police station. Moved by councilman Barker that the unanimous consent of the council be given to suspend the rules to take action in relation to the adoption of the report of the committee on finance. The motion was carried by unanimous vote. Moved by councilman Barker that all action taken by the council in regard to the appropriation report of the committee on finance be rescinded. The motion prevailed.

action of the council on appropriation bill rescinded

Councilman Dodge presented the following resolution. Resolved by the city council of the City of Rochester [illegible]

entire charges of the city of Rochester and the [illegible] maintenance of its various departments for the financial year beginning March 1st and ending December 31st 1892 the sum of sixty seven thousand five hundred dollars shall be the full appropriation of the city of Rochester for the above named financial year.

Sec 2 Said appropriation is hereby divided and allotted as follows

Schools by law	6.092
Schools in excess	9.000
Free Text Book	350
For Hydrant Service	3.500
Fire Department	4.000
Highways	10.300
Salaries	3.305.68
County Tax fixed by law	13.891.32
Miscellaneous	5.000
Police Department	3.000
Sampson Post	150
East Rochester Free Library	100
Rochester Reading Room	150
Street Lights	5.000
Dependent Sol[diers] aid and city poor	700
For Side Walks	2.000
	67.500.00

The state tax of $8.310 and 6.000 for the payment of notes and interest are provided for and appropriated out of money coming from the state

Sec 3 That the collector of taxes shall collect the [illegible] in money. By motion of councilman Varney voted that the report be accepted. On motion of councilman Barker voted that the resolution be referred to the committee on bills in their second reading. The committee asked leave to retire and report on the resolution which was granted. The committee reported the bill as drawn in proper form and was read the second time by its title. On motion of councilman Varney voted that the report be adopted. On motion of councilman Barker voted that the resolution be passed. On motion of councilman Dodge voted that we proceed to the election of assessor for two years, and as chairman of the committee to nominate a candidate presented the name of Henry S. Walker. Councilmen Woodward and Horn were appointed tellers

Appropriation bill passed

Election of Assessor

Whole number of votes	16
Samuel S. Page had	1
Henry S. Walker had	15.

and Henry S. Walker was declared elected. The following claims were withdrawn from the committee on claims and accounts, and with the claim of Geo. A. Rowe were referred to a special committee consisting of the city solicitor, and councilmen Willand and Warren. Claims of James Lessor S. D. Smith and Chas. L. Hodgdon. On motion of councilman Josselyn voted to adjourn to Thursday March [illegible] at seven o'clock.

Special Committee

Attest [illegible] record

[illegible]

City of Rochester
March 1[illegible] 1892.

Adjourned meeting of the council met according to adjournment with the mayor in the chair. Roll of council called and the following responded as their names were called

Tebbetts and Richards of ward one
Willand and Horn of ward two
Bickford and Warren of ward three
Bickford and Josselyn of ward four
Varney, Walden and Dodge of ward five
Barker and Woodward of ward six.

Record of minutes of last meeting read and approved. Petition of [illegible] O Smart for permission to make additions to his stable on Congress street read and referred to committee on Public Buildings. Councilman Flagg of ward three entered and was seated in the council. C. J. Smart Esq in behalf of John O Smart came before the council and requested that immediate action be taken on the petition as presented. Councilman Duncan of ward two now came in and joined the council. Communication of C. F. Rusk asking for the privilege of renting the town lot so called for the storage of [illegible] Referred to committee on Shade Trees Parks and commons. The mayor withdrew the petition of [illegible] and accounts which was referred to them February 17th and referred the same to a special committee consisting of the city solicitor, councilmen Willard and Warren. Warren declining to serve councilman Josselyn was appointed in his place. Communication from the Portsmouth Savings Bank in relation to a note held by them against the city was read. Councilman Dodge presented the following resolution Resolved by the city council of the city of Rochester. That the sum of one thousand be and the same hereby is taken from the unexpended balance of the sum appropriated for miscellaneous expenses. and appropriated as a fund for the support of County poor.

Resolution for Support of County Poor

Referred to committee on bills in their second reading. Councilman Dodge presented the following resolution. Resolution relating to proposals for the purchase of Hose for the fire department of the city of Rochester.

Resolution for purchase of fire Hose

Resolved by the city council of the city of Rochester as follows. That the committee on Fire Department be and are hereby instructed to solicit proposals for the furnishing of 2000 feet of hose for the use of said Department, and report at some future meeting, stating price quality &c. Referred to committee on bills in their second reading. Councilman Barker presented the following resolution. Resolved by the city council of the city of Rochester

Sec 1 That J. Frank Springfield, [illegible]

and Albert Wallace all of the city of Rochester be authorized at an expense not exceeding one hundred dollars to act as a committee to prepare and present for the consideration of the city council, alternative plans for sewerage for Rochester Village

Sec 2 That they present the same together with the estimated cost thereof to the city council as soon as practicable. Referred to committee on bills in their second reading.

Councilman Duncan presented the following resolution. City of Rochester March [illegible]

Whereas the habit of smoking in the council room be and hereby is prohibited

Edwin A. Duncan Simon S. Hanson Albert [illegible] Richards. D. V. [illegible] Geo. A. Bickford

Referred to committee on bills in their second reading. On motion of councilman [illegible] voted that the petition of John O. Smart be withdrawn from the committee on Public Buildings. for immediate action by the council. C. J. Smart [illegible] being called upon came forward and made a statement as to the change proposed proximity to other buildings &c. On motion of councilman Warren voted the petition of Mr Smart be granted.

Petition of Smart granted

On motion of councilman Varney, voted that the committee on supplies prepare suitable blanks for the use of parties desiring to [illegible] to erect or make [illegible] in buildings within the limits of the Fire Precinct. On motion of councilman Dodge, voted to adjourn to Wednesday March 23 at 7 o'clock p m.

A true record
Attest
Chas. W. [illegible]
City Clerk

City of Rochester
March 28 1892

Adjourned meeting of the city council met as per adjournment with the mayor in the chair Roll of council called and the following responded as their names were called.
Ward 2 Duncan & Horse
Ward 3 Bickford
Ward 6 Philbrick Barker & Woodward
No quorum being present. On motion of councilman Woodward voted to adjourn to Tuesday evening March 29 at seven o'clock
A true record
Attest
Chas W. Brown
City Clerk

City of Rochester
March 29 1892

Adjourned meeting of the city council met as per adjournment with the mayor in the chair Roll of council called. all responded except Allen of ward one Duncan of ward two and Philbrick of ward six. Councilmen Duncan and Philbrick came in later and joined the council. Record of last two meetings read and approved. Application of W. P. Neal for permit to build a house on Charles street was read and referred to committee on Shade Trees Parks and Commons. Petition of Chas C. Pickering and 41 others for a sidewalk on the south side of Portland street read and referred to committee on Roads Bridges and Drains. *Petition of C. C. Pickering for Sidewalk*

Committee on bills in their second reading made the following report on the resolution for the purchase of Hose for the Fire Department.
The committee on bills in their second reading report that the resolution is in proper form and ought to be passed. *Passage of resolution for Hose and Badge*

Charles S. Barker
Cyrille Pageott
Simon L. Horne
(Committee on bills in their second reading.)

On motion of councilman Barker voted that the resolution be amended by inserting after the word "hose" the words "and suitable pass as amended. Report of committee on bills in their second reading on the resolution for appointing a committee on sewerage. The committee on bills in their second reading report that the above resolution is in proper form

Charles S. Parker } Committee on
Simon L. Horn } bills in their
Cyrille Pageott } second reading.

Moved by councilman Warren that the resolution be laid on the table for future consideration. The motion did not prevail. On the question shall the bill be read a second time a division of the council gave eight yea and eight nay. the mayor voting nay the bill was refused a second reading.

Report of committee on bills in their second reading on the resolution appropriating money for the support of the county poor.

Resolution for Support of County Poor laid on the table

The committee on bills in their second reading report that the resolution is in proper form

Charles S. Parker } Committee on
Cyrille Pageott } bills in their
Simon L. Horn } second reading.

On motion of councilman Warren voted that the report of the committee be accepted and the resolution lay on the table

Committee on bills in their second reading asked for further time to consider the resolution introduced by councilman Duncan in relation to smoking in the [illegible]

granted The special committee to whom was referred the claim of George A. Rowe reported as follows. To His Honor the mayor and the Honorable council of the city of Rochester.

Report of committee on horse of Geo. A. Rowe

The committee to whom was referred the claim of George A. Rowe for injuries to his horse by reason of alleged defect in the highway leading from Rochester to Strafford Corner having attended to their duties report as follows. They are of opinion that the highway was not defective at the place where the accident occurred but in order to dispose of the claim and avoid the expense incident to the trial of the action of which notice was given by said Rowe the recommend the payment of Twenty five Dollars in full settlement provided said Rowe will accept said sum in full satisfaction

C. M. Willand

The report of the committee was accepted and on motion of councilman Duncan voted that the claim of George A. Rowe be left in the hands of the mayor to settle as reported by the committee

Councilman Warren introduced the following resolution, Resolved by the city council of the city of Rochester. That a special committee of two be appointed and instructed to purchase a pair of horses cart and harnesses for the use of the city. and

Committee to purchase pair of Horses

[illegible] dollars is

appropriated, or such part of it as may be needed to pay for the same Referred to committee on bills in their second reading with instructions to retire and report at this meeting. The committee complied and reported the bill as drawn in proper form. The resolution passed its second reading, and by vote of the council the resolution was passed. Councilman Barker introduced an ordinance for the election and definition of the duties of a civil engineer. Referred to committee on bills in their second reading. The mayor appointed as a committee to purchase the city team, Councilmen Abbott and Dodge. Councilman Abbott declined to serve, and councilman Flagg was appointed in his stead. On motion of councilman Barker voted that the board of trade be granted permission to hold a meeting in the council room next Wednesday evening. On motion of councilman Varney voted that the city clerk be required to furnish bonds in the sum of two thousand dollars. On motion of councilman Dodge voted that the committee on fire department with the chief engineer dispose of the hand engines at the best advantage to the city. On motion of councilman Barker voted to adjourn to two weeks from to night (April 12th) at seven o'clock.

A true record

Attest

Ordinance for election and duties of a civil Engineer

Bond of City Clerk

City of Rochester.

Rochester N.H. April 8-1892

There will be a meeting of the city council at their room on Saturday evening April 9-1892 at 7 o'clock P.M. Business. election of assessor

Per order of the mayor.

Chas. W. Brown.

City Clerk.

City of Rochester

April 9th 1892

Council met at seven o'clock tonight in accordance with the foregoing notice. The mayor being absent the clerk called the council to order, and after reading the call for the meeting, called for a ballot for chairman pro tem. Councilmen Josselyn and Varney appointed tellers.

Whole number of votes cast	14
C. H. Willand Esq.	3
William Flagg Esq.	1
J. T. Dodge Esq.	4

Councilman Flagg having a plurality of votes was declared elected. Roll of council called and all responded except councilmen Duncan, Warren and Bickford of ward 4. Resignation of Hiram Tilton as assessor was read and accepted. On motion of

Whole number of votes	14
John B. Frances had	1
Silas J Wentworth had	
Micajah H Wentworth had	8

and Micajah H Wentworth was elected. Vacation of councilmen. Barker voted to adjourn

A true record

Attest

Chas. W. Brown

City Clerk.

Adjourned meeting of the city council met according to adjournment. The mayor was absent and the council called to order by the clerk. Roll of council called. and all responded except Allen of Ward one, and Stagg & Warren of Ward three. Councilman Warren came in later and joined the council. The clerk called for a ballot for chairman pro tem and appointed councilman Waldron and Millard as tellers.

Whole number of ballots	16
J. C Dodge had	2
Charles S. Barker had	3
H. L. Richards had	11

and H. L. Richards was declared elected, and came forward and assumed the duties of his office. Record of last two meetings read and approved.

Petition for St Light at Willow Brook

Petition of John H Lord and six others for a street light near Willow brook bridge was read and referred to committee on street lights.

Petition of A W Richards

Petition of A. W. Richards & Co for permission to occupy and use as a steam planing mill box factory and general wood working job shop, the mill on Grove street East Rochester. was read and referred to committee on Fire Department. Communication from M. L. Sanborn in relation to sale of Fire Engine was read and to be accepted and placed on file. Communication of L. Vachon and Sarah Marquis of Somersworth, claiming damage on account of defective highway at the overhead bridge on the Great Falls road was read and referred to the special committee consisting of the city solicitor, councilmen Millard and Warren. Councilman Warren from the committee on Roads, asked for further time to consider the petition of C. C. Ricker, granted. Councilman Josselyn from committee on Fire Dept, asked for further time to consider the petition of Cocheco Engine Co. granted. By unanimous consent councilman Duncan was allowed to withdraw his resolution in relation to smoking in the council room introduced March 17th. Committee on bills in their second reading made the following report on the ordinance in relation to a civil engineer. The committee report that the above ordinance is in proper form and ought to be enacted

Claim: L. Vachon & Sarah Marquis for damages

Adoption of Ordinance relating to Civil Engineer

Charles S. Parker
Simon L. Stevens
Cyrille Pigeault

Committee on bills in their second reading.

The ordinance was read a second time by its title and on motion voted that the ordinance be adopted and enacted. Moved by councilman Parker that we proceed to elect three persons by ballot to serve as a committee on Sewerage. The motion being [illegible]

of councilman Waldron voted to proceed to ballot for the committee. The chairman appointed as tellers councilmen Philbrick and Duncan.

Selection of Committee on Sewerage.

Ballot for first member of the committee

Whole number of ballots 15
Charles S. Parker had 12
J. T. Dodge had 1
Geo. A. Bickford had 1

and Charles S. Parker was elected

Ballot for Second Member

Whole number of ballots 15
J. T. Dodge had 15

and was elected.

Ballot for third member

Whole number of ballots 15
Geo. A. Bickford of ward 3 had 1
Chas. C. Woodward had 2
John D. Philbrick had 12

and councilman Philbrick was declared elected. Councilman Varney presented the following resolution. Resolved by the city council of the city of Rochester that the committee on sewerage elected by the city council be authorized to employ such assistance as they may deem necessary for the purpose of preparing and presenting to the council alternative plans for sewerage for Rochester Village, referred to committee on bills in their second reading. On motion voted that the committee have

Resolution to prepare plans for Sewerage

the resolution at this meeting. The committee reported bill in proper form and should be passed. Bill read a second time by its title and on motion of councilman Barker voted that the resolution pass. On motion voted the expense shall not exceed one hundred dollars.

The chairman declared a recess of fifteen minutes for the examination of fire hose. After the council was called to order councilman Josselyn presented the following resolution.

Resolved by the city council of the city of Rochester that the sum of four hundred dollars to be received for the sale of the hand engine at East Rochester be and the same hereby is appropriated for the purchase of a Hose wagon to take the place of the hand engine and that the committee appointed to sell the hand engine act as a committee for the purchase of the hose carriage. The resolution was referred to committee on bills in their second reading. Voted that the committee have leave to retire and report at this meeting. The committee reported resolution as drawn in proper form and ought to pass. [illegible]

Resolution for the purchase of Hose wagon for E. Rochester

the Fire Department and the committee on said Department be authorized to purchase 2000 feet of 2½ inch "Eureka Surprise [illegible]" hose for the sum of $1700. Referred to committee on bills in their second reading. On motion voted that the committee have leave to retire, examine and report at this meeting. Committee reported resolution in proper form and ought to pass. Resolution read the second time and on motion of councilman Barker voted that the resolution be passed. On motion of councilman Dodge voted that when we adjourn we adjourn to meet one week from tonight April 19 at 7½ o'clock p.m. On motion voted to adjourn.

A true record

Attest

Chas. W. [illegible]

City Clerk

City of Rochester
April 19 - 1892

Adjourned meeting of the city council met according to adjournment, called to order by the clerk. Roll of council called and all were present except Allen of ward one and Bryant of ward 4. Councilman Flagg declined to serve as temporary chairman. On motion of councilman Barker voted to proceed to elect a chairman to serve during the disability of the mayor. Councilmen Dodge and Willand appointed tellers

Whole number of ballots 16
J. P. Dodge had 1
A. L. Richards had 15

and councilman Richards was elected.

Record of last meeting read and approved. Councilman Shelbirds, committee on street lights asked for further time to consider the petition of John H. Lord & others for a street light near Willow Brook bridge, granted. Petition of Edward Smart in relation to building on Congress Street presented and referred to committee on Fire Department. Petition of Ezekiel Wentworth for leave to build a store house in the rear of Goodrich Block presented and referred to committee on fire department. The committee on Fire Department made the following report on the petition of H. W. Richards & Co. The committee to whom the above petition was referred [illegible]

Petition of E. Wentworth

Submit that the same ought to be granted

Edward Josselyn / Committee on
Charles S. Barker / Fire Department

Petition of H. W. Richards granted

On motion of councilman Varney voted that the report be accepted. On motion voted that permission be granted H. W. Richards & Co to occupy and use the steam mill as set forth in their petition. Committee on highways made the following report on the petition of Charles C. Ricker and 49 others for sidewalk on Portland street. The committee to whom was referred the above petition would recommend a brick or concrete sidewalk commencing at the B & M railroad and ending near the store of D. W. Gerrish

Joseph Warren / Committee on
Geo. H. Bickford / Highways

On motion of councilman Barker voted that the report be accepted and placed on file. Councilman Josselyn from the committee on fire department asked for further time to consider the petition of Cocheco Engine Co., granted. On motion of councilman Barker voted that we proceed to elect a civil engineer. The chairman appointed councilmen Warren and Varney tellers.

Election of Civil Engineer

Whole number of ballots 15
J. Frank Springfield had 15

and was declared elected. On motion of councilman Barker voted that a committee [illegible] committee on police. On motion of councilman Varney voted to appoint a committee of three to act with the clerk in procuring suitable storage for the old town books. On motion of councilman Warren voted that the committee on Shade Trees Parks and Commons be instructed to employ some suitable person to act as superintendent of the old cemetery grounds. On motion voted that the city clerk be authorized to procure printed notices for Dog Licenses and blank notifications to jurors also jury boxes for the several Wards. Claim for damages on highway was presented and voted to lay on the table one week. The chairman appointed as committee on police Councilmen Duncan Barker and Dodge. Committee on Storage of books Councilmen [illegible] Abbotts and Willand. Mr Potter was allowed to address the council on the petition of John V. Smart. On motion of councilman [illegible] voted to adjourn to next Tuesday night April [illegible] at 7½ o'clock.

Committee on Storage of books

Appointment of Committee on Police

A true record

Attest.

Chas W. Bowen

City Clerk.

City of Rochester

April 26-1848

Adjourned meeting of the city council met according to adjournment with the mayor pro tem in the chair. At the roll call all responded except Allen of ward one Flagg and Warren of ward three and Bickford of ward four. Allen and Warren came in later and joined the council. Record of last meeting read and approved. Petition of J. Frank Reed and others to widen River street read and referred to committee on Roads Bridges and Drains. Petition of J. M. Varney to build a slaughter house referred to the Board of Health. Resolution for sewers at East Rochester referred to committee on Roads Bridges and Drains. Petition of Charles Blegs to disconnect stable from the house and move it back read and referred to committee on fire department. Petition of James Lord of [illegible] to have railing [illegible] in front of his house at Willow Brook and a passage way opened read and referred to committee on Roads Bridges and Drains. Petition of John V. Smart to amend his former petition for building on Congress street read and referred to committee on fire department. Petition of Frank C. Blackmar for leave to move a building presented and on motion of [illegible]

Petition of J. Frank Reed for widening of River street

Petition of Chas Blegs to make repairs

Petition of James Lord

Petition of John V. Smart

the petitioners. Committee on street lights made the following report. The committee to whom was referred the petition of John H. [illegible] and twenty four others, would respectfully recommend that the prayer of the petitioners be granted, and your committee would also recommend that there be an electric light placed at the turn in the road near the Willow Bridge so called.

John D. Philbrick } Committee
Simon L. Horn } on St. Lights.

Petition for Street Light at Willow [illegible] Granted

On motion of councilman Barker voted that the report be accepted and placed on file. Committee on fire department made the following report on the petition of Ezekiel Marchwith. The above named committee reports that the petition ought not to be granted.

Edward Josselyn
Geo. A. Brickford } Committee on
Charles S. Barker } Fire Department.

Refusal to grant petition of E. Marchwith

On motion of councilman Dodge voted that the report of the committee be accepted and adopted. The special committee to whom was referred the petition of Niger Engine Co. of Gonic made the following report. To His Honor the Mayor and the Honorable Council of the City of Rochester. The committee to whom was referred the communication from Niger Engine Co. No. 2 relative to their interest in the building used by them in Gonic Village report that from what information the [illegible]

Report of committee on the petition of Niger Engine Co.

said company did invest certain sums of money in the finishing and furnishing of the inside of said building under a certain understanding between the town and company. That said town began and erected a much larger building than was necessary for the housing of the machine and fixtures of said company or the use of its members as a fire company, and in the opinion of your committee certain rights of occupancy were gained by said company at the time of the erection of said building. Such as the right of holding public gatherings, and renting the hall for general purposes. but it is not clear that any legal claim exists against the city in favor of said company for [illegible] [illegible] made by them as it does not appear that such expenditures were made either under the direction of the town or to meet the general requirements of said organization as a Fire company. Your committee being unable to report in favor of the payment asked by said engine company and treating the communication referred to them as a petition, respectfully recommend its dismissal.

Report of committee on the petition of Niger Engine Co.

George E. Cochrane
Edward Josselyn } Com.
Charles H. Willand

On motion of councilman Barker voted that the report of the committee be accepted and adopted. Councilman Woodward of and Commons reported that the committee had secured the services of George D Richardson to act as superintendent of the old Cemetery grounds. Mr Potter asked for permission to be heard on the petition of John C Smart. Claim of Abby H. Whitehouse for damages on account of defective highway read and referred to the special committee. Claim of C. P. Stubbard for damages sustained on account of defective highway presented and referred to the special committee. An amendment of Sec 1 chapter 23 of the General ordinances read and referred to committee on bills in their second reading. Resolution authorizing committee on supplies to furnish desk and shelving for clerks office. On motion of councilman Barker voted that sec 39 of the Rules and Orders be suspended, and on motion of councilman Barker voted that the resolution pass. Harry Burquett declined to serve as clerk in ward six and on motion of councilman Woodward voted to proceed to the election of clerk in Ward Six. The chairman appointed as tellers councilmen Varney and Duncan.

Claim of Abby H. Whitehouse for dam.

Claim of C. P. Stubbard for damages

Amendment to Ordinance

Resolution to supply clerks office with shelving

Election of Clerk in Ward Six

Whole number of votes cast	15
A H Durgin had	10
N. C. Kimball had	5

and A H Durgin was declared elected. Councilman Warren presented the following resolution. Resolved that the sum of sixteen hundred dollars be paid to [illegible]

117 23

[illegible] of Gonic for their rights and interest in the building at Gonic known as the engine company's Hall, and that the above named amount of sixteen hundred dollars be and the same is hereby appropriated from any money in the treasury not otherwise appropriated. Referred to committee on claims and accounts. Report of committee on fire department on petition of John C Smart. The above named committee report that the petition of John C Smart dated March 17 1892 as amended by petition of April 26 1892 ought to be granted.

Resolution in favor of Gonic Engine [illegible]

Petition of J. C. Smart granted.

Edward Josselyn
George H. Bickford
Chas. S. Barker
Committee on Fire Dept.

Moved by councilman Dodge that we ballot on the report of the committee, the motion did not prevail. On motion of councilman Woodward voted that the petition of John C Smart be granted. On motion of councilman Barker voted that the committee appointed to procure storage for the books in the city clerks office be instructed to include the books and papers in the lobby. On motion voted to adjourn to Tuesday May third at 7½ o'clock at Council.

A true Record
Attest
Chas W. [illegible]
City Clerk

City of Rochester
May 3. 1892

Adjourned meeting of the city council met as per adjournment with the chairman pro tem in the chair. Roll of council called and the following named were present,
Tibbetts and Richards of ward one
Duncan of ward two.
Bickford Flagg and Warren of ward three
Pageotte and Josselyn of ward four
Varney and Dodge of ward five
Philbrick Barker and Woodward of ward six
Record of last meeting read and approved

Petition of
E. Wentworth
for permit
to build

Petition of Ezekiel Wentworth for permit to erect a building in the rear of Cocheco Block read and referred to the committee on fire department. Petition of Norway Plains Co. for permit to erect a shed in the rear of the "Old Tavern House" so called referred to committee on fire department.

Petition of
Norway Plains

The committee on fire department to whom was referred the petition of Chas. Flagg made the following report "That in the opinion of the committee the petition ought to be granted".

Petition of
Chas. Flagg
Granted

Edward Josselyn
Geo. A. Bickford
Silas S. Barker
} Committee

On motion of Councilman Dodge voted that the report be accepted . .

The amendment to the General Ordinances presented at the last meeting . not being in proper form, a new amendment was presented. On motion voted to lay the same on the table until new business was in order.

Amendment
to Ordinances

Councilman Warren of the committee on Roads Bridges and Drains asked for further time to consider the petition of Lord for removal of railings or of the petition of Reed for the widening of River Street and the resolution for sewers at East Rochester. The chairman recalled the petition of Lord and the resolution for East Rochester sewers, and referred to committee on bills in their second reading. On petition of the committee on police the chairman appointed Rodney Le Gross as special Police at Meaderbor Corner. Resolution in relation to paying members of the fire department for keys presented and referred to committee on bills in their second reading. Claims for damages on highway laid on the table for one week. Recommendation of the civil engineer and Supt. of water works for the extension of water works presented and on motion accepted and placed on file. The following resolution for the bonding of the water debt was presented by the finance committee.

Appointment
of Police at
Meaderbor

Recommendation
of the Civil
Engineer for
Extension of
water works

Resolved by the City Council of the City of Rochester.

Resolution
bond the
debt

Sec. 1. That the debt of the city of Rochester arising

and amounting to the Sum of Two Hundred Thousand Dollars now due and owing by the City of Rochester, be and the same hereby is funded. Said funded debt shall be known as the "City Water Works Loan"

Sec. 2. Bonds with coupons attached shall be issued for said loan which shall [illegible] date and of the denomination of one Thousand Dollars each. Said bonds shall be numbered from one to two hundred inclusive shall be made payable to bearer with interest at the rate of four per cent per annum payable semi-annually on the first day of June and the first day of December of each year at some bank in the City of Boston Commonwealth of Massachusetts.

Sec. 3 Said bonds shall be dated on the first day of June 188[illegible] and shall mature and be made payable in thirty years from the date thereof at the City Treasurer's office in the City of Rochester.

Sec. 4. Said bonds shall be signed by the mayor and City Treasurer and countersigned by the City Clerk and shall be under the seal of the City, and the coupons attached shall be signed by the Mayor or his name engraved thereon, and said coupons shall be orders upon the City Treasurer for the payment of the semi-annual interest on the day on which the same shall be made [illegible]

shall keep a record of the date [illegible] and amount of such bonds and the [illegible] of the purchaser of the same

[illegible] The Standing Committee on Finance is hereby authorized and [illegible] powered to carry into effect the provisions of this resolution, and to advertise for proposals for the purchase of said bonds and the same shall be sold to the highest bidder but not below their par value reserving the right to reject any and all bids therefor, and the proceeds arising from the sale of said bonds shall be applied to the within described indebtedness, and any [illegible] obtained on said bonds shall be applied as the City Council may determine. On motion of Councilman Dodge voted that the rules be suspended, and that we take action on the resolution at this time. On motion of Councilman Barker voted that the resolution be passed. The Electric Light Co asked for permission to erect a pole on [illegible] street in the rear of McDuffee Block. On motion of Councilman Dodge voted to refer to the Committee on Roads Bridges and Drains, and Councilman Dodge was added to the committee.

The following resolution for the extension of Water Works presented. Resolved by the City Council of the City of Rochester,

Sec. That the committee on water works together

to expend a sum not exceeding four thousand six hundred dollars in the extension of the public water works and for the purchase of materials therefor.

Sec 2. That the city civil engineer shall superintend the extension of said works and shall inspect all materials used for the same and shall report the cost thereof to the city council. On motion of councilman Barker voted that the rules be suspended that the resolution may be acted upon at this time. On motion of councilman Dodge voted that the resolution be passed.

On motion of councilman Barker voted that the committee on Supplies be authorized to furnish writing materials for the council room. — Committee on Supplies to furnish writing materials

On motion of councilman Dodge voted that the committee on Licenses be discharged and a new committee appointed. On motion of councilman Varney voted that the committee on claims and accounts act as committee on Licenses. — Committee on Claims and accounts to act as Com on Licenses

The amendment to Section one chapter twenty three of the General Ordinances was taken from the table, and on motion of councilman Barker voted that the rules be suspended in order to take action on the amendment. On motion of councilman Dodge voted that the amendment be adopted. — Amendment to Ordinances

On motion of councilman Barker voted that a committee of three be appointed by the chair to confer with the city engineer in relation to his sala... — Committee to confer ...

The chair appointed councilmen Barker Nutter and Warren as that committee.

The committee to whom was referred the petition of J W Varney asked for further time to consider, granted. On motion of councilman Dodge voted that when we adjourn we adjourn to one week from tonight at 7½ o'clock. Adjourned to the time specified

A true record

Attest

Chas W Brown

City Clerk.

City of Rochester

May 10 - 1898

Adjourned meeting of the city council met tonight with the mayor pro tem in the chair. Roll of council called and all were present except Barker of Ward six.

Record of last meeting read approved.

Petition of Sarah H. Hews for permit to make addition to her house at No 12 Wakefield street presented and referred to committee on fire department. — Petition of Sarah H. Hews

Petition of New England Telegraph and Telephone Co. for permit to erect poles on Main street presented and referred to committee on Roads Bridges and Drains. — Petition of N. E. Telegraph & Telephone Co.

... for permit to ... — Petition of

a sign across main street presented and referred to committee on Roads Bridges and Drains.

Petition of J. W. Varney with an amendment to former petition. referred to Board of Health.

Petition of Herbert C. Greenfield and others for a concrete sidewalk on Pleasant street referred to committee on Roads Bridges and Drains.

Petition of J. R. Grant and others for an amendment to the General Ordinances so as to charge a license to Fish and Meat peddlers referred to committee on bills in their second reading.

Remonstrance of C. P. Hayes and others against the erection of a slaughter-house as petitioned for by J. W. Varney. On motion of councilman Woodward, voted to lay on the table until the Board of Health make their report.

The committee on fire department made the following report on the petition of Norway Plains Co. "That in their opinion said petition ought to be granted.

C. Jusselyn } Committee
Geo. H. Bickford } on Fire Dept

On motion of Councilman Dodge voted that the report be accepted and adopted.

Councilman Philbrick from the committee on Street Lights reported that the Electric Light Co would furnish lights for the various city offices and the police station for the expense of [illegible] Councilman [illegible] asked

by Ezekiel Wentworth which was granted.

Councilman Woodward presented the following resolution. Be it resolved by the city council of the City of Rochester

That the Committee on street lights are hereby authorized to have the rooms in the building occupied by the city government and the police station supplied with electric lights at an expense not exceeding thirty five dollars. and a sum sufficient to pay the same is hereby authorized from the miscellaneous department. On motion of Councilman Dodge referred to committee on bills in their second reading. with leave to retire and report at this meeting. Resolution for an electric light near Willow Brook bridge presented and referred to same committee.

The committee reported both bills in proper form and ought to pass. Under a suspension of the rules, on motion of Councilman Dodge voted that the resolutions be passed.

The engineer submitted the following estimate of the cost for concreting Market street bridge and approaches.

For Roadway 667.23 sq yard @ .65 433.70
" Sidewalk 201.26 " .55 [illegible]
Removing surface materials etc [illegible]
[illegible]

Respectfully submitted

On motion of councilman Josselyn voted that
the committee on Roads Bridges and Drains with
the civil engineer receive proposals for the
concreting of Market street Bridge, and
report to the council. Recommendation of the chief — Recommendation
engineer for a fire alarm system referred to — for fire alarm
the committee on fire department. — System
Bill of Elmer J Smart for professional services
in the Hickey case referred to committee on — Bill of
claims and accounts, to settle on the best — E J Smart
terms possible. Claim of Clara A Brown
Lizzie J. Brown and Lillie B Brown for — Claim of
damages sustained on account of alleged — Clara A Brown
defect in the highway, presented and referred — Lizzie J Brown
to the special committee. On motion of — Lillie B Brown
councilman Dodge voted that when we adjourn — for damage
we adjourn to one week from to night May 17th
at 7½ o'clock On motion of councilman
Warren voted to adjourn to the time specified

A true record

Attest

Chas M. Brown

City Clerk.

City of Rochester

May 17–1892

Adjourned meeting of the city council met as
per adjournment with acting mayor Richards
in the chair. Roll of council called and the
following named responded as they were
called. Abbott and Richards of ward one
Duncan and Horn of ward two
Pingree & Josselyn of ward four
Varney Waldron and Dodge of ward five
Philbrick Barker and Woodward of ward six,
Bickford and Warren of ward three and Bickford
of ward four came in later and joined the
council. Record of the previous meeting read
and approved. Petition of L. H. Nute for permit — Petition of
to make an addition to his wood shed presen- — L H Nute
ted and referred to committee on Fire Department.
Petition of Leander P Pickering for permit — Petition of
to move a building from Adams corner to — L P Pickering
Sheridan Avenue was read and on motion
of councilman Varney voted that the petition
be granted. Petition of C. S. Berry and 24 — Petition of
others for an extension of side walk on — C S Berry
Charles street presented and referred to
committee on Roads Bridges and Drains.
Petition of Charles A Demeritt for lease of — Petition of
land near Market street Bridge and permit — C A Demeritt
to move a building thereon, referred to

The committee on Fire Department made the following report on petition of Isaiah H. Howe "That in their opinion said petition ought to be granted
Ed Josselyn } Committee
Chas S. Parker } on Fire Dept.

Isaiah H. Howe petition granted

On motion of councilman Woodward voted that the report be accepted and petition granted. Committee to whom was referred the petition of Ezekiel Wentworth asked for more time to consider, and also requested the members of the council to view the premises. On motion of councilman Dodge the report was accepted and adopted. The Board of Health to whom was referred the petition of J M Vassey made the following report.

Report on the petition of J M Vassey

To the Mayor and council of the city of Rochester N.H. The Board of Health have attended to the duties assigned them and report that the prayer of the petitioner ought not to be granted.
C. S. Hubbard }
J. S. Daniels } Board of
Geo. P. Wilkey } Health

On motion of councilman Josselyn voted that the report be accepted. Committee on bills in their second reading, to whom was referred the petition for sewer in East Rochester made the following report. "Your committee report that it is inexpedient to pass the above resolution until the city engineer has presented a plan for the same."

Charles S Parker }
Simon S. Horn } Committee
Cyrill Pageott }

On motion of councilman Dodge voted to lay on the table for one week. The same committee made the following report on the resolution to pay Tiger Engine Co. $100. "The above committee report that the resolution is indefinite"
Chas S. Parker }
Cyrill Pageott } Committee
Simon S Horn }

On motion it was voted the report be accepted and adopted. The same committee reported as follows on the petition of John R Grant and others "that it is inexpedient to amend the Ordinances as called for by the above petition"

J R Grant's petition not allowed

Chas S. Parker }
Simon S. Horn } Committee
Cyrill Pageott }

On motion of councilman Josselyn voted that the report be accepted and adopted. Voted that James Ford have leave to withdraw his petition. The committee on Roads Bridges and Drains asked permission for further time to consider the for sidewalk on Pleasant Street which was granted. The same committee made the following report on the petition of the New England Telegraph & Telephone Co. "That the petition be granted with the

Ford given leave to withdraw

N. E. Tel. & Tel. Co. granted

sawed tapered pole, planed and painted."

Joseph Warren
Geo. A. Bickford } Committee
J. Thorne Dodge

On motion of councilman Duncan voted the report be accepted. and on the petition of I. S. Howe the same committee reported "that the petition be granted"

I. S. Howe petition Granted

Joseph Warren
Geo. A. Bickford } Committee
J. Thorne Dodge

On motion of councilman Warren voted that the report be accepted and adopted. On motion voted that the C. E. present his plans for sewerage. Engineer Springfield being present made a report setting forth the need of sewerage and also presented plans for the same cost of construction &c. Councilman Barker presented the following Resolution for constructing a system of sewerage for Rochester Village and appropriating money therefor. Resolved by the city council of the city of Rochester.

Plans of Sewerage presented

Resolution – Sewerage

Sec. 1. That the plan recommended by J. Frank Springfield civil engineer for separate systems of sewerage be accepted and adopted as a plan of sewerage for Rochester Village.

Sec. 2. That the sum of Sixty five thousand dollars be raised and appropriated hereby creating a debt of Sixty five thousand dollars, for the purpose of constructing a system of sewerage for the Village of Rochester in accordance with the above named plan.

Sec. 3. That the city of Rochester hire the above named sum as a temporary loan for the purpose aforesaid.

Sec. 4. That the city civil engineer shall superintend the construction of said system of sewerage and shall inspect all materials used therefor.

Sec. 5. That the special committee on sewerage elected by the city council, together with the city civil engineer be authorized in behalf of the city to contract for the services of such other civil or sanitary engineers as they may deem necessary. to act as a committee to advertise for bids for furnishing materials and labor and to sign contracts therefor in behalf of the city, for the construction of said system of sewerage, said bids to be directed sealed to the city clerk and opened by him in the presence of the city council, and the city council shall determine what bids shall be accepted.

Sec. 6. That no bill contracted by or in behalf of the city of Rochester for the construction of said system of sewerage shall be paid until it shall have been approved by said committee, and after such approval it shall be paid in accordance with Section five chapter XV of the General Ordinances. On motion of councilman Duncan voted that rule 39 be suspended. Moved by councilman Barker that the resolution pass. The following is the vote of the council. Yeas Abbott ... those

Pay not. Bickford of ward four Josselyn Varney, Waldron Dodge, Philbrick, Barker and Woodward 18. Nays. Warren 1, and the resolution passed. Councilman Warren of the committee on roads, bridges and drains, stated only two proposals had been received for re[illegible] erecting Market street bridge and asked that further time be granted. The civil engineer presented the following estimate of cost of sewerage for Abbott & Highland streets East Rochester. — *Engineers estimate of cost for Sewers at E. Rochester*

Abbott Street

500 - 8" Pipe	@ .14 ¢		70.
50 - 6" "	.9 ¢		4.50
10 Y. Branches 8 x 6"	@	.60	6.00
3 Catch Basins	@ $20.		60.
2 Manholes	$30		60
Laying 500 ft	@ 30 ¢		160.
	Total		$365.50

Highland Streets

500' - 8" Pipe	@ .14 ¢	70.
50' - 6" "	9 ¢	4.50
10 - 8" Y. Branches	60 ¢	6.
2 Manholes	$30.	60.
5 Catch Basins	$20	100.
Laying 500'	@ 30 ¢	165.
	Total	$405.50

On motion of councilman Varney, voted that the committee appointed to confer with the [illegible] in relation to his salary be a committee to [illegible] what [illegible] made for a [illegible] for the water committee and [illegible] [illegible]. Councilman Barker presented the following resolution. Resolved by the City Council of the City of Rochester, that the committee on Police be authorized to expend a sum not exceeding thirty dollars for purchasing Lanterns and Belts and Policemens clubs for the City Marshal and members of the night watch. Referred to committee on bills in their second reading, with leave to retire and report at this meeting. The committee reported bill as in proper form and ought to pass. On motion voted the report be accepted, and under a suspension of the rules the resolution was passed. On motion of councilman Varney voted to adjourn to one week from tonight May 24 at 7½ o'clock adjourned. — *Resolution to purchase Lanterns and Belts for Police*

A true record

Attest

Chas W. Brown

City Clerk.

City of Rochester.
May 24 - 1892.

Adjourned meeting of the city council met
agreeably to adjournment with the mayor in
the chair. On the calling of the roll the follow-
ing councilmen were present.
Richards of ward one.
Duncan and Willand of ward two,
Pickford and Warren of ward three
Pagett and Bickford of ward four.
Nancy Waldron and Dodge of ward five
Barker and Woodward of ward six.
Record of previous meeting read and approved.
Communication from Sampson Post G. A. R.
extending an invitation to attend the services
on memorial day, also to join the procession.
On motion of councilman Dodge voted to
accept the invitation. Petition of S. H. Burnham Petition of
and others for extension of sidewalk on School S. H. Burnham
street referred to committee on Roads.
Petition of Edward Dyer and others for sidewalk, Petition on
on Spring street referred to same committee. E. S. Dyer
The mayor appointed councilman Richards
to act with the finance committee in auditing Richards
the book of the water commission. The commit- appointed on
tee to whom was referred the petition of A. H. Hale committee
reported favorably and on motion of councilman
Dodge voted that the report be accepted and
the petition granted. Committee to whom

was referred the petition of Herbert C. Greenfield
and others reported as follows: "that it is not C. Greenfield
advisable to grant the petition at present petition not
Joseph Warren } Committee allowed
Geo. A. Pickford } on Roads B. of.

On motion voted the report be accepted.
On the petition of Ezekiel Wentworth the committee reported favorably, and on motion voted C. Wentworth
the report be accepted, and the recommendation petition
adopted. The committee to whom was referred allowed
the petition of Chas. A. Demerit reported
"inexpedient to grant the petition" and on motion
of councilman Duncan voted the report be
accepted and the recommendation adopted.
The committee on Roads Bridges and Drains
asked for more time to consider the petition
of C. H. Berry and others for extension of
sidewalk on Charles street. Bond of the city
clerk read and referred to committee on Finance.
Petition for East Rochester sewerage taken from
the table and on motion voted to lay on the table
until next meeting. Councilman Warren
introduced the following resolution.
Resolved that the sum of Sixteen Hundred Resolution
Dollars be paid to the [illegible] members in favor of
of Tiger engine company No 3 of Gonic for Gonic Engine
their rights and interests in the building
at Gonic known as the Engine company
Hall. the money to be paid only to those
[illegible] contributed to

the building, and each ... the said member to receive such a proportionate part of the sixteen hundred dollars as his term of service in the company while the building was being paid for may entitle him to. The money to be paid to Geo. A. Pickford treasurer of the company and by him paid in accordance with this resolution. And the above named amount of sixteen hundred dollars be and the same is hereby appropriated from any money in the treasury not otherwise appropriated.

Referred to committee on bills in their second reading. Protest against the emptying of the proposed sewerage at Walker bridge from Gonic Manufacturing Co was read and one of similar import signed by Nahum Yeaton and 105 others, also one signed by G. W. Osborn and 6 others referred to committee on Sewerage. The committee on Roads Bridges and Drains asked for an extension of time for receiving proposals for erecting Market street bridge which was granted. The following resolutions were read. Be it resolved by the City Council of the City of Rochester that the sum of Fifty Six dollars be paid from the City treasury for sixteen Rubber coats for the use of the firemen of the city.

Protests against applying the Sewer at Walker Bridge

Resolutions for supplies for the Fire Dept

Be it resolved by the City Council of the City of Rochester that the sum of ten dollars

keys belonging to Engine House on Hanson street said keys having been paid for by the members of Resolute Hook and Ladder Co from the town of Rochester. Be it resolved by the city council of the city of Rochester that the sum of twenty two dollars and fifty cents be paid from the city treasury for fifteen badges purchased by the members of Pioneer Hose Co from the town of Rochester. Be it resolved by the city council of the City of Rochester that the sum of Fifty six dollars be paid from the city treasury for four Callahan Hose Nozzle for use of Fire Department. Be it resolved by the city council of the city of Rochester that the sum not to exceed \$200. be paid from the city treas. ... for the construction of wagon shed addition changes inside and lowering of Engine House on Hanson street, suitable for stabling city Horses. All referred to committee on fire department. On motion of councilman Dodge voted that when we adjourn we adjourn to May 31st at 7 1/2 o'clock. On motion of councilman Parker voted to adjourn.

Resolutions Fire Department Engine House on Hanson St.

A true record.

Attest

Chas W. Brown

City Clerk.

Meeting of the finance committee
May 24, 1892.

Committee met at City Clerks Office when the following bids for Water Works bonds were opened.

R. L. Day & Co	100.537
Brewster Cobb & Estabrook	101.88
Blake Bros & Co	100.77
Rochester Loan & Banking Co	102.85
Spencer Trask & Co	100.124
Third National Bank Boston	102.85
Geo. A. Fernald & Co	102.03
E. H. Rollins & Sons	102.93

On motion of J. Thomas Dodge it was voted to accept the bids of the Rochester Loan and Banking Co, and the Third National Bank of Boston, both bids being the same the bonds to be divided equally between them.

Attest
Chas. W. Brown
City Clerk.

City of Rochester
May 31st 1892.

Council met this evening at the time of adjournment with the Mayor in the chair. Roll called and the following members were present.
Ward One Libbey and Richards.
Ward Two Willand.
Ward Three Bickford.
Ward Four Pogent Bickford and [illegible].
Ward Five Varney and Dodge
Ward Six Philbrick. Councilmen Allen Seavey [illegible] [illegible] and Woodward joined the council before any business was transacted. Petition of C. A. Demeritt to move a building was read and on motion of councilman Varney the petition was granted. Petition of Dominicus Hanson for permission to make some additions to stable building on H[illegible] street read and referred to committee on fire department. Petition of S. J. Wentworth and others for extension of sidewalk on Chestnut street presented and referred to committee on Roads. Rochester Fair Association asked that a committee might be appointed to confer with them in relation to purchasing a piece of land on the westerly side of Cold Spring Park. referred to committee on Shade trees Parks and Commons. Committee asked

Petition of C. A. Demeritt

Petition of D. Hanson

Petition of S. J. Wentworth

Petition of Roch. Fair Asso.

presented at the last meeting against emptying the sewerage at Walker bridge granted.

The committee on Fire Department to whom was referred five resolutions at the last meeting reported favorably and recommended their passage and on motion of Councilman Dodge voted that the report be accepted and adopted, Councilman Warren asked for more time to consider the petitions for sidewalks in various parts of the city, granted.

The resolution for East Rochester sewerage taken from the table plans of the same presented and explained by engineer Springfield, On motion of Councilman Dodge voted that the rules be suspended and under the suspension of the rules the resolution passed. — *Passage of resolution for E. Roch. Sewerage*

Proposals for constructing Market street bridge read and referred to Committee on Roads.

Councilman Warren asked permission to withdraw the resolution in relation to Gonie Engine Co. presented at the last meeting. On motion of Councilman Dodge voted the permission be granted. — *Resolution in favor of Gonie Engine Co. withdrawn*

Councilman then presented the following resolution. Resolved by the city council of the City of Rochester:— That the sum of sixteen Hundred Dollars be paid to the members and ex members of Tiger Engine Co. No 3 of Gonie for their rights and interests in the building at Gonie known as the Engine Co. Hall, the — *Resolution in favor of Gonie Engine Co.*

ex members of the company who contributed to the building, and each member and ex member to receive such a proportionate part of the sixteen hundred dollars as his term of service in the company while the building was being paid for may entitle him to, the money to be paid to Geo H. Bickford treasurer of the company and by him paid in accordance with this resolution, and the above named amount of sixteen hundred dollars be and the same hereby is appropriated from any money in the treasury not otherwise appropriated. On motion voted that the rules be suspended so as to act on the resolution at this time. The resolution was then referred to committee on Fire Department. On motion voted to adjourn to one week from tonight June 7th at 7½ o'clock p.m.

A true record
Attest
Chas. W. Brown
City Clerk.

City of Rochester
June 7 - 1892

Council met at 7-30 this evening according to adjournment with the mayor in the chair. The following councilmen responded on the calling of the roll.

Ward one Bickett and Richards
Ward two Hassan and Duncan came in later
Ward three Bickford Flagg & Mason
Ward four Paycott and Josselyn
Ward five Varney and Dodge Waldron came later
Ward six Philbrick and Woodward.

Record of the previous meeting read and approved. Petition of J. F. Quinlan for permit to erect a shed in addition to his Stable on Hanson street, read and referred to committee on Fire Department. — *Petition of J. F. Quinlan*

Petition of Louis M Laplante and others for a new Highway in Gonic Village referred to Committee on Roads Bridges and Drains. — *Petition of L. M. Laplante*

The committee on Shade Trees Parks and Commons to whom was referred the request of Chas F. Trask to occupy a part of the City's land just below and adjoining the Box Factory, for piling lumber have attended to their duty and recommend that the same be granted at a yearly rental of Seventy-five dollars, said rental to begin the 1st day of June 1892, either — *Petition of C. F. Trask Granted*

143

three (3) months notice

Jabez S. Whitehouse } Committee
Chas E. Woodward }

On motion of councilman Dodge voted that the report be accepted and adopted.

The committee to audit the accounts of the Treasurer of the town board of water commissioners have attended to that duty and find vouchers for all expenditures. The accounts under their several heads are correctly cast and admirably tabulated. The following is a summary of the various accounts.

Receipts

From the Selectmen		59.500.00
Plumbing etc. Supplies Sold		59.01
Water etc.		2.10
Construction etc.		674.21
Services put in	2300.57	
Less abatements 37.66		2,262.91
Water Rents		5937.49
Total Receipts		64,450.32

Expenditures

For Construction etc.	60,614.57
Plumbing etc.	2,117.57
Maintenance	1,263.12
General expenses	83.21
Cash on hand	4,367.77
	64,450.32

justice to commend in the highest terms the admirable set of books which Mr H. W. Hayes the treasurer, has arranged, giving each department of the water service its proper place and every detail in its completeness. Nor can they withhold their admiration and appreciation of the excellent care and accuracy Mr Chas. S. Buck has shown in keeping the accounts and tabulating the many bills.

Respectfully submitted

Chas. S. Whitehouse, J. Thorne Dodge, Albert L. Richards } Committee to audit of Treasurer of Water Board

On motion voted that the report be accepted and placed on file. Committee on Shade Trees Parks and Commons to whom was referred the petition of the Rochester fair association recommended that the city convey to the association the acre and one eighth near the Grand Stand. On motion voted the report be accepted and placed on file.

Councilman Dodge introduced the following resolution. Resolved by the city council of the city of Rochester. That the city solicitor be instructed to draw up a proper conveyance of the land now enclosed by the Rochester Fair Association owned by the city conveying the same to the Rochester Fair Association said conveyance to be signed by the Mayor and City Cl [illegible]

Resolution in relation to land near Cold Spring Park

The consideration for the same to be Twenty five dollars.

On motion it was voted the resolution pass.

The Committee on Fire Department to whom was referred the petition of Dominicus Hanson reported that in their opinion it should be allowed

D. Hanson's petition allowed

Ed. Josselyn, W. H. Bickford } Committee

On motion voted that the report be accepted and the petition granted.

Moved by councilman Warren that the petition of Gonic Engine Co. be withdrawn from the committee on Fire Department and considered at this time. The motion did not prevail.

Councilman Warren demanded the yeas and nays which resulted 6 yeas and 8 nays and the motion did not prevail.

Councilman Warren presented the following resolution. Be it ordained by the city council of the city of Rochester. That the committee on sewers chosen at a meeting of the city council held April 12-1892 are hereby instructed and ordered to change the terminus of the main sewer as voted by the city council May 17-1892 so that instead of discharging at or near Walker's bridge so called the same be continued and the sewerage be discharged below the lower dam at Gonic Village.

Resolution Terminal Sewer Below Gonic Dam

resolution be referred to the committee on sewerage. Councilman Richards called to the chair, when the mayor took the floor and advocated the emptying of the sewerage at some other point than at Walker Bridge. Engineer Springfield being called upon stated that a sanitary engineer would probably be here and investigate the matter of sewerage during the coming week. On motion of councilman Horn voted that that the resolution lay on the table for one week. Councilman Warren presented the following resolution. Resolved that the Committee on Roads Bridges and Drains be and are hereby instructed to invite further proposals for the construction of a tar concrete roadway and side walk at and near the market Street Bridge. On motion it was voted that the resolution pass. Proposals for laying water pipe opened and read, and referred to committee on Water works. On motion of councilman Dodge voted that the matter of awarding the contracts be left with the Committee on Water Works. On motion of Councilman Dodge voted that when we adjourn it be to one week from to night June 21st at 7 1/2 o'clock and on motion voted to adjourn to the time specified.

A true record

Resolution instructing further proposals for concreting Market St Bridge

Laying of Water Pipe left with the Committee

City of Rochester

June 14. 1892

Adjourned meeting of the city council called to order by the mayor. The following responded to the roll call.

Ward Three Bickford & Warren.
Ward Four Josselyn.
Ward Five Varney Waldron & Dodge
Ward Six Philbrick Parker & Woodward.

There being no quorum present the mayor adjourned the meeting to one week from to night June 21st at 7.30 o'clock

A true record

Attest

Chas. W. Brown.
City Clerk

City of Rochester
June 21st 1892

Adjourned meeting of the city council called to order by the mayor. The following responded to the Roll call.
Ward one Allen Pebbles and Richards
Ward two Wiland and Horn
Ward three Bickford and Flagg
Ward four Pageott, Bickford and Josselyn
Ward five Varney Walden and Dodge
Ward six ~~Philbrick~~ Parker and Woodward
Councilmen Duncan Warren and Philbrick joined the council before the transaction of business. Record of last two meetings read and approved.

Report of committee on resolution to pay Tiger Engine Co

The committee to whom was referred the resolution to pay Tiger Engine Co Sixteen Hundred dollars made the following report. The committee on the Fire Department report that the above resolution ought not to pass. On motion of councilman Dodge voted that the report be accepted and adopted.

Report on petitions for sidewalks

The committee on Roads Bridges and Drains made the following report on the petitions of J H. Burnham and others, Edwin S Dyer and others, and S. J Wentworth and others for sidewalks. The committee on Roads Bridges and Drains to whom was referred the above petitions report that it is inexpedient to take action [illegible] be accepted and adopted.

Petition of Berry & others recommitted

On the petition of C. F. Berry and others for sidewalk on Charles street the committee on roads bridges and drains reported that it is inexpedient to take action. On motion of councilman Duncan it was voted that the petition be recommitted.

Report of committee on petition of J Frank Reed & Mr Laplante

The committee on Roads Bridges and Drains to whom was referred the petition of J Frank Reed and others for the widening of River street and the petition of Louis H Laplante and others for a new Highway at Gonic recommended that the petitioners and land owners interested be granted a hearing on the above petitions. It was voted that the report of the committee be adopted. The committee on Fire Department to whom was referred the petition of J. S. Quinlan reported that in their opinion it should be granted. Voted to adopt the report of the committee.

Appointment special Police

Thomas O'Neil John H Pooler and Moses St. Jacobs were appointed and confirmed as Special Police

Resolution in relation to Sewer referred

The resolution for the extension of the sewer below Gonic lower dam was taken from the table and considered. On motion of councilman Dodge it was voted to refer to committee on Sewerage. Communication from the Board of Health in relation to an open drain through the Hale field was read. Resignation of C. F. Hubbard City Physician was read. Councilman Parker the city council of the city of Rochester That John D Philbrick John W Tibbetts and Dudley B. Waldron act as a committee to see the heirs of Sarah Dodge deceased and ascertain for what price the city of Rochester can purchase the land and buildings on Central square between Wakefield street Market Street and Dodges Hotel.

Resol[illegible] to the Lodg. [illegible] [illegible]

That the above committee ascertain what portion of the purchase price of said property the owners of the neighboring or abutting estate will agree to pay. Voted that the resolution be adopted.

Councilman Warren presented the following resolution. Resolved by the City Council of the city of Rochester. That a sum of money not exceeding one hundred and fifty dollars be and the same hereby is appropriated from any money in the treasury not otherwise appropriated for the purchase of a drinking fountain suitable for man or beast to be placed on the square in Gonic Village. and that the Supt of the waterworks and the Supt of streets constitute a committee to purchase and erect the same. Referred to committee on bills in their second reading. Petition of A. H. Weare and others for the purchase of land of the Cocheco Manufacturing Co adjoining the School house lot. also the action of the School board in the matter was presented.

Resolution [illegible] East Rochester

Resolution for drinking fountain at Gonic

The following resolution was introduced by councilman [illegible] [illegible]

city of Rochester. That the recommendation of the School board to purchase a tract of land at East Rochester adjoining the School house lot be adopted, and the committee on Public Instruction are hereby authorized to negotiate with the Cocheco Manufacturing Co for the Same. Voted that the resolution be adopted. The councilman Waldron presented the following resolution. Be it resolved by the City Council of the city of Rochester. that a sum of money not to exceed three hundred dollars is hereby appropriated for the purchase of the tract of land at East Rochester adjoining the school house lot and owned by the Cocheco Manufacturing Co. the same to be expended from any funds not otherwise appropriated. Referred to committee on bills in their second reading. Bill of [illegible] W. Willey for board of A. S. Brown presented, and voted it be left in the care of the clerk.

Bids for sewerage pipe opened and read from Portland Stone Ware Co. Chas Miller and Son. M. G. Nash. Potomac Terra Cotta Co. Otis & Gorsleener all enclosed check except the latter. Referred to committee on Sewerage Committee to secure room for Committee on Water works made their report. On motion of councilman Dodge [illegible]

Bids for Sewer Pipe

Room for Water Board

in Grange Block be taken to expire at the same time as the other rooms hired by the city. Voted to adjourn to one week from to night June 28 at 7½ o'clock.

A true record
Attest
Chas. W. Brown
City Clerk

City of Rochester
June 28. 1892

Council met to night as per adjournment with the mayor in the chair The following named responded to the roll call.
Ward two Duncan Ham.
Ward four Pogett and Pickford
Ward five Varney Warren and Dodge
Ward six Philbrick Parker and Woodward.
Councilman Warren came in later and joined the council. The committee on bills in their second reading to whom was referred the resolution for drinking fountains at Gonic reported the resolution as in proper form and it was voted that the resolution pass. *Passage of resolution for drinking fountain*

The committee on bills in their second reading to whom was referred the resolution to purchase a ... of ... *Passage of Resolution*

of Cochecho Woolen Co at East Rochester reported the resolution in proper form on its second reading. Councilman Barker moved to amend the resolution by striking out the words "any funds not otherwise appropriated" and insert in place thereof the words "the sum appropriated for school purposes". Voted that the amendment be adopted. and it was then voted that the resolution be adopted as amended. The committee on sewerage reported on the bids for sewer pipe. W. S. Nash of Boston was reported by the committee as offering the best bid and recommended its acceptance. On motion of Councilman Barker voted that the bid of W. S. Nash of Boston be accepted. *Acceptance of bids for Sewer Pipe*

The committee on water works presented the following schedule of Rates. also Rules and Regulations *Schedule of Water Rates*

Rates.

Private Dwellings

Occupied by one family not exceeding four persons	* 5.00
" " " not exceeding eight persons single faucet	6.00
" " "	1.50
Each additional faucet	.50
Each additional [illegible]	
Occupied by two or more families supplied by same service pipe each family	5.00
More than one family using same faucet each family	3.50
	3.00

Schedule of Water Rates

Each additional tub	$2.00
Bath tub used by more than one family in same house each family	2.00
Set wash tubs, not exceeding three	1.50
Set wash bowls each	50
Water closet (Self closing)	3.00
Each additional closet (Self closing)	1.50
Urinals (Self closing) each	2.00
Urinals (not self closing) each	4.00
House heating apparatus	1.00

Boarding Houses

If family including Boarders does not exceed eight persons, same rate as in dwellings	
Exceeding eight and not ten	7.00
For each additional five persons	2.00
For first bath tub (number of persons exceeding eight and not ten)	5.00
Exceeding ten persons and not twelve	6.00
Exceeding twelve persons and not fifteen	7.00
Each additional tub	2.00
First water closet (Self closing) if number of persons exceed eight and not ten	4.00
Each additional five persons	2.00
Each additional closet (Self closing)	3.00
Urinals (Self closing) each	3.00
Set tubs, not exceeding three	2.00

Offices, Stores, Etc.

Each tenement occupied as store office or warehouse first faucet	4.00

Schedule of Water Rates

When two or more tenants are supplied with same faucet each	5.00
First water closet (Self closing)	3.00
Each additional closet	2.00
Set bowls each	50
Restaurants and markets, each	$6.00 to 20.00
Hotels, Blocks, etc., special contract or meter	
Barber shops first two chairs	6.00
Each additional chair	2.00
Photograph rooms, each	$7.00 to 20.00
Boilers, per H. P. (exhaust returned)	3.00
Laundries, greenhouses and for manufacturing purposes, by meter	
Building purposes, for each cask of lime or cement	07
For other purposes, per bbl of water	03
Bakeries	$6.00 to 10.00
Private Stables. In no case will the rate be less than $3.00 in connection with house service, otherwise not less than	5.00
Neat stock and horses less than twenty, each animal	60
More than twenty and less than thirty, each animal	50
More than thirty, each animal	40
Livery Stables, not exceeding ten horses	10.00
Each additional horse	60
Use of hose for washing carriages and harness in stable, each horse	50
Sprinkling carts, Special Rates	
Standpipe, Special rate	
Use of hose for washing windows, sprinkling	

and other similar purposes nozzle not to exceed 7/8 of an inch in diameter, limited to one hour per day, in connection with other service $3.00 otherwise $5.00

Schedule of Water Rates

One hose for each additional hour per day as above 2.00

Each additional hose as above per hour per day 2.00

Fixed fountains for ornamental purposes, in connection with house or other service jet limited to 1/4 inch in diameter, flowing not more than four hours per day. 6.00

More than four hours per day not exceeding ten hours 10.00

Movable fountains or lawn jets used in connection with hose as above 1.00

Meter Measurements.

Water metered or used for motor power and any mechanical purposes shall be paid for quarterly. If water is measured the consumer must provide a meter of pattern approved by the water board, and keep the same in repair at his own expense, and whenever a meter is put in the minimum annual rate shall in no case be less than $10.00. Should the water board so elect they may put meters in any service and an annual rent of ten per cent on the cost of the meter shall be charged the consumer.

Average from 1000 to 5000 gallons per day, for the year, per 1000 gallons .20

Average from ...

for the year per 1000 gallons. .15

Average from 5000 or more gallons per day for the year per 1000 gallons .10

Motors special rates.

Public Rates

Fire hydrants each $30.00

Fountains each 25.00

Regulations, Rules Etc.

Regulations and Rules of Water Board.

The following regulations shall be considered as being a part of the contract entered into by each person using the water.

1. The city will lay the service pipe from the main to the inside of the curb or walk and a charge of $300 will be made each consumer. This sum shall cover tapping the main furnishing all pipe and fixtures necessary for carrying the water to the curb including the corporation cock and suitable connections to the main together with a stop and waste cock and service box for same at the side walk. For all services larger than ordinary size and additional charge will be made. All repairs from the main pipe must be paid by the consumer.

2. All application for the use of water must be made in accordance with the prescribed form, and the various uses to which the water is to be applied must be fully

of the premises or his authorized agent will be required. Each taker shall be entitled to the use of water for such purposes only as are stated in his application.

3. Each service must be provided with a stop and waste cock inside the foundation walls, so arranged that the whole system of piping within the building can be drained, and all pipes must be fully protected against freezing, and the consumer will be held liable for any damage which may result from the neglect of such precaution.

4. Any plumber or other person who shall make any alteration in or addition to any water pipe or fixture, except so far as a written permit therefor has been given by the Water Board or Superintendent, shall be liable to a fine not exceeding twenty ($20) dollars.

5. There shall be no unnecessary waste of water and no fixture or faucet shall be allowed to be kept open at any time longer than is necessary for the proper use of water, neither shall the water be kept running to prevent freezing.

6. The Water Board or their duly authorized agents shall have the right to decide what shall be considered as a waste or improper use of water, and may restrict the use thereof whenever they deem it necessary, and should the consumer [illegible]

such directions as may be given then the water shall be shut off, and not again let on until the sum of $1.00 has been paid by said consumer.

7. The Superintendent or any authorized agent of the Water Board shall have the right to enter upon the premises of any water taker to examine the pipes or fixtures, and to ascertain the quantity of water used, and the manner of its use, and should any piping or fixture be considered as being unsuitable the same on their recommendation must be abandoned.

8. No person except an employee of the water department shall be allowed to make any connections, to set, repair or remove any piston or meter. And no person or persons except for the actual use of extinguishing fires shall open any hydrant without consent of the Water Board.

9. The water in no case shall be turned on until an examination has been made by the Superintendent, or an authorized agent of the Water Board, and the application signed by the proper party.

10. No consumer shall be entitled to damages or any rebate in water rates by reason of any stoppage for purposes of additions, extensions, or repairs, or non-use of the water on account of absence, or by reason of being deprived of the use of the water by a shut off for any purpose which the Water Board may deem

11. All water rates except meter and special shall be due and payable at the office of the City Clerk semi-annually and in advance on the first days of January and July in each year. In case of non payment of the same within ten days the water will be shut off, and not let on again until rates have been paid, and the additional sum of $1.00. All meter or special rates are due and payable quarterly on the first day of January, April, July and October. No discount will be made for vacant premises unless the Water Board has been previously notified and the water shut off. The Board shall have the right to attach seals to any fixture not in use and a fee of 50 cents shall be charged for the same.

12. All charges for laying service pipe or making connections or furnishing materials shall be due and payable in ten days.

13. The Water Board shall have the right to ascertain by meter the quantity of water used in any case, and the meter shall be attached whenever in their judgment it may be deemed expedient.

14. The above rates, regulations etc. are made subject to any changes [illegible]

by the Committee be adopted. On motion of Councilman Barker voted that the rules and regulations of the Water Board be adopted. The Committee on Roads Bridges and Drains asked for further time to consider the petition of C. F. B[illegible] and others which was granted. A communication was read from the owners of the Hale estate by their attorney, C. B. [illegible] in relation to the open drain in the Hale field. On motion of Councilman Varney voted to refer the matter to the Committee on Sewerage. Bids for erecting Market street Bridge opened and read and referred to Committee on Roads Bridges and Drains. On motion of Councilman Dodge voted that when we adjourn we adjourn to two weeks from tonight July 12 at seven thirty o'clock. On motion of Councilman Woodward voted to adjourn to the time specified.

A true record attest
Chas. W. Brown
City Clerk.

Adoption of Regulations and Rules of Water Board

Communication from Hale Estate Owners

City of Rochester
July 12 1892

The city council met as per adjournment with the mayor in the chair. The following named were present:
Ward One Allen
Ward two Duncan Willand & Horn
Ward three Pickford & Warren
Ward four Pagrett Bickford and Jusselyn
Ward five Varney and Dodge
Ward six Philbrick Barker Woodward
The record of the last meeting was read and approved. Petition of Geo H. Pitton to build on Summer street was presented and on motion of councilman Varney voted that the petition be granted. Petition of John S. Smart to remove a sign from the corner of Main and Arrow streets and erect the same at the corner of Main and Congress streets also to hang a wire sign across Congress street

Petition of Geo H. Pitton to build

Petition of John S. Smart to remove sign

the road was James Carson and on the 21st day of May 1890 a contract was entered into by said Carson with the town by which he agreed to build said road according to the specifications which were made a part of the contract for the sum of $4000.00 he to begin said work on the 26th of May 1890 and prosecute the same continuously until finished at a date not later than Sept 30 of the same year. A bond of the same date was given said town in the sum of $2000.00 for the faithful performance by said Carson of his contract and to indemnify said town for any loss or damage it might sustain by reason of any failure on the part of said Carson to meet the conditions of his said contract. According to the terms of said contract 80 per cent of 1/3 of the contract price was due and payable when 1/3 of the work was completed, and 80 per cent of 1/2 the remainder when the work was 2/3 completed, and the balance when work during the Spring and Summer and continued the work during the fall of 1890. The first payment of $1240.00 was upon estimate made in Oct. 1890 and the second of $1002.00 was upon estimates made in November of the same year. The road was not completed to the satisfaction of the Selectmen at any time during the year 1890, and on the 6th day of May 1891 a notice was served on Mr Carson to complete the building of said highway at once or a suitable person would be placed in charge to finish the same and the necessary expense thus incurred would be charged to his account. After this notice was served on Mr Carson your committee understand he did work on said road for which he charged the sum of $69.37 in his bill. The Selectmen not satisfied with the condition of the road as left by said Carson caused another notice to be served on Mr Carson on or about Aug 2/21 1891 in which he was informed the road would be completed at once by the town and the expense charged to him. This was done under or by direction of the Selectmen at the expense of $218.72 and charged to account of Mr Carson as appears from the annexed account. After this work had been done a tender of $1476.29 was made Mr Carson as the amount due him and he refused to accept the [illegible]

a claim similar to the one now presented was made against the town. A difference of $917.90 appears between the amount claimed by Mr Carson and the amount acknowledged as due by the town. The Selectmen have never recognized Mr Carsons claim except as under his contract. And it appears from copies of the annexed vouchers the payments made were based upon the estimates of the Engineer under said contract at or about the time such estimates were made and receipted for by Mr Carson as payments on said contract. Your committee find the sum due Mr Carson on said contract to be $1476.29 as tendered by the town and refused by him about Dec. 1891.

C. M. Willard
G. L. Cochrane
Joseph Warren

On motion of Councilman Varney voted that the report of the committee be accepted and adopted and that the amount reported by the committee as due Mr Carson be tendered to him by the Mayor.

The committee to whom was referred the purchase of the old building in Central Square owned by the Sarah Dodge heirs asked for further time to consider which was granted. The following report was [illegible] Roads Bridges and Drains to whom was referred the bids for constructing Market Street bridge have attended to that duty and would recommend that the bid of John D Parsley be accepted. The bid of the Worcester parties was a little lower but in the opinion of your committee inasmuch as they use solid rollers while Parsley uses heat we consider the latter to be the best method and therefore recommend the acceptance of Parsley bid.

Report of Committee on bids for Construction Market St Bridge

Joseph Warren }
Geo. A. Bickford } Committee on Road Bridges and Drains
Chas. W. Allen }

On motion of councilman Duncan voted that the report be accepted and adopted.

Councilman Parker of the committee on Sewerage made a verbal report in relation to the open drain through the [illegible] field. The committee on Sewerage asked for further time to consider the extending of the sewer below lower dam which was granted.

Proceeded to ballot for City Physician in place of Dr C J [illegible] resigned.

Selection of City Physician

Whole no of ballots	13
Stephen G. Kent	1
James [illegible]	1
R. V. [illegible]	1

that when we adjourn we adjourn to one week from tonight July 19 at 7.30 o'clock.

On motion of councilman Warren voted that the highway petitioned for at [illegible] leading from the westerly end of [illegible] Street be laid out and an award of one dollar be made to each land owner.

On motion of Parker voted to adjourn to the time specified.

A true record

Attest:
Chas. W. Brown
City Clerk

City of Rochester
July 19. 1892

Adjourned meeting of the city council met as per adjournment with the mayor in the chair. The following responded to the roll call. Richards & Tebbetts of ward one
Duncan & Wiland of ward two
Bickford and Warren of ward three
Josselyn of ward four
Dodge of ward five
Philbrick Parker and Woodward of ward six.
The mayor presented a communication in relation to the unveiling of the statue of John P Hale at Concord N. H. August 3. and introduced the following resolution
City of Rochester July 19 - 1892
In council. We the representatives of the city of Rochester in council assembled. recognizing the national reputation of John Parker Hale a native of this town his labor in the cause of human liberty his profound statesmanship and lofty standard of political citizenship, and appreciating the great honor conferred upon his native place therefor Resolved. That the Mayor and city clerk with such of the council as may join attend the public unveiling of of his statue at the State House on the

Communication from the mayor and Resolutions in relation to the unveiling of the statue of John Parker Hale
For Communication from the mayor See page 171

Resolved. That badges appropriate to the occasion be procured and worn by each member on that day.
Resolved. That the people of Rochester be invited to send a delegation of its citizens to join with the council in doing honor to the occasion and the family of their distinguished townsman
Resolved. That the city clerk arrange for railroad transportation for the city Government on that day the cost of the same to be paid for out of any money in the treasury not otherwise appropriated.
Resolved That a committee of three be appointed from the council to arrange all details necessary to carry into effect the above resolutions.
Resolved. That the City Clerk cause a copy of this preamble and resolutions to be suitably engrossed and sent to Hon William E. Chandler U.S. Senator from New Hampshire.
Resolved. That these resolutions be spread in full upon the city Records.
On motion of councilman Parker voted that the resolution pass and a committee be appointed to make the necessary arrangements. the mayor appointed

Willand as that committee.

Petition of Charles M. House for permit to construct a roll way to the cellar in the Willey building. also for permission to close the walk on Arrow Street a distance of four feet. On motion of councilman Barker voted that the petition be granted.

Petition of Chas M. [illegible] to construct a roll way

Petition of R DeWitt Burnham for permit to build an addition to the upper and back side of the Mansion House about 22 x 35 feet. On motion of councilman Dodge voted that the petition be granted, Semi Annual report of the city treasurer read and ordered to be placed on file. Councilman Philbrick of the committee to see about the purchase of the old buildings on the Square, known as the Dodge property, made a verbal report in relation to the same. Moved by councilman Warren that the report be made in writing. on a viva-voce vote the motion was declared carried. doubt being expressed the yeas and nays were ordered, which resulted in four voting in the affirmative and eight in the negative so the motion did not prevail.

Petition of R DeWitt Burnham

Report of Committee on purchase of Dodge property,

Councilman Barker presented the following resolution. Resolved by the city council of the city of Rochester.

Resolution for purchase of Dodge property,

Sec 1. That the sum of six thousand seven hundred dollars received as premium on the sale of the water bonds of the city of

Rochester together with a sum not exceeding three thousand three hundred dollars from any unexpended balance remaining in the city treasury. is hereby appropriated for the purpose of purchasing the land and buildings on Central Square owned by Sophia D. Hall,

Sec 2. That John D. Philbrick. John W. Tibbetts and Dudley P. Waldron act as a committee to purchase the same for the city of Rochester, and to take a deed from J. Thorne Dodge to the city of Rochester of all land lying between said property, and the sidewalk in front of Dodges Hotel, in a line running from Market St to Wakefield St.

Sec 3. That the above described premises are bought to be used for public purposes and shall constitute an extension of Central Square. Councilman Willand moved that the rules be suspended so as to take action at this time. objection being offered the motion was withdrawn, and on motion of councilman Barker voted, that the resolution lay on the table until the next meeting. The C. E. presented a plan for a fence around the Stand Pipe at Adams corner also the following estimate of the cost of additional extension to the water works. together with the improvements at the Stand Pipe. Estimate for water works extension

Estimate of cost of water Pipe extension

Extension of Rice St. 225' 6" Pipe
Harrison Ave 451' 6"
" " Seward St. 1010
Private way Seward & [illegible] 200
Superial St. 350
2350'

6. 6" Gates @ 12.00	150
6 " Boxes @ 3.25	19.50
4 Hydrants @ 25.00	100.
35 Tons Pipe @ 24	840
Laying	470.
1300 lbs Specials @ 2½	32.50
	1507.00

Estimate of work and material required at Stand Pipe

Wrought Iron Fence	164.00
Manhole & Ventilator	36.00
Estimate for Outlet and Repairs	200
	400.00

J. F. Springquist C. E.

Councilman Varney presented the following resolution. Be it resolved by the city council of the city of Rochester that such a proportion of the sum of $1907.00 as may be required for the extension of the water works upon the streets named in the report of the civil engineer, together with the improvements at the stand Pipe and reservoir be and is hereby appropriated from the unexpended monies in the hands of the water board. Referred to committee on Bills in their second reading.

Resolution to extend water pipe and for improvements at Stand Pipe

On motion of councilman Barker voted to adjourn to two weeks from tonight (Aug 2) at 7½ o'clock

A true record
Attest
Chas. W. Brown
City Clerk

City of Rochester
August 2. 1892

Adjourned meeting of the city council met according to adjournment with the mayor in the chair. The following named councilmen responded as their names were called. Tibbetts & Richards of ward one. Bickford Hagg Willand of ward two. Foyert Bickford and Warren of ward three. Varney and Dodge and Josselyn of ward four. Barker and Woodward of ward of ward five. Allen, Duncan Horne & Philbrick six. joined the council before the transaction of business. Minutes of previous meeting read and approved. The mayor reported making the tender of $1471.62 to James Lawson as

John Dunion for leave to build the proposed addition to his stable fifty feet instead of twenty four feet as originally proposed was referred to committee on fire department. *Petition of John D…*

Recess of ten minutes declared after calling the council to order the special committee made the following report on the claim of E. T. Hubbard. *Report of Special Com. on Claim of E. T. Hubbard*

To the mayor and council of the city of Rochester,

The committee to whom was referred the claim of Edwin T. Hubbard for injuries alleged to have been received on the 17th day of April 1892 to his team and person through and by reason of a defect in the highway in Gonic Village known as Main street near the Electric Light Pole at the junction of said Main street with the street leading past the school house having attended to their duties are of opinion that the claim is one that might be compromised to the advantage of both parties, and said claimant having offered to accept the sum of two Hundred ($200) Dollars in full settlement by way of compromise your committee would recommend the payment of said sum in adjustment of said claim.

E. M. Willand
G. E. Cochrane
Joseph Warren

On motion of councilman Dodge voted that the report be accepted and adopted.

The same committee made the following report [illegible]

Brown and Clara A. Brown *Report of Spcl. Committee on claims of Lillie B. Brown, Lizzie Brown, Clara A. Brown*

To the mayor and council of the city of Rochester;

The committee to whom was referred the claims of Lillie B. Brown, Lizzie S. Brown and Clara A. Brown for alleged injuries said to have been received by reason of a defective highway in said Rochester leading from Gonic Village to Rochester Neck on the twenty fifth day of April 1892 having attended to their duties report that in their opinion the city of Rochester is not liable and that said claim be disallowed.

E. M. Willand
G. E. Cochrane
Joseph Warren

On motion of councilman Jocelyn voted that the report be accepted and adopted.

The same committee on the claim of F. T. Smith reported as follows. *Report of Spcl. Com. on claim Frank T. Smith*

To the Mayor and Council of the City of Rochester.

The committee to whom was referred the claim of Frank T. Smith for alleged injuries to his team on Market street in said city on the 19th day of February 1892 having attended to their duties report that in their opinion said street was not defective insufficient or in want of repair at the time of the alleged injuries to his team and recommend the disallowance of his said claim. E. M. Willand

voted that the report be accepted and adopted.
also on the claim of Leonie Vachon and Sarah Marquis the following report was made — [Report of Spec. Com. on claims of Leonie V. & Sarah Marquis]
To the Mayor and Council of the City of Rochester.

The Committee to whom was referred the claims of Leonie Vachon and Sarah Marquis for injuries alleged to have been received to their team and persons on the highway leading from Rochester to Great Falls on the 5th day of April 1884 through certain defects in said highway at or near the covered bridge over the Northern Division of the Boston and Maine Railroad having attended to their duty report that in their opinion said highway was not defective as claimants allege and recommend the disallowance of their said claims.

L. M. Miland [?]
G. C. Cochrane [?]
Joseph Masseur [?]

On motion of councilman Dodge voted that the report be accepted and adopted.
On motion of councilman Abbotts [?] voted that the claim of Joshua G. Hall be referred to a special committee. [Claim of J. G. Hall]
On motion of councilman Josselyn [?] voted that the petition of John S. Dunlan [?] be considered at this time and it was voted to grant the prayer of the petitioner. [Dunlan petition granted]

following Resolution to [illegible] Hose Reel for Sturtevant Hose Co.
Be it resolved by the City Council of the City of Rochester.
That a sum not to exceed [illegible] be appropriated from the money already appropriated for the Fire Department for the purpose of purchasing a new Hose Reel for the Sturtevant Hose Co. to replace the one which they now have which in the opinion of the chief engineer and committee on Fire Department is not worth repairing. After voting that the rules be suspended in order to take action at this time the resolution was withdrawn at the request of the committee on Fire Department. [Resolution to purchase Hose Reel withdrawn]
The following resolution was presented,
Resolved that the City Solicitor be and hereby is instructed to proceed under Section 8 of chapter 114 Public Statutes in an action of debt against Gilman L. Marden for the non payment of license on two Billiard or Pool tables in his charge. Voted that the resolution be adopted. [Resolution instructing City Solicitor to prosecute Gilman Marden]
Communication from the Chief Engineer in relation to the new building of Ezekiel Wentworth in the rear of Cocheco [?] Block, was presented, and on motion of councilman Barker voted that the committee on fire department be instructed to see that the condition of the permit [Instructions to committee on fire department]

Finance presented the following resolution.
Resolution to appropriate for expenditures to the various departments to March 1st 1892. Resolution to appropriate for expenditures to March

Resolved by the city council of the city of Rochester, That the following sums be appropriated from the amount received from the town of Rochester to defray the expenses of the following named departments to March 1st 1892.

To Highway Department	2591.49
" Miscellaneous	307.68
" Fire	512.89
" Police	568.36
" Street Light	1500.
" Salary Department	568.
" Health	1.65
" Support of County Poor	176.96
" " Soldiers Aid	105.39
" " City Poor	157.75
" " City Soldiers Aid	166.88
" School Department	4106.90
Total	11,762.96

The committee on finance recommend the passage of the above resolution.

John S. Whitehouse
John W. Abbott
J. Thomas Dodge

On motion of councilman Varney voted that the resolution pass. On motion of councilman Warren voted that on the

for the widening of River street a hearing be granted to the petitioners three weeks from to night August twenty third at the council room at six thirty oclock p.m. Hearing on widening of River Street

The committee on bills in their second reading made the following report on resolution to appropriate money for the purpose of extending the Public Water Works. Report of Committee on bills in their second reading to extend water work.

The above named committee report that the resolution is in proper form.

Chas. S. Barker }
Simon A. Hoar } Committee

and after the resolution was read the second time it was voted that the resolution pass.

Moved by councilman Barker that Cole Bros Shoe Co be exempt from paying taxes for a period of ten years from this date. the exemption to include their machinery stock in trade and buildings occupied by them for manufacturing shoes referred to committee on Finance to report at the next meeting. Motion of Barker to exempt Cole Bros from taxation

Moved by councilman Woodward that we proceed to elect a Sanitary officer in the place of Geo. F. Willey deceased the motion did not prevail. On motion of councilman Dodge voted that a committee be appointed to nominate a candidate for Sanitary officer. On motion of councilman Barker voted that when we adjourn we adjourn

The mayor appointed as the committee to investigate the claim of Joshua G Hall, Councilmen Tibbetts, Horn and Woodward, and as the committee to nominate a candidate for Sanitary officer Councilmen Horn, Flagg & Duncan.

Committee on claim of J. G. Hall and Committee Sanitary officer

Voted to adjourn to time specified

A true record

Attest Chas W. Brown

City Clerk.

To the City Council

Gentlemen

Remarks from the Mayor in relation to John P. Hale

On Wednesday August 3 – at Concord in the State House grounds will be unveiled and dedicated to the people of New Hampshire with appropriate ceremonies a statue of John Parker Hale; a native of Rochester, a learned lawyer, a profound statesman, a heroic defender of human liberty, and a man of National reputation. Born in Rochester March 31st 1806 within a 'stones throw' of where we are sitting, educated in the common schools of this village and at Exeter Academy and graduated at Bowdoin College in 1827. He studied law with Jeremiah H Woodman of this town and with Daniel M Christie of Dover and began the profession of his life in the latter city where he ever after lived. He was elected to the state legislature from Dover in 1832, when but twenty six years old. In 1843 he was elected to congress and served one term; in 1846 again elected to the state legislature from Dover, chosen speaker of the house and by the same legislature elected a U.S. Senator for a full term of six (6) years. Again elected for an unexpired term of four (4) years in 1855, and for a full term of six years in 1859. Nominated as the in 1847 but declined, again nominated for the Presidency by the Free Soil convention in 1852. At the close of his senatorial term in 1865 he was appointed minister to Spain where he remained five (5) years, much of the time in ill health, and died in Dover November 19 1873. In the words of another distinguished son of Rochester Hon Jacob H Ela "bearing with him the blessings of millions who had been raised from the sorrow and degradation of human servitude, and of millions more who had admired his unselfish fidelity to the cause he had espoused, and his unswerving integrity" Such in the briefest manner possible I have named the dates and principle events in this distinguished man's career who shed lustre and honor on the nation, the state and his native town.

But to speak of his high rank as a lawyer, his power with a jury his skill in handling witnesses his "keen wit burning indignation and touching pathos" needs an abler tongue than mine. As a statesman loyal to his convictions of right undaunted when standing solitary and alone in the U S Senate fighting the encroachments of a domineering and arrogant slave oligarchy unmindful of the threats and persuasions of his (at that time) political associates thrusting aside the brilliant prospects

the faith of a prophet to the ultimate disenthralment of a race from human servitude he presents to this generation a figure heroic and grand such as no other state in the Union can show, and one which the people of his native town can do homage to with commendable pride. On the 3rd of August his statue the gift of his distinguished son in law Senator William E Chandler is to be publicly unveiled and formally dedicated to the people of New Hampshire whom he loved so well and served so faithfully. It seems to me eminently fitting that the people of his native place through this council should take cognizance of this important event by some official action. I therefore recommend the adoption of the following resolutions,

Chas S. Whitehouse
Mayor

For Resolution see page 168-169

City of Rochester August 9th 1892.

The council met tonight as per adjournment
The mayor in the chair
The following councilmen responded to the roll call
Duncan Willard and Horn of ward two.
Bickford Sloggy & Warren of ward three
Rogers Bickford and Joslyn of ward four.
Varney Warden and Dodge of ward five
Chesebro Barker and Woodward of ward six.
Record of last meeting read and approved
Petition for a new highway from Pine street to Abbott avenue signed by Alonzo R Reed and others presented and referred to the committee on Roads Bridges and Drains,

Petition for Highway Pine street to Abbott ave

The committee to whom was referred the petition of the electric light co for permission to erect a pole on Congress street, made the following report they have attended to their duty and would recommend that the prayer of the petitioner be granted

Joseph Warren
Rogers Bickford
J Thomas Dodge

Petition of Electric light co granted

On motion of councilman Varney voted the report be accepted and the petition granted
The special committee made the following report. To the mayor and council of the [illegible] refused the claim of Charles C Hodgdon for injuries alleged to have been received on the fifth day of December 1891 through and by reason of a defective highway leading from Rochester to East Rochester having attended to their duties Report they have been unable to agree with the claimant in negotiations looking to a settlement and recommend the disallowance of said claim

Joseph Warren
C. M. Willard.

On motion of councilman Dodge voted the report be accepted and adopted.
The committee on finance asked for further time to consider the motion to exempt the Nute Bros from taxation. Moved by councilman Barker that we consider the question of exempting Nute Bros from taxation at this time the motion prevailed then on motion of councilman Barker voted to exempt Nute Bros from taxation for a period of ten years the exemption to include their machinery stock in trade and buildings occupied by them for manufacturing shoes.
On motion of councilman Barker voted to take the resolution for the purchase of the Dodge property from the table when councilman Barker presented the

Whereas the public interest and convenience of the City of Rochester require that the land and buildings situate and lying between Wakefield street Market street and Dodges Hotel should be purchased by the City of Rochester. — *Resolution in relation to purchase of Dodge property*

Therefore resolved by the City council of the City of Rochester,

Sec. 1 That the sum of six thousand and seven hundred dollars received as premium on the sale of the water bonds of the City of Rochester, together with a sum not exceeding three thousand and three hundred dollars appropriated for the purpose of purchasing the land and buildings on Central Square owned by Sophia D Hall.

Sec. 2 That John D Philbrick John W. Tibbetts and Dudley B. Waldron act as a committee of the City council of the City of Rochester to purchase the same for the City of Rochester and to take a deed from J Thom Dodge to the City of Rochester of all the land lying between said property above mentioned and the sidewalk in front of Dodges Hotel [illegible] from Market Street to Wakefield Street on said sidewalk.

On motion of councilman Willand voted that the rules be suspended and that we take action at this time. On motion of councilman Barker voted that the resolution pass. — *Passage of the resolution*

resolution. Councilman Josselyn presented the resolution for the purchase of Hose reel for Sturtevant Hose Co. which was presented at the last meeting and withdrawn. — *Resolution for purchase of Hose [illegible]*

Referred to committee on bills in their second reading. Councilman Barker presented the following resolution for paying L. T. Hubbard for damage to person and horse received on the highway. — *Resolution to pay L. T. Hubbard for damage*

Resolved by the City council of the City of Rochester.

That the sum of two hundred dollars is hereby appropriated from the sum appropriated for miscellaneous expenses to the payment of the amount awarded to said L. T. Hubbard. On motion of councilman Dodge voted that the rules be suspended and that we take action at this time. When on motion of councilman Barker it was voted that the resolution pass. The following estimate for laying sidewalks was presented by the civil engineer.

For Sidewalk on Westerly Side of Market St. — *Estimate for sidewalk*

[illegible]	[illegible]	48.00
Digging		24.00
225' Edge Stone	[illegible]	78.75
Setting		5.75
[illegible]		7.00

Grading	35.00
Total	209.50

Estimate for Sidewalk on Easterly side of Portland St from Signal st to School.

30. m Brick a 6.00	180
Laying	90.
1125' Edge stone	393.75
Sillary	25.
Planking	30.
Driveway & additional	30.
Grading	25.
Total	773.75

Voted that the estimates lay on the table until the next meeting.

Voted that the clerk open the bids for the laying of Sewer pipe at this time. — *Bids for Sewerage opened*

Voted that the bids be referred to committee on Sewerage without reading.

On motion of Councilman Dodge voted that when we adjourn we adjourn to next Saturday night August 13th at 7.30 o'clock.

On motion of Warren voted that the committee on Sewerage be requested to report on the resolution to extend the sewer below Goric Dam at the next meeting.

The following amendments to the General ordinance was read and referred to committee on bills in their second reading. — *Amendment to Gen Ordinance*

An ordinance in amendment of Sect of the City of Rochester.

Be it ordained by the City Council of the City of Rochester that the sentence in chapter XXIII of the General Ordinances of the City of Rochester relating to the salary of overseer of the poor be amended to read as follows.

The overseer of the Poor including his service as member of the board of health two Hundred dollars.

On motion voted to adjourn to time specified.

A true record

Attest Chas W. Brown
City Clerk

City of Rochester August 13 1892

Adjourned meeting of the city council met
agreeably to adjournment with the mayor in
the chair
The following named councilmen responded to
the roll call Bebbatt and Richards of Ward one
Willard and Storm of Ward two
Flagg of ward three
Paget and Josselyn of ward four
Varney Waldron and Dodge of ward five
Philbrick Barker and Woodward of ward six
and the following named joined the council
before the transaction of business.
Allen of ward one Duncan of ward two and
Warren of ward three,
Minutes of last meeting read and approved.
Petition of G. J. Mether to have trees on
Summer and Wakefield streets trimmed
read and referred to committee on Shade
trees Parks and Commons. The committee on
Bills in their second reading asked for further
time to consider the resolution to purchase
Hose reel and also the amendment to the
General Ordinances which was granted
Also the committee on Roads Bridges and
Drains asked for further time to consider the
petition of Hiram R. Reed and others for a
new highway from Pine street to Bebbatt

Petition of G. J. Mether

On motion of councilman Barker voted
that the bid of Joseph Bruno for laying sewer
pipe be accepted and that H. F. McGee have
leave to withdraw. The bid of Bruno for the
entire job was $25,712 he to deposit a certified
check for three thousand dollars, and make an
assignment of insurance policies to the
city. The civil engineer being called upon
made a statement in relation to plans for
extending the sewer to some point below
Gonics The committee to whom was referred the claim of Joshua G. Hall asked for
further time to consider which was granted
Councilman Duncan of the committee to
nominate a candidate for sanitary officer
presented the name of Edgar F. Reynolds
Petition of G. L. Tebbetts for leave to move
a building from the Unity church lot to
the lower end of Charles street was read and
on motion of councilman Dodge voted to
grant the petition. Proceeded to ballot
for Sanitary officer with the following result

Whole number of votes cast	16
James C. Coyle had	1
G. W. Goodwin "	1
John Burgess "	1
Moses Stevens "	2
Edgar F. Reynolds "	11

and Edgar F. Reynolds was declared

Acceptance of bid of Joseph Bruno for laying Sewer Pipe

Report of Committee to nominate Sanitary officer

Petition of G. L. Tebbetts to move building

Ballot for Sanitary officer

Barker That the Rochester Enterprise association and Peoples Shoe Co be exempted from the payment of taxes for a period of ten years on their land buildings capital stock and stock in trade and the motion was carried.

Vote to exempt the Rochester Enterprise and Peoples Shoe Co. taxable

On motion of councilman Dodge voted to adjourn to next Saturday night Aug 20 at 7.30 oclock

A true record
Attest Chas W. Brown
City Clerk

City of Rochester August 20. 1892

Adjourned meeting of the council met according to adjournment the mayor in the chair. The following named councilmen responded to the Roll call.

Duncan and Horn of ward two.
Flagg and Warren of ward three.
Pageott Bickford and Josselyn of ward four
Varney Waldron and Dodge of ward five
Barker and Woodward of ward Six.

Minutes of previous meeting read and approved. Councilman Philbrick came in and took his seat with the council.

The mayor stated he had a communication to present to the council, when he returned the resolution for the purchase of the Dodge property giving his reasons therefor in the following message

To the city council of Rochester

Gentlemen.

Mayors veto of the resolution to purchase the Dodge property

I return the resolution passed by your board at its regular meeting Tuesday evening August 9th 1892 unsigned and disapproved.

This resolution contemplates the purchase of the Dodge property, so called on Central Square and appropriates ten thousand (10000) to pay for the same.

public square though there is no mention in the resolution what it is intended for and for all it says, the city may fit it up for any purpose it pleases and rebuild it or sell it again. This omission alone I consider an objection, and believe it should have stated in unmistakable language what it was intended for.

The scheme to buy this property and (presumably) create a public square ostensibly for the good and convenience of the public while it may not be altogether in contravention of the statutes, is in my mind in the way it originated and in the methods by which it has been enacted entirely different from what is intended by the statute.

While the right is given councils under chapter 50 Section 5 of the laws of 1891, to purchase real and personal property for certain purposes. I do not think it was intended that the methods to wit, by petition and public hearings should be dispensed with.

The people have not asked for this legislation by petition in the usual manner and no hearing has been had as provided in the case of highways. The laying out of highways, streets squares and parks in most if not all instances where they are referred to in the statutes are grouped

ally been the same in such cases, to wit, a petition by the people for the desired object then notice of a hearing when those in favor and opposed either by themselves or by council would be heard for and against the proposed proceedings, and finally a decision. This council has recognized this fact several times already in its brief existence of seven months as a city; and at the same meeting at which this resolution was passed a petition was received asking for a new highway or street to be laid out and the preliminary steps were taken to give the petitioners and subject a hearing. This council acting by itself or through a committee has already held hearings upon petitions for new streets or the extension of existing ones and acted upon them, and are continuing to act upon them in like manner as they arise. It seems to me that this matter should have followed the same course. Under the law prior to 1891 this would have been the proper and only course permissable; and while the law of 1891 allowed city councils to purchase etc I think it intended the methods should be the same as applied to towns and selectmen in the case of highways.

The resolution has for its authority Chapter 50 or Section 5 in the laws of 1891, shall have the care and superintendence of the city buildings, all city property and all public squares and streets, and the power to sell or let what may be legally so disposed of and to purchase property real or personal for the use of the city, whenever the interests or convenience of the city shall require it. This is plain, but does the public interest or convenience at this time require it? The expression "public interest" has a wide latitude I know, but it should be exercised in a wise and prudent discretion. What would be judicious to do under some circumstances and at some particular period, might under other circumstances be highly injudicious. Is it judicious at this time for the city just beginning a new career in its municipal form of government, its people not yet familiar with its requirements and needs, with many things more needed than beautifying individual localities to such beauty into the expenditure of ten thousand dollars or more which has no practical benefit to the public beyond getting rid of these old buildings and improving the looks of that locality. There are many ways that ten thousand dollars can be spent for the benefit and convenience of the whole people, better than beautifying any particu-

The community here have put up with those unsightly buildings for many years, and prospered. Isn't it more judicious for them to put up with them for a year longer or until the legislature passes a betterment law by which a part at least of the cost of such improvements as parks and squares can be assessed upon those in the immediate vicinity who are especially benefited? It certainly seems so to me.

Will the convenience of the public be greater? To people passing up and down Market or Wakefield, above or below these streets there can be no convenience or inconvenience by having a square instead of these buildings; and to those going to or from Wakefield and Market either way, they have a shorter and better way with the present thoroughfare in front of the hotel. I can see no difference in going round a building and going round a square. It resolves itself after all into a matter of looks. But granted that the removal of these buildings would improve the appearance of the locality, and I do not deny the fact that it would, is it a judicious time to bring about this improvement, is it not adding to the city debt too [illegible] the [illegible] of its business interest

people and their pocket books.
The city debt not including the old town debt of about fifty thousand dollars is already $200,000 dollars for its Water Works; an appropriation of $65,000 for Sewerage has been voted, with the almost certain probability of being increased $25,000 more before its completion. this "Dodge" purchase calls for $10,000 now and $5000 or $3000 more for prospective improvements for building fountains or statuary. and the same influences which are pushing this scheme so persistently. are foreshadowing another raid on the tax payers for a $100,000 City Hall and Opera House at the corner of Hanson street. Here we have a probable debt of quite $400,000 looming up before the city in the immediate future. and this too on a valuation of less than 4,000,000. Will not such a present and prospective debt as this do more to deter business men from locating in the city than all the efforts of the board of trade can offset! Isn't it about time to cry halt for a year or two! Isn't it better to put our streets and highways which all the people use, in complete condition before we indulge in parks and squares and City Halls and Opera

of the people ask for? Cannot we afford to wait a few years for such improvements however commendable rather than saddle the city with an unreasonable debt, and burden the people with excessive taxation to pay the interest!
Another objection I have to this purchase is, that the council made no effort to avail itself of the statute to obtain the property at a more reasonable price than ten thousand dollars. Chapter 40 Section 6 of the laws of 1891 says "Whenever any town cannot obtain any land required for public use (presumably for a reasonable price) such land may be taken. the damages assessed and the same remedies and proceedings had as in case of laying out highways."
If as the preamble to the resolution recites "the public interests and convenience require" this property, proper efforts should have been made to acquire it either by contract at a reasonable price or as the above section points out. Has any such effort been made! The council are the agents of the people chosen to do the public business for the best interest of the city, as their unbiased judgement may dictate and common prudence for their individual reputation should make them [illegible] careful that no

by any possibility attach to their action. Is ten thousand dollars a reasonable price for the property for the purposes for which it is "required" or for any business purposes for which it is available? I have asked this question of several of the leading business men in the city and they invariably have said, it is more than it is worth. The lot contains approximately about 5000 square feet, which is equivalent to $2 per square foot. Nobody considers the buildings of any value. They would barely pay for their removal and clearing up the ground. The lot is irregular in shape and consequently not so valuable for a business block. It is true the property as it stands to day pays a fair rental on the sum asked but remove the buildings by fire or otherwise would any business man with the necessary capital to erect a block, be wise to give ten thousand dollars for the land for permanent improvements? I doubt it very much. I know of but one to whom such an investment might appear judicious and he is the present proprietor of Dodge's Hotel and his decision might and probably would be contingent somewhat upon the rights the city may have in the passage way in front of his hotel; anyway this passageway is an important factor to any one else buying

legal authority on behalf of the city examined the title and boundaries of this property. If there has been I have not heard it mentioned in the council. Has the city Solicitor the chosen advisor of the council been asked to give an opinion upon this matter or been consulted officially regarding it? Does any member know of his own knowledge or has he sought to know whether or not the city is already the owner of some parts of it. If he or they have I have not heard it mentioned here where it properly should be known. The last deed of these lands was executed June 25 189[illegible] less than two months ago and four days after this resolution was first introduced into this body. This deed (which is a quitclaim) gives no more definite starting point other than, "Beginning at the corner of Wakefield Street and Central Square." What the width of Wakefield street is at this point becomes an important question in connection with the property, and would require a thorough examination of the old town records as far back as 1740 probably. One of the oldest citizens of the city who has known this property for sixty years, says that the part occupied by John B [illegible] encroaches upon Wakefield street a number of feet.

Wakefield street would seem to confirm this opinion. Any way it would be a sensible thing to find out before buying something the city already owns. A well read lawyer has raised the point whether the omission of "metes and bounds" in the resolution itself may not complicate the title, and whether the council having voted a section or to purchase and take a deed without such provision being first mentioned in the resolution, the present owner may not be at liberty to convey more or less than is vaguely understood and make restrictions and the city be obliged to accept or pay damages. I am no lawyer but the point is worth considering. Again I cannot bring myself to believe it is right or just, or good policy at this time that a majority of the tax payers of the city should be compelled to pay for a benefit which is at best but a benefit to a few fortunate real estate owners in the immediate vicinity. The outside community have been generous in the past in complying with the appropriations for water works, street lights, fire department, sewerage, police protection and many other things incident to the compact parts of the city, but I doubt very much if it is proper or just that they should be assessed to pay for "the love of the beautiful" of the few who [illegible]

and if I am any judge of public opinion as expressed daily on the streets there is a very respectable number of the tax payers of this village itself who do not approve this expenditure of the peoples money while outside this village there is hardly a voice to commend it. And well may the public hesitate to commend this project when they consider the undue haste with which it has been enacted; for it was proposed, the ordinances suspended and the resolution passed in less time than it requires to read it. No deliberation, no suggestion as to its future use, no discussion upon its merits, no hint given of any possible or probable complication by reason of adverse interest of any one, not a twentieth part of the time given the consideration of spending ten or twelve thousand dollars that was given the matter of whether John Smart should build an addition to his stable or another party should build one with brick walls or sheet iron, and the other fact: that the whole thing has been worked up by a few individuals and plainly in the interest of a few individuals, and which when completed will doubtless be a very pretty front lawn for a popular hotel. Will the people look upon such ill considered methods and hasty legislation, if it and confidence. better infinitely better that the whole matter should be wiped out and started anew, than it should be tainted with even the suspicion of "jobery" or rest under the cloud of being pushed through in the interests of any person or persons. No man in this city has less personal selfish considerations of economy in the city affairs than myself and I would gladly approve of any and every scheme that would benefit my native place. But as Mayor it is my duty as it is my inclination, to protect so far as I can those who are differently constituted or conditioned. this I shall do while I hold the honorable position of mayor, uninfluenced by any private spleen or prejudice. With these views I cannot consistently approve of the action of a majority of the council in this matter. I have arrived to this conclusion after careful thought and a sincere desire to do my duty as I see it. I am well aware that I am going counter to the wishes of some citizens who are friends to me and for whose opinions I have great respect. I shall be censured and criticised by some but I am content to trust to the sober judgement of the people for approval or disapproval of these objections to this resolution.

Charles S. Whitehouse
Mayor

Rochester N. H.
August [illegible]

After reading the message councilman Warren moved that the resolution be reconsidered. councilman Barker moved that the resolution lay on the table. the mayor declared councilman Barkers motion as not in order. councilman Flagg seconded Warrens motion and the affirmative being called for the motion was declared carried. After a recess of ten minutes, moved by councilman Barker that the resolution pass the mayors veto to the contrary notwithstanding, and that this matter lay on the table until the next meeting. ~~[illegible]~~.

On motion of councilman Duncan voted that when we adjourn we adjourn to one week from next Tuesday night Aug 30. at 7-30 o'clock.

Petition of S. B. Folsom and others for an electric light on Cohn street, referred to the committee on Street Lights. *Petition of S. B. Folsom and others for Street light*

The committee on roads bridges and drains asked for more time to consider the petition of A. R. Reed and others, granted.

The committee on bills in their second reading made the following report on the amendment to chapter XXXIII of the General Ordinances. *Com on bills in their 2nd reading report on amendment to Gen Ordin*

"The committee on bills in their second reading report that the above amendment is in proper form. Charles S. Barker Com
Ivan S. Horne

that the amendments be adopted and market. Committee on the purchase of Dodge property asked for further time which was granted. Claim of J. G. Morrill & Co for damage on account of alleged defect in the highway referred to a special committee consisting of the city solicitor councilmen Horn and Pagent. *Claim of J. G. Morrill for damage*

Claim of Joshua G. Hall for $ — referred to the special committee appointed at a previous meeting to investigate the claim. *Claim of J. G. Hall*

Estimate for sidewalks on Market and Portland Streets taken from the table. Voted that the plans and grades for the sidewalks as presented by the civil engineer be adopted as the plans of the city. Voted to adjourn to the time specified. *Adoption of plans and grade of sidewalks Portland and Market St*

A true record

Attest

Chas. W. Brown

City Clerk

City of Rochester August 30 1892

Adjourned meeting of the city council met as per adjournment. The mayor in the chair. The following councilmen responded to the roll call. Allen and Tibbetts of Ward one Duncan Willand and Horn of Ward two, Bickford Flagg and Warren of Ward three Pagett Bickford and Josselyn of Ward four Varney Waldron and Dodge of Ward five Whitehouse Barker and Woodward of Ward six. Record of last meeting read and approved. The committee to whom was referred the claim of Joshua G. Hall made the following report.

To the Mayor and Council of the City of Rochester

The committee to whom was referred the claim of Joshua G. Hall for salaries and services rendered as attorney for the water works having considered his claim are of opinion that payment for a part or all of the same could be enforced against the city and would respectfully recommend its adjustment.

John W. Tibbetts

Chas. L. Woodward

Simon L. Horn

The committee to whom was referred the claim of Abbie Whitehouse for alleged injuries to her arm by reason of defective highway having attended to their duties, report that in their opinion the claimant will accept the sum of thirty dollars in full settlement.

Report of committee on claim Abby Whitehouse

Your committee further understand that immediately after the alleged injuries were received the road in the vicinity of the accident was extensively repaired which of not and admission of its lack of repair at the time of the accident has invariably proved an element of weakness for the defendent in the trial of this class of actions. Your committee in view of all the facts recommend the payment of such sum not exceeding thirty dollars as will effect a settlement of this case.

C. H. Willard
Joseph Warren
B. C. Cochrane

On motion voted to refer to the same committee for adjustment. The committee on Fire department made the following report.

"The committee to whom was referred the matter of Ezekiel Wentworth in regard to his

Report of Committee on Wentworth

Mayor who is governed by the laws of the State see that the City Ordinances is complied with by the said Wentworth.

C. Josselyn for the committee on Fire Dept.

On motion voted that the report be placed on file, and that the Mayor see that the ordinances in relation to this matter be enforced. The mayor brought before the council several bills for expenditures on side walks in Lorraine which the committee on claims and accounts had declined to approve. On motion voted that the committee on claims and accounts be instructed to approve these bills.

Mayor instructed to see the laws are enforced

Committee on claims and accounts instructed to approve bills on sidewalk at Lorraine

On motion of councilman Barker voted that the motion to pass the resolution for the purchase of the Dodge property over the mayors veto be continued on the table to the next meeting.

Motion to purchase Dodge property continued on the table

On motion voted to adjourn for one week to Sept. 6th.

A true record
Attest Charles W. Brown
City Clerk

City of Rochester

September 6th 1892

The council met as per adjournment with the mayor in the chair

The following named councilmen responded to the roll call. Tebbetts and Richards of ward one

Duncan and Willand of ward two

Bickford and Flagg of ward three.

Pugsley Bickford and Jesselyn of ward four.

Varney Waldron and Dodge of ward five

Philbrick Barker and Woodward of ward six.

Hoxie of ward two and Warren of ward three joined the council later in the evening

Minutes of the last meeting read and approved.

The mayor read the following communication from Hon Wm. E. Chandler

Waterloo N. H. Sept 1. 1892 — *Letter from W. E. Chandler*

To Mayor Whitehouse

and the City Government of Rochester

Gentlemen

Not the least of my pleasures on the occasion of the unveiling of the Hale statue at Concord on August third was the presence of the delegation from Rochester, Mr Hale's birthplace. The ceremony would have been incomplete without some recognition by Rochester of her interest in the memory of her most distinguished son who ever [illegible]

and old Strafford county with an[illegible] affection. Please accept my grateful thanks for your contribution to the success of the ceremonial, and believe me to be with sentiments of the highest respect

Your obedient Servant

W. E. Chandler

It was ordered that the communication be placed on file. Petition of J. C. Nichols and two others for an electric light on Prospect St referred to committee on street lights. *Petition of J. C. Nichols for an electric light*

Petition of Kessel Fire Brick Company for the [illegible] and extension of Orchard street. referred to committee on Roads Bridges and Drains. *Petition of Kessel Fire Brick Co [illegible]*

Petition of Peter Poisson and 37 others for a sidewalk on the southerly side of Tebbetts lane referred to committee on Roads, Bridges and Drains. *Petition for sidewalk on Tebbetts lane*

The committee on water works asked for permission to lay a small pipe on Maple Street in Gonic to extend about eight hundred and fifty feet from the main pipe *Permission to water com. to lay a small pipe*

On motion of Councilman Dodge voted that the request of the water committee be granted. a request that the committee on Street lights look up the old street lights and place some price on them, was referred to the committee on street lights. *Committee on Street lights to look up the old street lamps*

The following communication from the board

Mayor and ~~City~~ Council of the City of Rochester N.H.

We respectfully represent that the Board of Health having directed the Street Commissioner to flush or wash out all the sewers now in use in said City, and having been informed by him that proper hose for that purpose has been denied him by the Chief Engineer of the Fire Department, and that he is unable to comply with the order.

We regard the order given to the Street Commissioner as conducive to the continued good health of the public and having in view the strict sanitary conditions observed by other cities having in view the dreaded approach of cholera and other contagious diseases. We recommend to the City Council such action as will enable the street commissioner to comply with the order at the earliest possible moment.

Rochester N.H. Sept. 5 1892

J. S. Daniels
D. L. Stokes
C. P. Twombly
} Board of Health

On motion of councilman Barker voted that the Chief Engineer turn over to the Street Commissioner [illegible] hose.

On motion of councilman Barker voted that the motion to pass the resolution to [illegible]

Communication from B. of Health

mayors veto be now taken from the table

Recess of 15 fifteen [illegible] was declared, after the council was called to order on the question shall the motion to pass the resolution the mayors veto to the contrary notwithstanding prevail, the yeas and nays were ordered with the following result. Yea Councilmen Tebbets Richards [illegible] Willand Sloane [illegible] [illegible] Varney Waldron Dodge Kimball Barker and Woodward 13

Nay Bickford of Ward three Clegg Warren and Bickford of Ward 4. 4

The necessary two thirds having voted in the affirmative, the resolution to purchase the Dodge property was passed over the mayors veto

Passage of the resolution to purchase Dodge property over the mayors veto

Resignation of Chas H. Seavey as supervisor of check list was read and accepted.

Resignation of Chas Seavey as supervisor

The committee on Roads Bridges and Drains made the following report.

To the Mayor and Council of the City of Rochester. The committee to whom was referred the petition of [illegible] Reed and others for a new highway leading from Pine Street in an easterly direction on the easterly side of Tebbetts avenue

Respectfully [illegible] [illegible] [illegible]

[illegible] [illegible]

Report of com. on the petition for new highway

On motion of Councilman Barker voted to lay the report on the table.

Moved by councilman Dodge that a special committee of three on Sidewalks be elected by the City Council to [illegible] the [illegible] of the appropriation on sidewalks — [illegible]

after some discussion the motion was laid on the table, and on motion voted to proceed to ballot for supervisor of check list in place of Chas [illegible] resigned — Election of Supervisor

Whole no of ballots	17
[illegible]	2
Stephen D Wentworth	15

and Stephen D Wentworth was declared elected.

On motion of councilman Barker voted to adjourn to one week from tonight Sept 15 at 7 30 o clock.

A true record

Attest Chas W Brown

City Clerk.

City of Rochester

September 15 1892

The City Council met tonight as per adjournment with the mayor in the chair.

The following councilmen were present

Allen and Richards of Ward one

Duncan Willand and Ham of ward two

Bickford and Warren of ward three

Bickford and Josselyn of ward four

Varney Walcher and Dodge of ward five

Philbrick Barker and Woodward of ward six.

Record of the last meeting read and ordered to be corrected so as to read "laid on the table" instead of "the motion was withdrawn" having reference to the motion of councilman Dodge that a special committee of three on sidewalks be elected. — Correction of record of last meeting

Petition of Chas S Barker for permission to temporarily obstruct a portion of the sidewalk on Railroad Ave and Main Street in contemplating building on his premises near the junction of the above named streets. — Petition of [illegible] to obstruct sidewalk

On motion of councilman Dodge voted that the petition be granted.

The following report of the committee on Roads Bridges and Drains — Report of Com on [illegible]

Fire Brick Company for the opening of Orchard St. would recommend that a hearing be held by the council

Joseph Warren
Geo A. Bickford
Chas W. Allen

On motion of Councilman Barker voted the report be laid on the table

The same committee made the following report. Report of [illegible]

The committee on Roads Bridges and Drains to whom was referred the petition of Peter Poison and 27 others for sidewalk on Ribbetts Ave have attended to their duty and report that in their opinion all that is necessary is to have the sidewalks graded which can be done at a small expense

Joseph Warren
Chas W. Allen
Geo A. Bickford

On motion of Councilman Dodge voted the report be accepted.

Report of Com on Fire Department on Engine House at [illegible]

The committee on Fire Department made the following report:

"The committee on Fire Dept. wish to report that the Engine House at [illegible] is considered by them dangerous as regards to fire that windows have been put in so very close to chimneys, windows high as the chimney and think that there is great danger of fire and suggest that the committee on public that in their [illegible] will make building safe

to Jossely.. } Committee
George A. Bickford }

Referred to committee on Public buildings.

Report of Com on Street Lights on petition of J. B. Folsom

The following report from the committee on Street Lights was read

Your committee to whom was referred the petition of J. B. Folsom and 36 others have attended to their duty and would recommend that a light be placed at the corner of Jennes St instead of the upper end of the hollow as asked in the petition

John D. Philbrick
Simeon L. Hoar

On motion of Councilman Dodge voted that the report be accepted.

Petition of Simeon Bros for removal of sign

Petition of Simeon Bros and others for the removal of the livery stable sign from the corner of Main and Congress streets was read and referred to a special committee consisting of Councilmen Woodward Varney and Willand.

Claim of Theresa S. Hussey for damages

Claim of Theresa S. Hussey for damages on account of alleged defect in the Highway referred to the special committee consisting of the City Solicitor Councilmen Warren and Willand

Report of Com on [illegible]

Councilman Philbrick of the committee on Street Lights reported

93 Glass tops. and 82 wire frames and
9 iron posts.

On motion of councilman Dodge voted that further time be granted the committee to obtain prices &c.

The committee to purchase Dodge property made the following report — *Report of comm. to purchase the Dodge property*

"Your committee that was directed to take the deeds of the Dodge property so called of Mrs Daniel Hall of Dover and also of J. Thorne Dodge of Rochester have attended to that duty, and that the deeds are now ready to be delivered to the city of Rochester."

J. D. Philbrick } Committee
D. B. Waldron }

Moved by Councilman Barker that *acceptance of deeds of the Dodge property* the deeds presented by the committee on purchasing the Dodge property on Central Square be accepted by the city and that the same be paid for at once and in connection with the motion the following resolution was introduced.

Resolved by the city council of the city of Rochester.

Sec 1 That the deed presented by J. Thorne Dodge *Resolution in relation to the deeds* be accepted by the city of Rochester as the deed intended to convey to said city the land lying between Wakefield St. Market St. Dodge's Hotel and land of Sophia D. Hall.

City council hereby tender to J. Thorne Dodge a vote of thanks for the above conveyance

The motion prevailed and the resolution passed.

On motion of councilman Barker voted that *Electric lights to be placed in rooms of Supt of water works.* the committee on Street lights be instructed to have electric lights placed in the room occupied by the Sewerage committee and Supt of water works.

Voted that the committee on Roads Bridges and Drains be requested to examine into the condition of the guide posts throughout the city. *Guide Posts*

The following resolution introduced by councilman Barker

Resolution for changing the plans adopted *Resolution to change plan for outlet of Sewerage* by the city of Rochester for an outlet for sewerage at Walkers bridge

Resolved by the City Council of the City of Rochester.

That so much of the plan for sewerage for the Village of Rochester as contemplated an outlet for sewerage at Walkers Bridge the same having been already abandoned by the special committee on sewerage be eliminated from the plan for sewerage for Rochester Village and that the outlet for the same be at some point where it will not interfere with the rights of the

On motion of Councilman Willand voted that the rules be suspended and that the resolution pass.
On motion of councilman Barker voted that we adjourn to three weeks from tonight Oct 4th at 7.30 o'clock

A true record
Attest Chas W. Brown
City Clerk

City of Rochester N.H.
October 4th 1892

Council met as per adjournment with the Mayor in the chair.
Roll of council called and the following responded.
Tibbetts and Richards of Ward one
Duncan Willand and Ham of Ward two
Pickford Flagg & Warren of Ward three
Pickford and [illegible] of ward four
Waldron and Hodge of ward five.
Hitchcock and Woodward of ward six.
Allen of ward one & Varney of ward five and Barker of ward six
Joined the council before the transaction of business.

Petition of G. C. Foss and others for an electric light on Seward street read and referred to committee on street lights — *Petition of G. C. Foss for Electric Light*

Petition of [illegible] Salinger et al. for permission to erect an addition to the rear of the McDuffee Block. On motion of councilman Woodward voted that the petition be granted. — *Petition of [illegible] Salinger et al. for permit. Granted*

Resignation of John [illegible] as supervisor of check list — *Resignation*

Thomas H. Gotts had 6 | Selection of Supervisor
Joseph V. Hayes 10

and Joseph V Hayes was declared elected.

Resignation of Arthur A. Brach as clerk in ward two read and accepted. On motion voted to proceed to ballot for clerk in ward two. | Resignation of clerk in ward 2

Whole number of ballots cast 16 | Selection of clerk in ward two
Eugene C Ross had 6
Albert L Hall 10

and Albert L Hall was declared elected.

The following named were appointed and confirmed as inspectors for the several wards | Appointment of inspectors

	Republicans	Democrats
Ward 1	James M. Wilder	Joseph Shaw
	George H Knap	James Dixon
Ward 2	Royal M Sargent	W. F. Emmons
	Henry L. Osborn	Chas. H Leave
Ward 3	Stephen B Seaton	C D Potter
	Chas H. Barkley	Frank P Preston

The following resolution presented by councilman Josselyn.

Be it resolved by the city council of the city of Rochester.

That the Selectmen of the several wards where there are no regular polling places be ordered to provide the same. | Selectmen to prepare polling places

On motion of councilman Dodge voted the resolution pass.

Letter read from Globe Gas Light Co making an offer for the old lamp posts lanterns &c.

On motion it was voted that the disposition of the old street lamps and posts be left with the committee on street lights to dispose of to the best advantage to the city. | Sale of old street lights left to committee

Bill of Vernon Horn

taken from the table
Councilman Barker seconded the motion of councilman Dodge the mayor ruled the motion as not in order. Councilman Barker appealed from the decision of the chair the yeas and nays being called the result was as follows. To sustain the mayors decision Yea Councilmen Allen Abbott. Richards Duncan Stone Bickford of ward three Clapp. Wilson Bickford of ward four Josselyn 10
Nay Councilmen Millard. Varney Dodge: Chelbrook Barker and Woodward 6
and the mayors decision was sustained.

Appeal from the mayors decision

The city engineer made the following estimate for the extension of Abbott St sewer to connect with brick sewer on Main St. E. Rochester =

Engineers estimate of cost of sewer at E. Rochester.

200'	12" Pipe	@	.25	50.
200'	6" do		.09	18.
2	Manholes		30.00	60.
2	Catch Basins		20.00	40.
Laying 200'	12" Pipe		.45 ft	90.
200	6"	"	.30 "	60
				318

Rochester N.H. Oct. 4. 1892

that the sum not exceeding $318. be and is hereby appropriated from and out of any money not otherwise appropriated for the extension of Abbott St. proposed sewer at East Rochester. the same being designed to connect with the existing sewer on Main street.

Resolution Extend Abbott St. Sewer E. Roch.

Referred to committee on bills in their second reading with leave to retire for examination and report at this meeting.
On motion of councilman Dodge voted that the engineers report and estimate of cost of sidewalks for Portland and Market Streets be accepted and that the sidewalk be built in accordance with the plan as presented by the city engineer.

Vote to build sidewalks on Portland and Market Street

On motion of councilman Dodge voted that when we adjourn we adjourn to two weeks from tonight Oct. 18th and on motion of councilman Barker voted to adjourn.

A true record
Attest: Chas. W. Brown
City Clerk.

City of Rochester
October 18 1892

Adjourned meeting of the city council called to order by the Mayor.
The following councilmen were present.
Allen of ward one
Duncan Willand and Horn of Ward two,
Bickford and Warren of ward three.
Pratt and Josselyn of ward four.
Varney Waldron an Dodge of Ward five.
Philbrick Parker and Woodward of Ward six.
Record of last meeting read and approved.

Petition of C. H. Demeritt and others for an electric light on Walnut street referred to the committee on street lights, — *Petition of C.H. Demeritt for El. Light*

Petition of D. W. Gerrish and others for a new Highway from Portland to Leonard street; referred to committee on Roads, Bridges & Drains. — *Petition of D.W. Gerrish for Street*

The committee on street lights made the following report.
"Your committee to whom was referred the petition of Eugene Foss and four (4) others have attended to their duty and would recommend that the request of the petitioners be granted.
John D. Philbrick
Simon L. Horn.
Voted that the petition be granted. The committee to whom — *Street light voted for [illegible]*

asked for further time to consider which was granted.

On motion of councilman Philbrick voted that the thanks of the council be extended to Sophia D. Hall for her generous gift of Five Hundred dollars for the improvement of the Dodge property, recently purchased by the city. — *Vote of thanks to Sophia D Hall*

On motion of councilman Warren voted that a committee of three be appointed to investigate the matter of Winter street. one to be from the committee on Roads Bridges and Drains. one from Committee on Shade Trees. Parks and Commons. and one other councilman. they to investigate and report at some future meeting. — *Committee to investigate Winter street*

The mayor appointed councilmen Warren Willand and Josselyn as that committee.

The Special committee on the petition of Pineman Bass made the following report. — *[illegible] removed*

The committee to whom was referred the within petition would report that the said Livery Stable sign has been removed satisfactory to the petitioners.
Chas. E. Woodward
C. H. Willand
I. H. Varney

the following resolution.

Be it resolved by the city council of the City of Rochester, — *Resolution to ______ Smart*

That the sum of two dollars be paid to John U Smart to recompense him for moving his sign.

Referred to committee on bills in their second reading.

On motion of Councilman Barker voted to proceed to elect a janitor in place of Geo. S. Welley deceased. — *Election of janitor*

Whole no of ballots 12
James Coyle had 12

and was declared elected.

A. S. Hall having declined to serve as clerk in ward two, on motion of Councilman Duncan voted to proceed to elect. — *Election of clerk in ward two*

Whole no. of votes 14
Eugene ______ 2.
Mike Donahue 3
George V Severance 9

and Geo. V Severance was declared elected.

On motion of Councilman Dodge voted that when we adjourn we adjourn to one week from tonight October 25.

On motion of Councilman Duncan voted to adjourn to the time specified.

A true record
Attest Chas. M. Brown

Mayors Office
City of Rochester
October 20 1892

To
Chas. M. Brown

You will please notify the city councilmen that a special meeting of the council will be held at the council Rooms Saturday evening October 22 1892 at 7 30 p.m. to consider the matter of sewerage by reason of the refusal of the contractor to complete his contract.

Chas. S. Whitehouse
Mayor

Agreeably to the above order the following notice was sent to each member of the council.

Rochester N H Oct. 20 1892

There will be a meeting of the City Council at their room on Saturday evening October 22 1892 at 7 30 o'clock p.m.

Business. Matter of Sewerage.

Per order of the Mayor
Chas. M. Brown
City Clerk.

City of Rochester
October 22 1892

The council met in accordance with the foregoing notice. The mayor in the chair. order of the mayor and notice of the meeting was read

The following councilmen responded to the roll call.
Duncan and Weiland of ward two.
Flagg and Warren of ward three
Bickford of ward four
Varney Woodson and Dodge of ward five
Barker and Woodward of ward six.

Councilman Barker chairman of the committee on Sewerage read the following communication.

Communication from Jos Bruno

To Chas. S. Barker J. Thomas Dodge and John D. Philbrick Sewerage committee of the city of Rochester.

I hereby notify you that I am unable to proceed further with the work of putting in the sewers of the city of Rochester, and have stopped work thereon.

Dated Oct 19 - 1892 Joseph Bruno

After some remarks by Councilman Barker in relation to the Sewerage councilman [illegible] called Mr Bruno. It was voted a recess be taken during the reading of the contract.

After the reading of the same It was moved by Councilman Varney. that the committee on Sewerage be requested to confer with Mr Bruno or any other contractor, and see if any plan for the completion of the sewerage can be devised. and report at the meeting next Tuesday evening. and the motion prevailed. Voted to adjourn.

Sewerage committee to confer with Bruno and report

A true record
attest Chas W Brown
City Clerk

City of Rochester
October 25-1892

City council met this evening as per adjournment with the mayor in the chair.

The following named councilmen responded to the roll call.

Ward one Allen Abbotts and Richards.
Ward two Duncan Maitland and Stover
Ward three Bickford and Warren
Ward four Pageott Bickford and Josselyn.
Ward five Varney and Dodge
Ward six Woodward
Dodge of ward five. Philbrick and Parker of ward six joined the council later in the evening.

Minutes of last regular meeting and also special meeting read and approved.

Petition of Martha A Jones to put a wooden addition on the rear of the store occupied by Martin L. Luce and referred to committee on fire department. — *Petition Martha A Jones to make addition to Luce store*

The committee on Roads Bridges and Drains made the following report. — *Report of Com on petition of D W Daniels for street*

Rochester October 25-1892

The committee to whom was referred the petition of D W Daniels and others for a highway from Portland street to Summer street would recommend that a hearing

Joseph Warren | Committee
George A Bickford | on Roads
Chas. W. Allen | Bridges drains

On motion of councilman Duncan voted that the report of the committee be accepted and adopted.

Resignation of C E Sampson as selectman in ward five read and accepted and on motion proceeded to ballot to fill the vacancy. — *Selection of Selectman in ward five*

Whole No of Ballots 13
H V Sanborn had 13

and was elected

Committee on bills in their second reading made the following report.

Report of committee on bills on second reading, on resolution appropriating money for extension of sewer pipe at East Rochester. — *Passage of resolution of appropriation to Rochester sewer*

The committee on bills in their second reading report that the above resolution is in proper form

Chas. S. Parker | Committee
Simon L. Stover | on bills in
Cyril Pageott | Second reading

The resolution having had two separate readings, on motion of councilman Warren voted that the resolution pass.

the same committee was read.

Report of committee on bills in their second reading on resolution to pay John O Smart two dollars.

The committee on bills in their second reading report that the above resolution is in proper form

Chas S Parker } Committee
Simon L Horn } on bills
Cyrille Pageotte } in second reading

The resolution having had two separate readings, on motion was passed.

Voted that the committee on public buildings be authorized to let the unoccupied rooms in the Dodge building and the city clerk to collect the rents. — *authorized D W Dodge building*

The mayor appointed Silas H Dame as weigher of hay and coal and surveyor of wood also appointed Frank M Carson as constable both appointments were confirmed by the council. — *Appointment S H Dame*

A Recess was declared during the session of the water committee.

After calling the council to order councilman Parker read the following communication from Joseph Bruno. — *Bruno's bill to complete sewers*

To Chas S Parker, Drew B Dyer and John W Dirilrick, sewerage committee of the city council of the city of Rochester N.H.

of Boston Mass make the following proposition for the completion of the sewerage system of said city of Rochester to wit

I will lay the pipes at the following prices per linear foot to wit:

18 in pipe at	90 cents
15 " " "	90
12 "	90
10 " "	60
8 "	50 "
6 " "	40
4 "	25 "

I will construct the manholes at two & 50/100 dollars per perpendicular foot. I will blast the rocks at four dollars per cubic yard

Joseph Bruno

I will lay the pipes wherever they are to be laid at or above the water line at the following rates per linear foot.

18 in pipe at	50 cts
15 " " "	47 "
12 " " "	47
10	40
8 " "	38 "
6 "	28 "
4 " " "	25

and wherever the pipe is to be laid below the water line I will lay it at double .... [illegible]

water line I mean the lower side of pipe
is at the said water line
I will construct the manholes at two [illegible]
dollars per perpendicular foot.
I will blast the rock at four dollars per cubic
yard.
Dated at Rochester Oct 22 1892
Joseph Bruno
Thos. McShanahan

Figures for this work from [illegible] to the
council.

Councilman Warren presented the
following resolution,

Resolved by the City
council of Rochester — Resolution
That, whereas Joseph Bruno — to suspend
contractor for laying Sewerage pipe in Rochester — work on the
having refused to complete the same according to — Sewer
his contract entered into with the city and
having ceased work on the same it is hereby

Willard Horn Bickford of ward three [illegible]
[illegible]ford of ward four Josselyn 9
Nays. Councilmen Duncan Pagett Dodge
Philbrick Barker and Woodward 6
So the resolution was carried
Moved by councilman Barker that the committee on Sewerage be discharged from any further
work on the sewerage the motion did not
prevail.

On motion of councilman Josselyn — Petition of
voted that the petition of Martha A Jones — Martha A Jones
be taken from the committee on Fire Depart- — granted
ment and considered at this time
On motion voted that the prayer of the
petitioner be granted
On motion of councilman Josselyn voted
that we adjourn to two weeks from tomorrow
night November 9th

A true record
Attest Chas. M. Brown
City Clerk

City of Rochester
November 9th 1892

City council met to night as per adjournment with the mayor in the chair

Roll called to which the following councilmen responded.
Allen Abbott and Richards ward one
Duncan Willand and Storm ward two
Bickford and Stagg of ward three
Josselyn of ward four
Varney Waldron and Dodge of ward five
Barker and Woodward of ward six
Chadwick of ward six joined the council before the transaction of business.

Record of last meeting read and approved

On motion of councilman Dodge voted that further work on Portland and Market Street sidewalks be deferred for the present — *Work on sidewalk suspended*

On motion of councilman Dodge voted that the unexpended balance appropriated to purchase the city team be used to purchase a single harness and set of sleds, and any deficit therefor be paid from appropriation to the miscellaneous departments — *Purchase sleds and harness*

On motion of councilman Barker voted that the mayor tender to Mr Mason the sum of fifty dollars for land — *Tender to Mr Mason*

Winter street.
Councilman Barker presented the following resolution

Resolved by the city council of the city of Rochester.

That the moneys released by released by Biagio Pireo from the assignment made to him by Joseph Bruno being or to become due to said Bruno from the city of Rochester be applied by the committee on sewerage to the payment for labor and materials furnished for the sewerage system of the city of Rochester. But the amounts so applied by them shall not exceed the twenty per cent held in reserve by the city of Rochester in its contract with said Joseph Bruno. And this resolution shall not be construed to in any way impair the contract between the city of Rochester and Joseph Bruno. The labor shall be paid for in full and the materials furnished shall be paid for pro rata from the remainder of the sum due as above and the resolution passed. — *Resolution to pay sewer bills*

On motion voted to proceed to ballot for Supervisor — *Election of Supervisor*

Whole number of ballots	15
Fred C. Small	5
Nahum Berry	10

and Nahum C. Berry was elected.

On motion of councilman Josselyn voted that the committee on report on the lay out of River street whether to be on a curve or straight line.

The city engineer presented two bids for laying sewer at East Rochester one from R D Shanahan and one from Moore & Co.

On motion of councilman Abbotts voted that the committee on sewerage be authorized to sign a contract with Moore & Co to put in sewer at East Rochester according to the plans of the city engineer.

Moore & Co. to construct E. Rochester sewer

Councilman Duncan presented the following amendment to the General ordinances.

Amendment to ordinances

City of Rochester Nov 9th 1892

Be it ordained by the City Council of the City of Rochester;

That chapter nine of the ordinances of the City of Rochester whereby a fire precinct was established be and hereby is repealed.

On motion of councilman Jasselyn voted to adjourn to Tuesday November 22.

A true record

Attest: Chas W. Brown
City Clerk

City of Rochester
November 22 1892

Council met as per adjournment with the mayor in the chair. The following responded to the roll call.

Ward one Abbotts and Richards.

Ward two Duncan Willand and Horne

Ward three Bickford Hogg and Mansion

Ward four Pagett Bickford and Josselyn

Ward five Varney Waldron and Dodge

Ward six Barker and Woodward

Record of last meeting read and approved.

Petition of James Kay to remove tree in front of his house referred to committee on Shade Trees, Parks and Commons.

Claim of Mrs C. H. Bassett for injuries received by a fall on the steps at the High School.

Claim of Mrs C. H. Bassett

On motion of councilman Parker voted to refer to the special committee on claims

The mayor reported he had tendered Mrs Mason fifty dollars in gold for damages from the widening of Winter street which she declined to accept.

Tender to Mrs Mason

Councilman Varney made a verbal report on the claim of Susan Sanborn for land damage. On motion of councilman Dodge voted that the water committee ... to the ...

Claim of Sue Sanborn

judgement

The mayor brought up the matter of supervisors in ward three. Edgar Stone was the Democratic nominee the ballots were printed Edgar J. Stone and he was declared elected no such person living in the ward the office was declared vacant. Councilmen Barker moved that inasmuch as the Democrats failed to elect their supervisor in Ward three that the council proceed to elect one for them.

Supervisor in ward three

Whole number of ballots cast 15

Edgar J. Stone had 15

and was elected.

Councilmen Barker presented the following resolution,

Resolved by the City Council of the City of Rochester.

Appropriation for School Books & Supplies

That the school committee of the City of Rochester be authorized to expend a sum not exceeding two hundred and twenty five dollars in addition to the amount already

Be it resolved by the City Council of the City of Rochester,

That so much of the unexpended money appropriated for the Fire Department as is necessary be used in purchasing a new Hose Wagon for for Hanson Street Engine House.

Moved by Councilman Richards that the rules be suspended and that the resolution pass without reference to a committee the motion did not prevail and the resolution was referred to the committee on bills in their second reading they to report at the next meeting.

On motion of Councilman Warren voted that S. D. Felker be allowed to make some remarks in relation to the street leading from Pine st to Abbott Ave.

On motion of Councilman Barker voted that land damages on the street between Chestnut and Pine streets be referred to committee on Roads Bridges and Drains.

Councilman Richards presented

Highland Street.

The city engineer presented his estimate of the cost of the same.

On motion of councilman Dodge voted that the rules be suspended and the resolution without reference to any committee.

Tax bills of Barrington and Stafford presented and referred to committee on Water works.

Tax bills of Barrington and Stafford

The amendment to the ordinances presented at the last meeting brought up for consideration.

On motion of councilman Josselyn voted that the resolution lay on the table.

On motion of councilman Varney voted that the tax bills of Barrington and Stafford be paid.

On motion of councilman Barker voted to adjourn to one week from tonight.

A true record
Attest Chas. M. Brown
City Clerk

City of Rochester
November 29. 1892

Council called to order by the mayor.
Roll called to which the following responded.
Allen of ward one
Duncan of ward two
Bickford of ward three
Pageau and Josselyn of ward four
Varney of ward five
Woodward of ward six
No quorum being present the council adjourned to Wednesday Dec. 7 at 7.30 o'clock.

A true record
Attest Chas. M. Brown
City Clerk

City of Rochester
December 7. 1892

Council called to order by the mayor.
The following members responded to roll call.
Duncan and Stevens ward two
Bickford and Clapp of ward three
Pageau and Josselyn of ward four
Varney Waldron and Dodge of ward five
Philbrick Barker and Woodward of ward six.
On motion of councilman Barker voted to
[illegible] A true record

City of Rochester
December 8th 1892

Council met at two oclock P.M.
The mayor in the chair
The following councilmen responded to Roll call
Duncan of ward two
Bickford and Blygg of ward three
Pyzotto and Josselyn of ward four
Varney Walden and Dodge of ward five
Philbrick Barker and Woodward of ward six

The mayor stated the object of the meeting to be to canvas the votes for Mayor. The vote as returned by the several ward clerks was referred to the committee on elections. — *Object of Meeting*

The committee on shade trees Parks and Commons made the following report — *Report of Committee on Shade Trees Parks and Commons*

The committee on Shade trees Parks and Commons to whom was referred the petition of James Kay would report that they have examined the tree referred to in said petition and would recommend that the petition be granted,

Chas. E. Woodward } Com.

On motion of councilman Philbrick voted that the report be accepted and the recommendation carried out,

The committee on elections

The undersigned Standing committee on elections ... have this day canvassed the returns of the several ward clerks of the votes cast for Mayor at the Municipal election held December 6th 1892 and find the result to be as follows. — *Report of Committee on Elections*

In Ward one
Robert V Sweet had 69 votes
Orrin H. Hoyt " 121 votes

In Ward two
Robert V Sweet had 68 votes
Orrin H Hoyt had 129 votes

In ward three
Robert V Sweet had 140 votes
Orrin H. Hoyt had 77 votes
Nathaniel Burnham had 1

In Ward four
Robert V. Sweet had 168 votes
Orrin H. Hoyt had 121 votes

In Ward five
Robert V Sweet had 152 votes
Orrin H. Hoyt " 140 votes

In Ward six
Robert V Sweet had 144 vote
Orrin H. Hoyt had 166 votes

and Robert V. Sweet had in all 745 vote
and Orrin H. Hoyt had in all 770 votes
and Nathaniel Burnham had in all 1 vote
and Orrin H. Hoyt has a majority of all the votes cast for mayor, Edward Josselyn Councilman ... of

and the mayor then declared Quin A. Hoyt elected Mayor in the City of Rochester for the ensuing year

Pay of Inspectors.

On motion of councilman Dodge voted that the pay of the election inspectors be twenty cents per hour of actual service

On motion of councilman Josselyn voted to adjourn to Tuesday Dec 20 at 7 30 o'clock p m

A true record

attest Chas W. Brown
City Clerk

City of Rochester
December 12 - 1892

Council met as per adjournment with the mayor in the chair. The following councilmen were present: Bickford of ward three
Bickford and Josselyn of ward four
Varney and Dodge of ward five
Barker of ward six.
No quorum being present the council adjourned to Tuesday Dec 20 - 1892.

Attest

Chas W. Brown City Clerk

City of Rochester
December 20 - 1892

Council called to order by the mayor and on calling the Roll the following responded: Duncan and Willand of ward two
Blagg of ward three
Bickford and Josselyn of ward four
Chadwick & Woodward of ward six.

No quorum being present adjourned to Friday December 23 - 7 - 30 p m.

Attest

Chas W. Brown
City Clerk

City of Rochester
December 20. 1892

Council met tonight as per adjournment with the mayor in the chair. Roll of council called and the following responded:

Ward one Allen
Ward two Willand and Stone
Ward three Bickford and Stagg.
Ward four Josselyn
Ward five Varney Waldron and Dodge
Ward six Philbrick Barker and Woodward

Petition of C. I. [illegible] and others for an electric light in [illegible] referred to committee on street lights. — *Petition for an electric light [illegible]*

S. S. Shaw asked permission to move a building. And on motion of councilman Varney voted that the petition be granted. — *Petition of Shaw to move building*

Communication from the chief engineer in relation to the change of name of some of the fire companies also in relation to pay of clerks treasurers and stewards referred to committee on Fire Department.

The Special committee made the following report. — *Report on claim of J. H. Hanson*

To the Mayor and City Council of the City of Rochester.

The Special committee to which was referred the claim of J. H. Hanson by reason of certain alleged defects and want of repairs in a certain public highway in said city called Prospect street having considered the same would respectfully recommend the payment of the sum of Thirty five dollars in full settlement of the same according to the terms of the bill herewith rendered.

C. M. Willand } Special
G. E. Cochrane } Committee

On motion of councilman Woodward voted that the recommendation be adopted and the bill paid.

On motion of councilman Josselyn voted that the pay roll of Cocheco [illegible] C. Whitehouse [illegible] and [illegible] Harrington [illegible] be paid and that the Steward clerks and treasurer be paid the amount recommended by the chief engineer. — *[illegible]*

The following resolution presented by councilman Barker.

Resolved by the City Council of the City of Rochester.

That the sum of Seventy five dollars is hereby appropriated from the sum already appropriated for miscellaneous expenses to the expense of the department of street lights. — *Appropriation for street lights*

On motion of councilman Dodge voted that the rules be suspended and motion of councilman Verney voted that the resolution pass.

The following resolution presented by councilman Barker,

Resolved by the City council of the City of Rochester,
That the sum of one hundred and twenty five dollars is hereby appropriated from the sum heretofore appropriated for miscellaneous expenses for the expense of the Board of Health.

Appropriation to Board of Health

On motion of councilman Dodge voted that the rules be suspended and that we take action at this time. Whereupon motion of councilman Woodward voted that the resolution pass.

On motion of councilman Barker voted that a special committee be appointed by the mayor to report some necessary changes to be made in the ordinances.

Special Com to Amend Ordinances

The mayor nominated as that committee councilmen Barker, Williams

voted that when we adjourn we adjourn to meet on Tuesday Dec 21st at 7-30 o'clock p.m.

On motion of councilman Woodward voted to adjourn to the time specified.

Attest

Chas. N. Brown

City Clerk

City of Rochester

December 27. 1892

Council met as per adjournment with the mayor in the chair.

Roll of council called to which the following responded

Ward one Allen

Ward two Duncan Willand and Stone

Ward three Bickford Slagg & Warren

" Four Pagent Bickford & Josselyn

" Five Vesey Waldron and Dodge

" Six Woodward

Minutes of last meeting read and approved.

The mayor nominated as the committee to make arrangements for the inauguration ceremonies.

Councilmen Barker of ward 6.

" Waldron of Ward 5

" Josselyn of ward 4

" Bickford of ward 3

" Allen of ward 1.

Committee of arrangements for inauguration

Sub Registrar at East Rochester be paid 10 cents for each death card returned.

Pay of Sub Registrar

The mayor made a verbal statement of the expense he had incurred in securing the adoption of the city charter and asked a reimbursement of $20 for such expenses.

Statement of Mayor in regard to his expenses in securing charter

On motion of Councilman Duncan voted to..

City of Rochester

January 2. 1893

Council met as per adjournment with the mayor in the chair.

The following councilmen responded as their names were called.

Allen Tebbetts & Richards of ward one

Duncan and Stone of ward two

Bickford of ward three

Bickford and Josselyn of ward four

Vesey and Dodge of ward five

Philbrick Barker and Woodward

Record of last meeting read and approved.

The committee on street lights to whom was referred the petition of J. L. Nichols made the following report: "The committee does not recommend this light."

J. D. Philbrick }
Simon L. Stone } Committee

Report of committee on street lights on petition of J. L. Nichols

Also the same committee reported on the petition of C. H. Demerritt and others for an electric light on Walnut St. reported "the committee does not recommend this light."

John D. Philbrick }
Simon L. Stone } Committee

and C. H. Demerritt

The report of the committee

Protest of J. G. Abbott by his attorney J. G. Hall against the emptying of the sewer into Rochester River. — *Protest of J. G. Abbott*

Report of the Sanitary officer read and on motion of Councilman Barker voted to be accepted and placed on file. — *Report of Sanitary Officer*

Report of the overseer of the poor read and voted to be accepted and placed on file.

Report of the Board of Health presented accepted and voted to be placed on file.

Report of the City Solicitor read and voted it be accepted and placed on file.

Councilman Barker presented the following resolution

Resolution for appropriating money for Hydrant Service

Resolved by the City Council of the City of Rochester,

That the sum of six hundred and fifty three dollars and thirty three cents is hereby appropriated from the unexpended balance of the last financial year for the support of the Hydrant Service for the financial year ending Jan 1 1893. On motion of Councilman Barker voted that the resolution pass under a suspension of the rules.

Report of the Committee for establishing the salary of the city [illegible]

establishing the salary of the city civil engineer report that they have consulted with Mr J. Frank Springfield city civil engineer and that they are satisfied that his salary should be sixty cents per hour for services rendered the city — *Report of Committee on [illegible] civil engineer*

Charles S. Barker } Committee
John W. Tibbetts } Salary City Engineer

On motion of Councilman Dodge voted the report be adopted.

On motion of Councilman Barker voted that when we adjourn we adjourn to Tuesday night Jan 3 at 7.30 o'clock

Councilman Barker made a verbal report in relation to the inaugural [illegible]

The following resolution presented by Councilman Barker

Resolved by the City Council of the City of Rochester.

That the sum of two hundred and eighty two dollars and thirty five cents ($282.35) heretofore appropriated for the support of the county poor is hereby appropriated for the support of the city poor. On motion of Councilman Dodge voted that the resolution pass under a suspension of the rules. — *Resolution of appropriation*

On motion of Councilman Dodge voted to adjourn to the time specified.

City of Rochester
January 3 - 1893

Council called to order by the mayor at the hour of adjournment. Roll of the council called to which the following responded. Abbott and Richards of ward one — Duncan and Willand of ward two, Bickford of ward three, Hodgdon of ward four, Varney and Walden of ward five, Barker and Drowne of ward six.

Reports. Report of city physician read. Voted it be accepted and placed on file.

Report of the city marshall presented and voted it be accepted and placed on file.

Report of the clerk of the police court presented accepted and placed on file.

Report of the city [illegible] engineer was accepted and placed on file.

Report of the committee on [illegible] [illegible] and on motion of Councilman Richards voted to accept and place on file.

Report of the city treasurer [illegible] and on motion of Willand voted to

Communication from the chief engineer in relation to pay of the chief clerk of the fire department read, and referred to the committee on fire department.

On motion of Richards voted to adjourn.

Attest.
Chas. W. Brown
City Clerk

City of Rochester
January 4th 1898

The city council met at ten oclock A.M. called to order by the mayor.
The certificates of election of the following councilmen were presented Jas B Stevens ward six
Chas. W. Howe of ward five,
Ernest Duval of ward four.
Geo. W. Robbins of ward two,
Also the vote for mayor was read.

The oath of office was administered to mayor elect O. A. Stoyles by Chas. S. Whitehead justice of the peace and he assumed the duties of his office. The councilmen elect who were present viz Stevens of ward six Howe of ward five Duval of ward four Robbins of ward two came forward and took the oath of office as by law prescribed. — *Oath of office to mayor* — *Qualification of councilmen*

On motion of councilman Barker voted to proceed to the election of clerk.

The mayor appointed councilmen Woodward and Walden as tellers, — *Election of city clerk*

Whole number of votes cast	13
Chas. W. Brown had	13.

and was declared elected, came forward and took the oath as prescribed by law.

Councilman elect Chas. [illegible] Allen of ward one came in and was
[illegible]

On motion of councilman Barker voted to proceed to ballot for a member of the School Board for three years.

Whole number of ballots cast	14	*Election of*
C. C. Woodward	1	*member of*
Dudley B Walden	4	*the School*
Willis McDuffee	9	*Board*

and Willis McDuffee was declared elected a member of the School board for three years.

On motion of councilman Willard voted to proceed to ballot for City marshal.

The vote being disputed the yeas and nays were demanded the voting 7 in favor 4 nay, and the motion of councilman Willard prevailed and the council proceeded to ballot for a marshal

Whole number of ballots cast	14	*Election of*
C. M. D. Hussey	1	*City marshal*
Joseph S. Harris	4	
Chas. W. Sleeper	9	

and Chas. W. Sleeper was declared elected.

On motion of councilman Willard voted to proceed to ballot for an assistant Marshal

Whole number of ballots	10	*Election of asst marshal*
John Burke had	1	
Edgar M. Coats had	9	

and Edgar M. Coats was declared elected

Stevens voted to proceed to ballot for a
night watch, councilman Waldron declined
to serve as teller and the mayor appointed
councilman Rollins to serve in his place

Whole number of ballots cast 8
Chas W Sleeper had 1
Ferdinand Sylvain " 7

no person voting, and the roll being called
and a quorum not present the mayor
declared the council adjourned to meet
at Hayes Opera House at 7.45 this evening.

Attest

Chas W. Brown
City Clerk

City of Rochester.

January 5 1893

The council met at Hayes Opera House
at 7.45 to night a large number of citizens [illegible]
being present The meeting called to order [illegible]
by Ex Mayor Whitehouse who after a few
appropriate remarks, called upon Rev O S Danforth
to offer prayer after the prayer, Mayor Hoyt
was introduced and delivered his inaugural
address after which on motion of councilman
Willand voted to adjourn to Saturday
[illegible]

City of Rochester.

January 7. 1893

City council met as per adjournment with
Mayor Hoyt in the chair
Roll of council called to which the following
named councilmen responded
Ward one Tibbetts Richards and Allen
Ward two Willand Ham and Rollins
Ward six Barker Woodward and Stevens.
9 councilmen present on motion of councilman
Barker voted to adjourn to Friday Jan 13
at 7.30 P M

A true record

Attest Chas. W. Brown
City Clerk

Rochester January 10 1893

Personally appeared Frank
R. Hayes councilman elect from ward
three presented his certificate of election
and took the oath of office as by
law prescribed -

Before me.
Chas W. Brown
Justice of the Peace

City of Rochester

January 13 - 1893

Adjourned Meeting of the City Council [illegible] called to order by the mayor when the following named councilmen answered to their names as the roll was called. Ward one Tebbetts Richards and [illegible] Ward two Walland Stone and Rollin Ward six Barker [illegible] and Stevens. No quorum being present the mayor adjourned the council to Friday January 20 at 7-30 p.m.

A true Record

Attest

Chas W. [illegible]

City Clerk

City of Rochester

January 20 1893

Adjourned meeting of the City Council called to order by the mayor.

Roll of council called to which the following responded. Ward three Slagg [illegible] and Hayes Ward four Bickford [illegible] and [illegible] Ward five [illegible] and [illegible]

No quorum being present the mayor adjourned the meeting to Friday January 27 at 7-30 p.m.

A true Record

Attest

Chas W. Brown

City Clerk

City of Rochester January 27 1893

City Council met tonight as per adjournment with the mayor in the chair.

Roll called to which the following responded.
Ward one Abbott Richards and Allen.
Ward two Willand Hanson and Rollins.
Ward three Flagg Warren and Hayes.
Ward four Bickford Josselyn and Duval
Ward five Waldron Dodge and Howe
Ward Six Barker Woodward and Stevens.

The minutes of previous meetings read and approved.

Communication from E. J. Mathes in relation to Shade trees on Summer St. read and referred to committee on Shade trees Parks and Commons. — Communication of E. J. Mathes

Petition from the fire department for an increase of pay was presented and on motion of Councilman [illegible] voted that the committee appointed to revise the city ordinances be instructed to present an amendment to the council relating to the pay of [illegible]. — Petition for increase of pay Fire Dept.

Petition of [illegible] and others for a new highway at [illegible] Rochester presented and referred to Committee on Highways. — Petition for Highway at [illegible] Rochester

The committee on Finance [illegible]

Resolution of Appropriation.

Resolved by the City Council of the City of Rochester

That the following sums be and hereby are appropriated for the various departments for the ensuing year viz:

For Schools including the amount required by law	18000 [illegible]
For Free Text Books and Supplies	600
" Hydrant Service and Drinking Fountains	4,360
Fire Department	4,500
Highways	8000
Sidewalks	1,000
Salaries	3,300
Miscellaneous Dept	3,000
[illegible] Department	2,000
[illegible] Post G. A. R.	150
East Rochester Free Library	150
Street Lights	6,000
" Dept Sold. Aid and City Poor	1000
" Minor City Officers to be denominated The Political Department	600

County tax, the amount to be assessed by the Assessors.

The State tax and the amount necessary to the payment of notes and interest are provided for and appropriated out of money coming from the State. And that the [illegible] Thousand five hundred raised by taxation, and the balance of any be paid from any money in the treasury not otherwise appropriated.

Rochester January 20 1873

C. H. Hoyle
J. Shaw Dodge
John M. Pebbles.
} Committee on Finance

On motion of Councilman Barker the resolution was read a second time and then it was voted to waive the reference to the committee on Bills in their second reading, and that the resolution pass.

City Solicitor added to the Committee to amend ordinances

On motion of Councilman Barker voted that the City Solicitor be added to the Special committee appointed to amend the ordinances.

The mayor announced the following as the Standing Committees for the ensuing year:

Standing Committees

On Finance

The mayor Dodge and Pebbles

On Shade Trees Parks and Commons

The mayor [illegible] and Woodward

On Public Buildings

Councilmen [illegible] Hayes and Allen.

On Roads Bridges & Drains

Councilmen Stevens Warren and Bickford

On Sewerage

Councilmen Barker Dodge and Stone

On Water Works

Councilmen [illegible] Pebbles and Warren.

On Fire Department

Councilmen [illegible] Barker and Hayes

~~[illegible]~~

On Street Lights

Councilmen Dodge Barker and Hayes

On Printing

Councilmen Woodward Waldron and Rollins

On Adams Street and Old Cemetery Street

Councilmen Richards Bickford & Stevens

The mayor also made the following nominations for Special Police. [illegible] Street. [illegible] [illegible] Wing. Leslie [illegible] ~~Fred E. Wentworth~~ [illegible] James E. [illegible] [illegible] Sidney [illegible] [illegible] Higgins Michael [illegible] [illegible] Charles [illegible] James [illegible] [illegible] W. Daggett. Orvil Leavitt.

Nominations of Special [illegible]

On motion of Councilman Parker voted that the confirmation of the Special Police be deferred one week.

The following officers were appointed and confirmed by the council

Appointments

Sealer of Weights and Measures, [illegible]
Surveyors of wood and Lumber [illegible] [illegible] James [illegible] [illegible] Woodman [illegible] James [illegible] Sidney B. Hayes. [illegible] Ezra [illegible] John [illegible]
Fish and Game Wardens. [illegible] [illegible] ~~Fred E. Wentworth~~
Measurer of ~~Stone~~ [illegible]
Weigher of Hay Straw and Coal [illegible] Albert [illegible] John [illegible]
Field Drivers. [illegible] [illegible] [illegible] and [illegible] Wentworth.
Pound Keeper. John [illegible]

On motion of Councilman [illegible] proceed to ballot for Street Commissioner. The mayor appointed [illegible]:

Whole number of votes	18
[illegible] Wentworth had	1
[illegible] had	5
[illegible] McDuffee had	8

and there was no choice

2nd ballot

Whole number of votes	18
[illegible] Wentworth had	1
[illegible] Hubbard [illegible]	5
Geo. [illegible] McDuffee [illegible]	9

and there was no choice.

[illegible] by Councilman [illegible] that we proceed to new business. On a division of the council 9 voted [illegible] and 9 nay, and the mayor voting in the negative the motion did not prevail. and the council proceeded to the 3rd ballot for St. Commissioner

Election of Street Commissioner

Whole number of ballots	18
[illegible] Wentworth	1
Edward [illegible]	7
Geo. [illegible] McDuffee	10

and Geo. [illegible] McDuffee was declared elected.

On motion of Councilman Parker voted to proceed to ballot for City Solicitor

Election of City Solicitor

Whole number of ballots	18
Leslie [illegible]	1
Geo. [illegible] [illegible] had	17

[illegible] elected

1st ballot for Treasurer.

Whole number of votes	18
Geo D Stowell	1
Simon Wolf had	8
John L Clapp "	9

and there was no choice

2nd Ballot

Whole number of votes cast.	18
Geo D Stowell had	2
Simon Wolf	8
John L Clapp "	8

and there was no choice,

3rd Ballot

Whole number of votes	18
Leslie M Snow had	1
Simon Wolf "	8
John L Clapp	9

and there was no choice.

4th Ballot

Whole number of votes	18
Leslie M Snow had	1
S. Wolf "	8
J L Clapp "	9

and there was no choice

5th Ballot

Whole number of ballots.	18
Leslie P Snow had	1
Simon Wolf	8
John L Clapp	8

6th Ballot.

Whole number of votes cast	18
Leslie P Snow had	1
Simon Wolf	8
J L Clapp	9

and there was no choice

7th Ballot

Whole number of votes cast	18
Leslie P Snow had	1
Simon Wolf had	8
John L Clapp had	9

and there was no choice

8th Ballot

Whole number of votes cast	18.
John L Clapp had	9
Simon Wolf had	9

It being a tie vote the mayor cast his vote for John L Clapp and he was declared elected.

On motion of councilman Storm voted to proceed to ballot for collector of taxes.

Whole number of votes cast	18
S J Wentworth had	1
Wm Ranel had	8
Marvin L Blaisdell had	9

and there was no choice. 2nd Ballot

Whole number of ballots	18
S J Wentworth had	1
Wm Ranel	8

3^d Ballot

Whole number of ballots 18
S. J. Wentworth 1
Wm Rand 8
Marvin S. Blaisdell 9

and there was no choice

4th Ballot

Whole number of votes were 18
S. J. Wentworth had 2
Marvin S. Blaisdell had 8
Wm Rand had 8

and there was no choice.

5th Ballot

Whole number of votes 18
S. J. Wentworth had 1
Wm Rand had 8
Marvin S. Blaisdell had 9

and there was no choice.

6th Ballot

Whole number of votes 18
Wm Rand had 1
S. J. Wentworth " 8
M. S. Blaisdell " 9

and there was no choice

7th Ballot

Whole number of votes 18
Wm Rand had 1
S. J. Wentworth 8
M. S. Blaisdell 9

8th Ballot

Whole number of votes 18
Wm Rand had 1
S. J. Wentworth " 8
M. S. Blaisdell " 9

and there was no choice

9th Ballot

Whole number of votes 18
Wm Rand had 1
S. J. Wentworth " 8
Marvin S. Blaisdell " 9

and there was no choice

10th Ballot

Whole number of votes 18
Wm Rand had 1
S. J. Wentworth had 8
Marvin S. Blaisdell " 9

and there was no choice

11th Ballot

Whole number of votes 18
Wm Rand had 1
S. Wentworth had 8
Marvin S. Blaisdell had 9

and there was no choice

12th Ballot

Whole no votes 18
Wm Rand had 1
S. Wentworth " 8
Marvin S. Blaisdell " 9

13th Ballot

Whole number of votes 18
Wm Rand had 1
S. J. Wentworth " 8
Marvin P. Blaisdell 9

and there was no choice

14th Ballot

Whole number of votes 18
Wm Rand had 1
S. J. Wentworth " 8
Marvin P. Blaisdell " 9

and there was no choice.

15th Ballot

Whole number of votes 18
Wm Rand had 1
S. J. Wentworth had 8
Marvin P. Blaisdell " 9

and there was no choice

16th Ballot

Whole number of votes 18
Wm Rand had 1
S. J. Wentworth had 8
Marvin P. Blaisdell had 9

and there was no choice

17th Ballot

Whole number of Ballots 18
Wm Rand had 1
S. J. Wentworth " 8
Marvin P. Blaisdell 9

18th Ballot

Whole number of ballots 18
Wm Rand had 1
S. J. Wentworth had 8
Marvin P. Blaisdell " 9

and there was no choice

19th Ballot

Whole number of votes 18
Wm Rand had 1
S. J. Wentworth " 8
Marvin P. Blaisdell " 9

and there was no choice

20th Ballot

Whole number of votes 18
Wm Rand had 1
S. J. Wentworth " 8
Marvin P. Blaisdell " 9

and there was no choice

21st Ballot

Whole number of votes 18
Wm Rand had 1
S. J. Wentworth " 8
Marvin P. Blaisdell " 9

and there was no choice

Moved by Councilman

Resolved that we take a recess for 20 minutes on a division of the council it being a tie vote the mayor voted in the affirmative and a recess of 20 minutes was declared proceeded to take the 22nd Ballot for Tax Collector

Whole number of votes 18

Wm Rand had 1

S. J. Wentworth " 8

Marvin J. Blaisdell " 9

and there was no choice

23 Ballot

Whole number of votes 18

Wm Rand had 1

S. J. Wentworth 8

Marvin S. Blaisdell 9

and there was no choice

On motion of Councilman Barker voted that we suspend the election of officers for 15 minutes and take up new business, when the same councilman presented the following resolution.

Resolved by the mayor and City council of the City of Rochester *Resolution relative to salaries of officers of Police Court*

That whereas there is now a bill before the legislature providing for more than doubling the salaries of the officers of the Police court of said City and whereas the Statutes of the State provide that the City council shall fix the salaries of all officers of the Police court in the same manner they fix the salaries of all other officers, and whereas the salaries [illegible] [illegible] fixed by the council for the officers of said court are ample for [illegible]

committee of five including the City Solicitor be appointed by the mayor to appear before the members of the legislature from Rochester and oppose said bill.

On motion of Councilman Warren voted that the resolution pass. The mayor appointed the following named councilmen to act with the City Solicitor as the committee. Barker, Warren, Tibbetts, and Hayes. On motion of Councilman Barker voted that the committee on printing have 200 copies of the list of committees printed. *200 copies of Committees to be printed*

On motion voted to proceed to the election of officers.

24th Ballot for Tax Collector

Whole number of votes 18

Wm Rand had 1

C. W. Emerson " 1

S. Wentworth " 8

Marvin S. Blaisdell 8

and there was no choice

25th Ballot

Whole number of ballots 18

Wm Rand had 1

S. Wentworth had 8

Marvin S. Blaisdell 9

and there was no choice

26. Ballot

Whole number of votes 18.

Wm Rand had votes 1

A. D. Hall " 1

S. J. Wentworth " 8

Marvin F. Blaisdell " 8

and there was no choice

27. Ballot

Whole number of votes 18

Wm Rand had 1

S. J. Wentworth had 8

Marvin F. Blaisdell " 9

and there was no choice.

28. Ballot

Whole number of votes 18

Wm Rand had 1

A. W. Emerson " 1

M. F. Blaisdell " 8

S. J. Wentworth " 8

and there was no choice,

29th Ballot

Whole number of votes 18.

Wm Rand had 1

S. J. Wentworth " 8

Marvin F. Blaisdell " 9

and there was no choice

30th Ballot

Whole number of votes 18

Wm Rand had 1

and there was no choice

31st Ballot

Whole number of ballots 18

Wm Rand had 1

A. W. Emerson had 1

S. Wentworth " 8

Marvin F. Blaisdell 8

and there was no choice,

32nd Ballot

Whole number of votes 18.

Wm Rand had 1

S. J. Wentworth 8.

Marvin F. Blaisdell 9

and there was no choice

33. Ballot

Whole number of votes cast 18

Wm Rand had 1

S. J. Wentworth had 8

M. F. Blaisdell 9

and there was no choice

34. Ballot

Whole number of votes 18

Wm Rand had 4

S. J. Wentworth 5.

M. F. Blaisdell 9

and there was no choice

35th Ballot

Whole number votes 18

Wm Rand 1

and there was no choice

36th Ballot

Whole number of votes 18
Wm Rand [illegible] 1
S. J. Wentworth 8
M. P. Blaisdell 9

and there was no choice

37th Ballot

Whole no of votes 18
Wm Rand [illegible] 1
[illegible] 1
[illegible] Wentworth 8
[illegible] Blaisdell 8

and there was no choice

38th Ballot

Whole number of votes 18
Wm R[illegible] 1
S. J. Wentworth 8
M. P. Blaisdell 9

and there was no choice

39th Ballot

Whole number of ballots 18
Rand [illegible] 1
S. [illegible] Wentworth 8
[illegible] Blaisdell 9

and there was [illegible]

40th Ballot

Whole [illegible] of votes 18
W[illegible] 1

41st Ballot

Whole number of votes 18
Wm Rand 1
S. Wentworth [illegible]
M. Blaisdell 9

and there was no choice

42nd Ballot

Whole [illegible] of Ballots 1[illegible]
J. P. [illegible] 1
Wm [illegible] 1
S. J. Wentworth [illegible]
M. P. Blaisdell.

and there was no choice

43 Ballot

Whole no of votes 18
Wm Rand [illegible] 1
S. J. Wentworth 8
M. P. Blaisdell 9

and there was no choice.

44th Ballot

Whole no votes 18
Wm Rand [illegible] 1
S. J. Wentworth 8
M. P. Blaisdell 8

and there was no choice.

4[illegible] Ballot

Whole number votes 18
Rand 1
S. J. Wentworth [illegible]

46th Ballot

Whole number of votes 18
Wm Rand had 1
S. Wentworth " 8
M. J. Blaisdell " 9

and there was no choice,

47 Ballot

Whole number of votes 18
Wm R[illegible] had 1
S. Wentworth " 8
M J Blaisdell " 9

and there was no choice

48th Ballot

Whole number of votes 18
Wm Rand had 2
S. Wentworth " 7
M. J. Blaisdell 9

and there was no choice,

49th Ballot

Whole number votes 18
Wm Rand had 1
S. J. Wentworth " 8
M. J. Blaisdell " 9

and there was no choice

50th Ballot

Whole number of votes 18
Wm Rand had 1
S. Wentworth " 8
M. J. Blaisdell 9

51st Ballot

Whole number of votes 18
Wm Rand had 1
S J Wentworth " 8
M. J. Blaisdell " 9

and there was no choice

52nd Ballot

Whole number of Ballots 18
Wm Rand had 1
S J Wentworth " 8
M J Blaisdell " 9

and there was no choice

53rd Ballot

Whole number of votes 18
Wm Rand had 1
S J. Wentworth " 8
M J. Blaisdell " 8

and there was no choice

On motion of [illegible] Butler voted that when we adjourn we adjourn to meet at 7,30 o'clock tomorrow (Saturday) night at 7,30

54th Ballot

Whole number of votes 18
Wm Rand had 2
S. J. Wentworth " 7.
M. J. Blaisdell 9

and there was no choice

55th Ballot

Wm Rand had 2
S. J. Wentworth 7
M. S. Blaisdell 9

and there was no choice.

56th Ballot

Whole number of votes 18
Richard Abbot had 1
Wm Rand 1
S. J. Wentworth 8
M. S. Blaisdell 8

and there was no choice.

57th Ballot

Whole number of votes 18
Wm Rand had 1
S. J. Wentworth 8
M. S. Blaisdell 9

and there was no choice.

58th Ballot

Whole number of votes 18
Wentworth Rand had 1
John S. Parker 1
Wm Rand 1
S. J. Wentworth 7
M. S. Blaisdell 8

and there was no choice.

59th Ballot

Whole number of votes 18
Wm Rand had 1
C. W. Hanna 1

and there was no choice.

6[illegible] Ballot

Whole number votes 18
Wm Rand had 1
John Pr[illegible] 1
S. J. Wentworth 7
M. S. Blaisdell 9

and there was no choice.

61st Ballot

Whole number of ballots 18
Wm Rand had 1
C. W. Allen 1
S. J. Wentworth 8
M. S. Blaisdell 8

and there was no choice.

62nd Ballot

Whole number of votes 18
Lewis D. [illegible] had 1
Wm Rand 1
S. J. Wentworth 7
M. S. Blaisdell 9

and there was no choice.

63 Ballot

Whole number votes 18
Wm Rand had 1
S. J. Wentworth 8
M. S. Blaisdell 9

and there was no choice.

64th Ballot

Asher Ward had 1
Wm Rand 1
S J Wentworth 7
M T Blaisdell 7
and there was no choice
15th Ballot
Whole number of votes 18
A T Rand had 1
Wm Rand 1
S J Wentworth 8
M T Blaisdell 8
16th Ballot
Whole number of votes 18
Wm Rand had 1
S J Wentworth 8
M T Blaisdell 9
and there was no choice,
17th Ballot
Whole number of votes 18
Wm Rand had 1
S J Wentworth " 8
M T Blaisdell " 9
and there was no choice
18th Ballot
Whole number of votes 18
Wm Rand had 1
S J Wentworth " 8
M T Blaisdell 9
and there was no choice.

19th Ballot
Whole number of votes 18
Wm Rand had 1
S. Wentworth 8
M. T. Blaisdell 9
and there was no choice.
20th Ballot
Whole number of votes 18
Wm Rand had 1
S J Wentworth " 8
M T. Blaisdell 9
and there was no choice.
21st Ballot
Whole number of votes 18
Wm Rand had 1
S. J Wentworth " 8
M. T. Blaisdell " 9
and there was no choice
22nd Ballot
Whole number of votes 18
Wm Rand had 1
S. Wentworth " 8
M. T. Blaisdell " 9
and there was no choice.
23rd Ballot
Whole number of votes 18
Wm Rand had 1
S J Wentworth 8
M T Blaisdell 9.

74th Ballot

Whole number of votes	18
Wm Rand had	1
S. J. Wentworth "	8
M. T. Blaisdell	9

and there was no choice

75 Ballot

Whole number of votes	18
Wm Rand had	1
S J Wentworth "	8
M. T. Blaisdell "	9

and there was no choice

76th Ballot

Whole number of votes	18
Wm Rand had	1
S J. Wentworth	8
M. T. Blaisdell	9

and there was no choice

77th Ballot

Whole number of votes	18
Wm Rand had	1
S J Wentworth	8
M. T. Blaisdell	9

and there was no choice

78th Ballot

Whole number of votes	18
Wm Rand had	1
S. J. Wentworth	8
M. T. Blaisdell	9

79th Ballot

Whole number of votes	18
Wm Rand had	1
S J Wentworth "	8
M. T. Blaisdell "	9

80th Ballot

Whole number of votes	18
Wm Rand	1
S. Wentworth	8
M. T. Blaisdell	9

and there was no choice

81st Ballot

Whole number of votes	18
Wm Rand had	1
S J Wentworth "	8
M. T. Blaisdell "	9

and there was no choice

82nd Ballot

Whole number of votes	18
C. Rehm had	1
Wm Rand	1
S. J. Wentworth	7
M. T. Blaisdell "	9

and there was no choice

83rd Ballot

Whole number votes	18
Wm Rand had	1
S J Wentworth	8
M. T. Blaisdell	9

84th Ballot

Whole number of votes	18
Wm Rand had	1
S. Wentworth	8
M. J. Blaisdell	9

and there was no choice

85th Ballot

Whole number of votes	18
Wm Rand had	1
S. J. Wentworth	8
M. J. Blaisdell	9

86th Ballot

Whole number of votes	18
Wm Rand had	1
S. J. Wentworth	8
M. J. Blaisdell	9

and there was no choice

87th Ballot

Whole number of votes	18
Wm Rand had	1
S. J. Wentworth	8
M. J. Blaisdell	9

and there was no choice

88th Ballot

Whole number of votes	18
Wm Rand had	1
S. J. Wentworth	8
M. J. Blaisdell	9

and there was no choice

89th Ballot

Whole number of votes	18
Wm Rand had	1
S. J. Wentworth	8
M. J. Blaisdell	9

and there was no choice

91 Ballot

Whole number of votes	18
Wm Rand had	1
S. J. Wentworth	8
M. J. Blaisdell	9

and there was no choice

91th Ballot

Whole number of votes	18
Wm Rand had	1
S. J. Wentworth	8
M. J. Blaisdell	9

and there was no choice.

92nd Ballot

Whole number of votes	18
Wm Rand had	1
S. J. Wentworth	8
M. J. Blaisdell	9

and there was no choice

93 Ballot

Whole number of votes	18
Wm Rand had	1
S. J. Wentworth	8
M. J. Blaisdell	9

94th Ballot

Whole number of votes 18
Wm Rand had 1
S. J. Wentworth " 8
M. J. Blaisdell " 9

and there was no choice

95 Ballot

Whole number of votes 18
Wm Rand had 1
S. J. Wentworth " 8
M. J. Blaisdell " 9

and there was no choice

96th Ballot

Whole number of votes 19
Wm Rand had 1
S. J. Wentworth " 8
M. J. Blaisdell 9

and there was no choice

97th Ballot

Whole number of votes 18
Wm Rand had 1
S. J. Wentworth " 8
M. J. Blaisdell 9

and there was no choice

98. Ballot

Whole number of votes 18
Wm Rand had 1
S. J. Wentworth " 8
M. J. Blaisdell " 9

99th Ballot

Whole number of votes 18
Wm Rand had 1
S. J. Wentworth 8
M. J. Blaisdell 9

and there was no choice

100th Ballot

Whole number of votes 18
Wm Rand had 1
S. J. Wentworth " 8
M. J. Blaisdell 9

and there was no choice

101st Ballot

Whole number of votes 18
Wm Rand had 1
S. J. Wentworth " 8
M. J. Blaisdell 9

and there was no choice

102d Ballot

Whole no of votes 18
Wm Rand had 1
S. J. Wentworth " 8
M. J. Blaisdell " 9

and there was no choice

103d Ballot

Whole number of votes 18
Wm Rand had 1
S. J. Wentworth " 8
M. J. Blaisdell 9

104th Ballot

Whole number of votes	18
Wm Rand had	1
S. J. Wentworth	8
M. S. Blaisdell	9

and there was no choice

105th Ballot

Whole number of votes	18
Wm Rand had	1
S. J. Wentworth .	8
M. S. Blaisdell .	9

and there was no choice

106th Ballot

Whole number of votes	18
Wm Rand had	1
S. J. Wentworth	8
M. S. Blaisdell .	9

and there was no choice

107th Ballot

Whole number of votes	18
Wm Rand had	1
S. J. Wentworth	8.
M. S. Blaisdell	9

and there was no choice

108 Ballot

Whole number of votes	18
Wm Rand had	1
S. J. Wentworth .	8
M. S. Blaisdell	9

and there was no choice

110th Ballot.

Whole number of votes	18
Wm Rand had	1
S. J. Wentworth .	8
M. S. Blaisdell .	9

and there was no choice

111th Ballot

Whole number of votes	18
Wm Bell had	1
S. J. Wentworth .	8
M. S. Blaisdell .	9

and there was no choice.

112th Ballot

Whole number of votes	18
Wm Rand had	1
S. J. Wentworth	8
M. S. Blaisdell	9

and there was no choice

114th Ballot

Whole number of votes 18
Wm Rand had 1
S. J. Wentworth " 8
M. J. Blaisdell 9

and there was no choice

115 Ballot

Whole number of votes 18
Wm Rand had 1
S. J. Wentworth " 8
M. J. Blaisdell " 9

and there was no choice

116th Ballot

Whole number of votes 18
Wm Rand had 1
S. J. Wentworth " 8
M. J. Blaisdell " 9

and there was no choice

117th Ballot

Whole number of votes 18
Wm Rand had 1
S. J. Wentworth " 8
M. J. Blaisdell " 9

and there was no choice

118th Ballot

Whole number of votes 18.
Wm Rand had 1
S. J. Wentworth " 6
M. J. Blaisdell [illegible]

119 Ballot

Whole number of votes 18
Wm Rand had 1
S. J. Wentworth " 8
M. J. Blaisdell 9

and there was no choice.

120 Ballot

Whole number of votes 18
Wm Rand had 1
S. J. Wentworth " 8
M. J. Blaisdell 9

and there was no choice

121st Ballot

Whole number of votes 18
Wm Rand had 1
S. J. Wentworth " 8
M. J. Blaisdell " 9

and there was no choice

122 Ballot

Whole number of votes 18
Wm Rand had 1
S. J. Wentworth " 8
M. J. Blaisdell " 8

and there was no choice.

123 Ballot

Whole number of votes 18
Wm Rand had 1
S. J. Wentworth 8
M. J. Blaisdell 9

124th Ballot

Whole No. of votes	18
Wm Reed had	1
S. J. Wentworth "	8
M. T. Blaisdell	9

and there was no choice

125th Ballot

Whole number of votes	18
Wm Reed had	1
S. J. Wentworth "	8
M. T. Blaisdell	9

and there was no choice

126th Ballot

Whole number of votes	18
Wm Reed had	1
S. J. Wentworth	8
M. T. Blaisdell "	9

and there was no choice

127th Ballot

Whole number of votes	18
Wm Reed had	1
S. J. Wentworth	8
M. T. Blaisdell "	9

and there was no choice

129th Ballot

Whole number of votes	18
Wm Reed had	1
S. J. Wentworth "	8
M. T. Blaisdell	9

and there was no choice.

130th Ballot

Whole number of votes	18
Wm Reed had	1
S. J. Wentworth "	8
M. T. Blaisdell	9

and there was no choice

On motion of [illegible]
Abbott voted to adjourn to the time
specified.

A true record
attest Chas M. [illegible]
City Clerk

City of Rochester

January 28 1892

Council met as per adjournment with the mayor in the chair.

Roll of the council called to which the following responded

Ward 2 Flagg Warren and Hayes

Ward 4 Bickford Jusselyn and Daniel

Ward 5 Warren Dodge and Howe

Ward 6 Barker

Reading of the record of last meeting dispensed with.

Petition of the W.C.T.U. asking for an appropriation for the reading room and on motion of councilman Dodge voted to lay on the table. — Welcome W.C.T.U.

Councilman Warren presented the following resolution

Resolved by the City Council of the City of Rochester. —

That all printing to be done for the City of Rochester during the year be done by contract and the City Clerk is hereby authorized to ask for proposals for that purpose. the contract to be let to the lowest bidder. — Resolution in regard to Printing

and on motion the resolution

New Hampshire for raising the salaries of the officials of the Police Court of the City of Rochester

Resolved by the City Council of the City of Rochester. —

That the committee appointed by the mayor to meet the representatives of the City of Rochester in regard to the passage of the above bill be hereby instructed to lay before the Senate and House of Representatives of the State of New Hampshire the action of the City Council of the City of Rochester in regard to the same and the proceedings held in [illegible] thereof.

On motion of Councilman Warren voted that the resolution pass.

On motion of Councilman Barker voted to adjourn to Monday Jan 30. at 7-30 p.m.

A true record

attest Chas W. Brown

City Clerk.

City of Rochester

January 30 189[illegible]

Adjourned meeting of the city council called to order by the mayor.

The following councilmen responded to the roll call.

Ward one Abbott Richards & Allen
Ward two Willard Howard Rollins
Ward three Bigg[?] Warren and Hayes
Ward four Bickford Josselyn and Daniel[?]
Ward five Waldron[?] Dodge and Stowe
Ward six Barker Woodward and Stevens.

Petition of H. H.[?] Otis and others for the establishment of a Free Public Library presented and referred to the Committee on Public Instruction. — *Petition of H. H. Otis and others for Library*

Petition of Geo. C.[?] Cochran for the appointment of a Special Committee to be known as the Committee on Legal affairs. On motion of Councilman Willard voted the mayor with councilmen Barker and Dodge be the committee. — *Appointment of Special Committee on Legal Affairs*

The Bond of the City Treasurer presented and referred to councilmen Barker and Dodge. The committee reported the Bond in proper form and should be accepted, and on motion of councilman Barker voted the Bond be accepted. — *Acceptance of Treasurer's Bond*

The mayor nominated Louis Lachance[?] and John Lacasse[?] as special police in addition to those already nominated. — *Special Police nominated*

On motion of councilman Barker voted to reconsider the vote whereby the confirmation of the Special Police was deferred one week. When on motion of the same councilman it was voted that the nomination for special Police as made by the mayor be confirmed. — *Special Police confirmed*

The following resolution presented by Councilman Barker.

Resolution in regard to the opening of Liquor Saloons. — *Resolution in regard to Liquor Saloons*

Resolved by the City Council of the City of Rochester.

That the mayor of the City of Rochester is hereby respectfully requested to instruct the City marshall to prevent the opening or establishment of Saloons or places for the sale of intoxicating liquors in addition to the Saloons or places now existing for that purpose.

On motion of councilman Josselyn voted that the resolution pass.

On motion of Councilman Barker voted to proceed to the election of City

The mayor appointed councilman Stivens and Hayes as tellers

Whole number of votes 18
C. P. Hubbard had 1
Chas. Blagg 8
D. L. Stoker 9

and there was no choice

2nd Ballot

Whole number of votes 18
C. P. Hubbard had 1
D. L. Stoker 8
Chas. Blagg 9

and there was no choice.

3rd Ballot

Whole number of votes 18
Chas. Blagg had 8
D. L. Stoker 10

Election of City Physician

and D. L. Stoker was declared elected.

On motion of councilman Barker voted to proceed to ballot for Supt. of Water Works.

Election of Supt. of Water Works.

Whole number of votes 18
Leander Pickering had 1
Leander P. Pickering 6
L. P. Pickering 11

and L. P. Pickering was elected.

On motion of councilman [illegible] voted to proceed to ballot for [illegible] for three years.

Uriajah Wentworth had 1
Silas Wentworth 1
Chas. H. Seavey 8
John Parsley 8

and there was no choice

2nd Ballot

Whole number of votes 18
Silas Wentworth had 1
Chas. H. Seavey 8
John D. Parsley 9

and there was no choice

3rd Ballot

Whole number of votes 18
S. Wentworth had 1
J. D. Parsley 9
Chas. H. Seavey 8

and there was no choice

4th Ballot

Whole number of votes 18
S. J. Wentworth had 1
Nathan [illegible] 1
John D. Parsley 8
Chas. H. Seavey 8

and there was no choice.

Moved by councilman Woodward that we postpone the election of Assessor for the [illegible] and proceed to the election of Chief Engineer of the Fire Department a [illegible] of the council in the negative the motion did not prevail.

On motion of Baker voted a recess of twenty minutes, after which the council called to order and proceeded to take the 5th Ballot for Assessor

Whole number of votes	18
S. J. Westcott had	1
Chas H Seeney "	8
John D Parkley "	9

and there was no choice.

Moved by councilman Baker that we postpone the election of assessor for the present. It being a tie vote the mayor voted yea and the motion prevailed.

On motion of councilman Woodward voted to proceed to the election of night watch.

Whole number of votes	18
Moses L Stevens had	1
Etienne Jacques	8
Ferdinand Sylvain	9

and there was no choice

2nd Ballot

Whole number of votes	18
Moses L Stevens had	1
Etienne Jacques	8
Ferdinand Sylvain	9

and there was no choice,

3rd Ballot

[illegible] Stevens [illegible]	1
Eti[illegible] [illegible]acques,	8
Ferdi[illegible] [illegible]	9

and there was no choice

4th [illegible]allot

Whol[illegible] [illegible] of votes	18
Moses L Stevens had	1
Etienne [illegible]acques	8
Ferdinand Sylvain	9

and there was no choice

5th Ballot

Whole number of votes	18
M L Stevens had	1
Etienne Jacques	8
Ferdinand Sylvain	9

and there was no choice,

Moved by councilman Woodward that we post[illegible] the election of night watch for the present [illegible] proceed to the election of chief engineer of the Fire Dept. Nine voting in the affirmative and nine in the ne[illegible] the ma[illegible]or voted [illegible] and the motion prevailed,

Whole number of votes	18
John W Thompson had	1
G. H Webster "	8
Samuel S. Sleeper "	9

and there was no choice.

2nd Ballot

John W. Thompson had 1
Geo. H. Webster 8
Samuel S. Stringer 9

and there was no choice.

On motion of Councilman [illegible] voted that when we adjourn, adjourn to Monday February 6 [illegible] at 7 o'clock

3rd Ballot

Whole number of votes 18
John W. Thompson had 1
Geo. H. Webster 8
Samuel S. Stringer 9

there was no choice.

4th Ballot

Whole number of votes 18
John W. Thompson had 1
Geo. H. Webster 8
Samuel S. Stringer 9

and there was no choice.

Moved by Alderman [illegible] that we adjourn to the time specified the motion did not prevail

5th Ballot

Whole number of votes 18
John W. Thompson had 1
Geo. H. Webster 8
Samuel S. Stringer 9

and there was no choice.

6th Ballot

John W. Thompson had 1
Geo. H. Webster had 8
Samuel S. Stringer 9

and there was no choice.

7th Ballot

Whole number of votes
John W. Thompson had 1
Geo. H. Webster 8
Samuel S. Stringer 9

and there was no choice.

On motion of Councilman [illegible] voted a recess of fifteen minutes, after which proceeded to the

8th Ballot

Whole number of votes 18
John W. Thompson 1
Geo. H. Webster
Samuel S. Stringer 9

and there was no choice.

9th Ballot

Whole number of votes 18
Edwin Hoyt had 1
John W. Thompson 1
Geo. H. Webster
Saml S. Stringer

and there was no choice

10th Ballot

Whole number of votes
John W. Thompson had 1

Geo H. Webster had 8

Samuel S. Stringer [illegible] 8

and there was no choice

11th Ballot

Whole number of votes 18

Michael Donahue had 1

[illegible] 1

Geo H. Webster 8

Samuel S. Stringer 8

and there was no choice

Moved by Councilman [illegible] that we now adjourn to the time [illegible] [illegible] the mayor [illegible] the council adjourned

[illegible]

Attest

Chas W. [illegible]

City Clerk

City of [illegible]

February [illegible]

Adjourned meeting of the City Council called to order by the mayor [illegible] which the following [illegible] and two. [illegible]

[illegible] Woodward [illegible]

[illegible] quorum

the mayor adjourned the meeting [illegible] February [illegible] [illegible] p.m.

[illegible]

[illegible]

City Clerk

City of Rochester
February 17 1892

Adjourned meeting of the city council called to order by the mayor.

The following councilmen answered to their names as called

Ward One Pibbetts Richards and Allen.
Ward two Willard Stanwood Rollins.
Ward three Warren
Ward Four Josselyn and Duval.
Ward Five Meldron Dodge and Stowe
Ward Six Barker Woodward and Stevens.

Record of last meeting read and approved.

Petition of C. H Sinclair and 108 others for a Free Public Library read and referred to committee on Public Instruction. — *Petition for Free Library*

Petition of Jennie L. Pennington for a permit to build an addition to her house on land near the City Hotel read and referred ~~to the Committee~~ on Fire Department. — *Petition of Jennie L Pennington*

Councilman Barker, chairman of the committee to meet the legislative committee made a verbal report, which on motion of councilman Richards was accepted and laid on the table for future action. — *verbal report of legislative com*

The mayor appointed as additional Special Police Ross I Hutchins — *additional Police appointed*
Amos [illegible]

and it was voted they be confirmed

Bill of S. I Smith for damage to sledge presented and on motion of councilman Dodge voted to refer to the street commissioner. — *Bill of S I Smith damage to sledge*

The City marshal's report for January read and voted to be placed on file — *City marshal's report for January*

The following resolution presented by councilman Barker

Resolution for establishing a Fire Alarm System for the city of Rochester — *Resolution to purchase a Fire Alarm*

Resolved by the City council of the City of Rochester.

That twenty five hundred dollars of the sum appropriated for the fire department for the current year is hereby set apart for the establishment of a fire alarm system for said City of Rochester, the same to be expended under the direction of the mayor, chief engineer of the fire department and the committee on fire department of the city of Rochester.

On motion of councilman Josselyn voted the rules be suspended and the resolution pass.

By the same councilman the following Resolution for purchasing badges for members of the fire department of the City of Rochester — *Resolution to purchase Badges*

City Council of the City of Rochester.

That the sum of one hundred dollars is hereby appropriated from the sums heretofore appropriated for the fire department for the current year for the purchase of suitable badges for the members of the fire department of said City of Rochester the same to be expended under the direction of the Mayor, chief engineer of the fire department and the committee on fire department of said City of Rochester.

On motion of Councilman Josselyn voted the rules be suspended and the resolution pass.

Councilman Woodward presented the following

Resolution for the sale of the buildings on Central Square

Resolved by the City Council of the City of Rochester. — *Resolution to sell buildings on Central Square*

That the committee on Public Buildings are hereby instructed to sell immediately the buildings on Central Square by public auction, the said buildings to be moved within

and the council then adjourned to the time specified.

A true record

Attest

Chas. W. Brown

City Clerk.

City of Rochester
March 3 1892

Council met as per adjournment with the Mayor in the chair
Roll of council called to which the following responded
Ward one Abbott, Richards and Allen
Ward two. Willard and Rollins.
Ward three Morris
Ward four Josselyn and Duval.
Ward five Dodge and Stevens
Ward six Barker and Woodward and Stevens

Petition for a Public Library from Ward 3. Also one signed by W.W. Allen and others. Also one signed by C.H. Meader and others, and the vote of the Board of Trade in favor of a Free Public Library were read and referred to the committee on Public Instruction

Report of Com on petition of Jennie Luring[?]

The committee on Fire Department made the following report

The committee to whom was referred the Petition of Jennie Luring[?] report that in their opinion judgements it ought to be allowed

D Josselyn } Committee
Chas S. Barker }

On motion of Councilman adopted,

Report of Committee on Claim of C.A. Bennett

The Special committee to whom was referred the claim of Caroline A Bennett made the following report:
To the Mayor and City Council of the City of Rochester

The special committee to which was referred the petition of Caroline A Bennett for compensation for expenses incurred and time lost by reason of injuries received June 24 1891 caused by defective steps leading into the Rochester High School Building where she was employed as a teacher, having considered the same report that in their opinion Mrs Bennett was injured through no fault or negligence on her part while in the discharge of her duties as a public servant that the steps before mentioned were defective out of repair and unsafe for use that by reason of the unsafe condition of the steps Mrs Bennett received such injuries as rendered her unable to continue her labor as a teacher since said injuries and from the best information we can obtain will be unable to resume her duties for a year at least from the time of the accident. She has expended considerable money in trying to effect a cure and evidently has suffered and is still suffering from injuries received. Mrs Bennetts salary as teacher

been lost to her. In addition to this she has employed local medical attendance and has been treated by an oculist in Boston for injuries received to her eyes at the time of her fall. Under the foregoing statement of facts your committee believe Mrs Bennett has a just and equitable claim against the city for one year's salary with such further allowance as would be reasonable for medical attendance and they would recommend the payment of Six Hundred Dollars to the claimant in full settlement of all claims against the city by reason of her injuries sustained as hereinbefore mentioned set forth.

George E. Seabury[illegible]
C. H. Willand

On motion of Councilman Dodge voted the report be accepted.

The committee on public instruction asked for further time to consider the petitions for a free Public Library.

Silas H. Dame appointed and confirmed as weigher of hay and coal.

Appointment of S.H. Dame as weigher

Bills of C. J. Smart were presented and permission being granted Mr Smart made an explanation of the bills.

Smart's bills to be paid

On motion of Councilman Josselyn voted that the bills be paid.

Bill of Wm. W. Hall for referred to committee on Highways.

Bill of Geo. W. Willey for Board of A S Brown read and referred to the Overseer of the Poor.

Bill of G. W. Willey

Bill of Nahum Keaton and M H Wentworth for use of teams in taking inventory read and on motion of Councilman Rollins voted to indefinitely postpone.

Bills of N. Keaton & M.H. Wentworth

Report of the City Marshal for the month of February read and was accepted and placed on file.

Report of treasurer for February read, accepted, and placed on file.

Councilman Barker presented the following resolution.

Resolved by the City Council of the City of Rochester

That an order be and hereby is passed that the White Bull Dog owned by Elmer W Rogers called Jack licensed by the City of Rochester as number 319 be restrained from running at large at any time between the passage of this order and the first day of May 1890.

Order to restrain Dog

On motion of Barker voted the resolution pass.

By the same councilman Resolution to pay Caroline A. Bennett for injuries.

of the City of Rochester

Resolution [illegible] Mrs Bennett

That the sum of five hundred dollars is hereby appropriated from the sum appropriated for miscellaneous expenses to settle the claim of Caroline A Bennett for personal injuries received on the steps of the High School building in said city while in the discharge of her duty as a servant of the above city.

On motion of councilman Rollins voted that the rules be suspended and the resolution pass.

Sale of Lodge Building

On motion of councilman Woodward voted the resolution for the sale of the old buildings on Central Square be taken from the table and acted upon at this time. On motion of councilman Barker voted that the resolution pass.

Petition of W.C.T.U. referred

On motion of councilman Barker voted that the petition of the Womens Christian Temperance Union be taken from the table ~~and~~

On motion of councilman Woodward voted to refer to the Finance Committee. On motion of councilman Woodward voted that when we adjourn we adjourn to two weeks from next Saturday night March 18 at 7.30 o'clock,

On motion voted to adjourn to time specified.

City of Rochester

March 18 1893

Adjourned meeting of the City Council met as per adjournment with the mayor in the chair.

The following councilmen responded to the roll call

Ward two Rollins

Ward three Clogg and Hayes

Ward four Josselyn and Duval

Ward five Walsh Dodge and Stone

Ward six Barker Woodward and Stevens

Record of last meeting read approved.

Communication read from C.H. Carroll in relation to the bill on Highways pending before the ~~same~~ Legislature.

On motion of councilman Dodge voted a resolution of approval be drawn up and as many of the council sign as will.

Petition of physicians to open Drug Stores

Petition of the physicians for the opening of the Drug stores on Sundays presented and referred to the committee on the revision of the ordinances.

Petition of E. Wentworth for permit to move buildings

Petition of Ezekiel Wentworth for permits to move the old buildings on Factory court was granted. also a permit to temporarily obstruct the side walk on Market street and a portion of Factory Court.

made the following report on the claim of Geo W. Willey.

[Report of the Overseer of the Poor on bill of Geo W. Willey]

To the Mayor and Council of the City of Rochester N. H.

I return herewith a claim referred to the Overseer of the Poor in favor of Mr and Mrs George W. Willey, amounting to $156.00 for boarding a dependent soldier Mr A. S. Brown.

Mr Willey has been informed when presenting this claim to me on several occasions that I would not approve any bills unless ordered by me. He has also been informed that if Mr A. S. Brown wished the City to provide boarding and lodgings for him I would do so at his request a request which Mr Brown has never made.

I know of no reason why the City should allow persons to take dependent soldiers to their homes and provide boarding and lodging for them and charge the City for the same without an order from the Overseer of the Poor.

I would recommend that this claim be referred to the committee on Claims, and that Mr and Mrs George W. Willey be requested to appear before said committee and prove their claim.

J. S. Daniels
Rochester N. H. March 16th 1892 Overseer of the Poor

On motion of Councilman Dodge voted the report be accepted and adopted.

The finance committee to

reported as follows.

[Report of Finance Com on the petition of the W. C. T. U.]

We the Committee on Finance to whom the within petition from W. C. T. U. was referred, would recommend that in view of the establishment of a free Public Library in a short time that the sum of fifty dollars be appropriated for the use of the W. C. T. U to cover the time from now until the first of July 1893.

C. A. Hoyt } Committee
J. Thorne Dodge }

On motion of Councilman Waldron voted the report be accepted and adopted.

[Report of Com. on Public Instruction on the Free Library]

The committee on Public Instruction made the following report.

The Committee on Public Instruction to whom the petitions in regard to a Free Public Library were referred report favorably on the same and recommend that it be established.

C. A. Hoyt } Committee
D. B. Waldron }

On motion of Councilman Dodge voted that the report be accepted.

James B. [illegible] having tendered his resignation as Special Police

[C. S. Osgood appointed Special Police]

Chas. S. Osgood was appointed and confirmed as Special in his stead.

Councilman Baker

running through this Deal field, and the request of the attorney for the estate that the damages therefor should be adjusted. [Damages through [illegible]]

On motion of Councilman Woodward voted to refer to the committee on Legal affairs. Claim of John S Hobbs for damages to horse and sleigh on account of defective highway was referred to the same committee, as was also the claim of Charles W Dame for damage to horse from the same cause. [Claims of John S Hobbs] [C W Dame]

Bill of Joseph Shaw for damage to sleigh referred to committee on claims and accounts. [and Joseph Shaw]

Assessors bill for use of team was on motion of Councilman [illegible] referred to the committee on claims and accounts. [Assessors bill referred]

Councilman Barker presented the following resolution.

Resolution for appointing a committee to receive subscriptions for improving Central Square. [Resolution for a Com. to improve Central Square]

Resolved by the City Council of the City of Rochester.

That a committee consisting of the mayor and Councilmen Dodge and Stevens and such others citizens as the above named may join with them are hereby appointed a committee to receive subscriptions for the

resolution passed.

Thomas Richardson asked for permit to temporarily obstruct sidewalk during the erection of his building on Union St.

After a recess of ten minutes the following resolution introduced by Councilman Barker.

Resolution for contributing to the support of the Reading Room maintained by the Womens Christian Temperance Union [Resolution of appropriation for the W.C.T.U.]

Resolved by the City Council of the City of Rochester.

That the sum of fifty dollars is hereby appropriated from the sum heretofore appropriated for miscellaneous expenses towards defraying the expenses of maintaining the reading room managed by the Womens Christian Temperance Union from March 1st current to July 1st next.

On motion of Councilman Rollins voted that the rules be suspended and the resolution pass.

On motion of Councilman Barker voted that when we adjourn we adjourn to one week from next Monday March 21 at 7.30 p.m. On motion of Councilman Dodge voted to adjourn to the time specified.

A true record.

City of Rochester
March 27 1888

Council met as per adjournment with the mayor in the chair.

The following named answered to the roll call.

Ward Three Warren and Hayes
Ward Four Bickford Josselyn and Duval
Ward Five Waldron Dodge and Hanson
Ward Six Barker Woodward and Stevens.

Record of last meeting read and approved.

Petition of Joseph Hanson for permit to erect a sign at the corner of Barker court and Wakefield street was referred to committee on Roads Bridges and Drains.

Petition of Jos. Hanson to erect a Sign

Remonstrance from the Lodge of Good Templars and also from the Free Baptist Congregational Methodist and Advent churches against an increase in the number of hours for opening Drug stores on Sunday was presented and referred to the committee on revision of the Ordinances.

Remonstrance against opening Drug Stores

Bill of S. E. Wentworth for balance due for collecting taxes in 1886 presented and on motion of Councilman Warren voted to refer to committee on Claims and Accounts and if found to be justly due to be paid.

Bill of S. E. Wentworth

establishment of a Free Public Library read and referred to Com. on Bills in their second reading.

Ordinance for Free Public Library

On motion of Councilman Barker voted that the tax collector of the City of Rochester is hereby directed on the first day of April next to give notice to all parties owing taxes to the City of Rochester of the amount of the same, the fee for such notices to be paid into the city treasury.

Tax collector to issue notice to tax payers

The civil engineer presented an estimate of the cost for extension of water pipes, and Councilman Hanson presented the following resolution.

Estimate Cost of Extension Water Pipe

Resolution for extension of Water System City of Rochester.

Resolution for extension of Water Works

Resolved by the City Council of the City of Rochester. That the sum of $2127.23 of the amount remaining unexpended from the sale of the water Bonds of the City of Rochester is hereby appropriated for the extension of the water System of said City in accordance with estimates presented herewith. On motion of Councilman Barker voted the rules be suspended and the resolution pass. On motion of Councilman Barker voted that when we adjourn we adjourn to one week from tomorrow night April 4) at 7.30 p.m. Voted to adjourn to time specified.

A true record

City of Rochester

April 4th 1893

The City council met this evening as per adjournment with the mayor in the chair. Roll of the council called to which the following responded,

Ward 2 Brown and Rollins
Ward 3 Hayes.
Ward 4 Josselyn and Duval,
Ward 5 Dodge and Brown
Ward 6 Barker Woodward and Stevens

Minutes of the previous meeting read and approved

Councilman Barker presented the following.

Resolution for completing the Sewerage System of the City of Rochester — *Resolution to complete Sewerage*

Resolved by the City council of the City of Rochester.

That the committee on Sewerage are hereby authorized and directed to contract for the completion of the Sewerage System adopted by the City of Rochester and to employ all necessary superintendents, engineers and assistants by them deemed necessary.

On motion of councilman Rollins voted the rules be suspended and the resolution pass

matter of the sale of the real estate of Paul A. Stuard deceased

Resolved by the City Council of the City of Rochester.

That the mayor of the City of Rochester is hereby authorized to institute and prosecute such proceedings as may be necessary to fully protect the interests of said city and all other parties interested in the final distribution of said estate — *Mayor to institute proceedings in sale of Stuard property*

On motion of councilman Barker voted that the rules be suspended and the resolution pass.

Report of the City treasurer for March read and on motion of councilman Dodge voted it be accepted and placed on file. — *Report of treasurer for March*

City Marshals report for March read and on motion of councilman Dodge voted it be accepted and placed on file — *Report of Marshal for March*

An amendment of Chapter 22 Sec 1 of the General Ordinances was offered by Councilman Josselyn and referred to the committee on the revision of ordinances. — *Amendment to Ordinance*

Councilman Barker presented the following.

Resolution for printing City reports. — *Resolution for printing City Report*

Resolved by the City council

That the committee on License of the City of Rochester are hereby authorized to expend a sum not exceeding twenty five dollars in publishing and binding copies of the annual city report for exchange or for the use of members of the council.

On motion of councilman Dodge voted the rules be suspended and the resolution pass.

Moved by councilman Woodward that when we adjourn we adjourn to the first Wednesday in May. the motion did not prevail

On motion of councilman Dodge voted that when we adjourn we adjourn to one week from tonight April 11th at 7-30 p.m.

Councilman Bickford presented the following.

Resolution for the purchase of a hose wagon. *Resolution to purchase Hose wagon*

Resolved by the city council of the City of Rochester.

That the committee on Fire Department are hereby authorized to expend a sum not exceeding five hundred dollars of the money appropriated for said department for the purchase of a hose wagon for the use of the city of Rochester. On motion of councilman Dodge voted the rules be suspended and the resolution pass.

City of Rochester

April 11 1893

Meeting of the City council tonight agreeably to adjournment.

The following councilmen responded to the roll call.

Ward two Stone

Ward three Hayes

Ward four Bickford Josselyn and Durrell.

Ward five Weldon Dodge and Stone.

Ward six Woodward and Stevens

Record of last meeting read and approved.

Petition of A D Whitehouse & others for an increase of pay [illegible] and referred to the committee on revision or Ordinances. *Petition of A.D. Whitehouse & Hose Co*

P. H. Hartigan asked for permission to place a sign temporarily across the sidewalk in front of his store which was granted. *Petition of P.H. Hartigan street sign*

Petition of J. D. Megrahan for license to move a small building from Charles to Washington Street which on motion of councilman Woodward was granted. *Petition of Megrahan to move building*

Petition of O. W. Ramsey for leave to temporarily obstruct the sidewalk on Market Street while repairs on his buildings were being made. On motion of councilman *Petition O.W. Ramsey to obstruct*

Petition of John Bickford for leave to move a building from Foster Court to Union Street was presented and on motion voted the petition be granted.

Petition of J. S. Twombly for leave to build a Slaughter House on his land near the old Town Farm Cemetery was on motion of councilman Dodge referred to the Board of Health.

Petition of J. S. Twombly to build Slaughter House

On motion of councilman Dodge voted the land owned by the city of Rochester where the old "Pest House" formerly stood be rented to Micajah H. Wentworth at an annual rental of four dollars.

Land rented to M. H. Wentworth

The committee to whom was referred the claim of Wm. W. Hall reported as follows

Your committee on the bill of William Hall against the city of Rochester for damage to his Horse and Sleigh on February 14 1893 would recommend that the mayor appoint a committee to buy a second hand Sleigh for said Hall not to cost over eight dollars, in settlement of said claim in full.

James B. Stevens
George A. Bickford

Report on bill of Wm. Hall

On motion of councilman Dodge voted the report be accepted and adopted.

The mayor appointed the committee on roads Briggs and Davis to ...

The same committee made the following report.

Your committee on the petition of Joseph Hanson to erect a post and sign at the junction of Barker Court with Wakefield Street would report unfavorably.

James B. Stevens
George A. Bickford

Report on Petition of Jo. Hanson

On motion voted the report be accepted.

The committee on claims and accounts to whom was referred the bill of Geo. W. Willey returned the same endorsed "Not allowed." which was on motion of councilman Josselyn accepted by the council.

Claim of Geo. W. Willey not allowed

On motion of councilman Josselyn voted that the committee on Shade Trees Parks and Commons be instructed to investigate the advisability of removing the elm tree near the store of H. D. Sanborn.

Tree near H. D. Sanborn Store

On motion of councilman Woodward voted that Mr. Geo. W. Anderson be instructed to remove the flag pole on Hanson Street.

Flag pole on Hanson St. to be removed

On motion of councilman Josselyn voted that a new Janitor be elected. Also that the janitor be under the authority of the City Marshal. Voted to proceed to elect a janitor by ballot.

Whole number of ballots 10
James Doyle had 8

Election of Janitor

and Edgar S. Barnaby was declared elected.

On motion of Councilman Dodge voted that there be a public hearing on all the road petitions now before the council in the council room on Wednesday May 3 1893. *Hearing on Road petitions*

On motion of Councilman Stone voted that Ex Mayor Whitehouse be invited to present his portrait to be hung in the council chamber. *Portrait of Mayor Whitehouse*

On motion of Councilman Dodge voted that when we adjourn we adjourn to two weeks from to night April 20.

On motion voted to adjourn to the time specified.

A true record
attest
Chas W. Brown
City Clerk

City of Rochester
April 20. 1893

Council met at the time of adjournment with the mayor in the chair.

The following councilmen were present

Ward one Roberts Richards and Allen
Ward two Stone and Rollins
Ward three Hayes
Ward four Josselyn
Ward five Waldron Dodge and Stone
Ward six Barker Woodward and Stevens

Record of last meeting read and approved.

Petition of S. B. Martin for permission to erect an overhead sign on Arrow street presented and referred to the Committee on Highways. *Petition of Martin for sign*

Petition of S. H. Hartigan and others to widen Portland Court was on motion of Councilman Josselyn referred to Committee on Highways and the mayor. *Petition to widen Portland Court*

Petition of Chas S. Barker for leave to prune the trees in front of his block was on motion of Councilman Dodge voted to be granted. *Petition of Barker to prune trees*

Statement from Dominicus Hanson in relation to extending the water pipes from Charles Ave to Hanson street read and on *Statement D. Hanson* the Board of Health.

To the Mayor and Council of the City of Rochester N.Y.

Report of Board of Health on Slaughter H.

The Board of Health to whom was referred the Petition of J. L. [illegible] to erect a slaughter house on his premises on [illegible] road leading from St. [illegible] paint shop, have attended to the duty assigned them and recommend that the prayer of the petitioner be granted.

J. S. Daniels } Board of
D. A. Stokes } Health.

Moved by Councilman Woodward that the report of the Board of Health be accepted and the petition granted. The motion did not prevail.

The committee on legal affairs made the following report.

Report on Claim of C. C. Hodgdon

To the Mayor and Council of the City of Rochester.

On the 5th day of January 1891 Charles C. Hodgdon of this City was thrown from his carriage while traveling on the public highway leading from Rochester to East Rochester at a point about 19 rods easterly from Adams corner and his right ankle was sprained and injured so as to render him unable to leave his house for several weeks and was unable to resume work for three months or more. Notice of the injury and a claim for damages was duly filed and who after careful investigation reported their inability to approve the claim in the sum demanded by Mr Hodgdon and no further action was taken by the Council. At the Sept term of court 1892 suit was brought against the City on this claim which was continued at that and the last City Term.

Mr Hodgdon and his counsel recently met your committee on legal affairs, and after a full consideration of the case the committee decided to recommend the payment to Mr Hodgdon of $295.31 in full settlement of damages and costs in this suit which sum is less legal expenses, the sum the former com. on claims would have recommended had Mr Hodgdon signified his willingness to accept. Your com is informed and believes Mr Hodgdon will release the City from all claims on payment of $295.31 and in view of the condition of the highway at place of accident and Mr Hodgdon unquestioned injuries they would recommend the payment of such sum in full settlement of his claim.

C. A. Hoyt
Geo. W. Cochrane } Com.
W. S. Barker
J. Warren Dodge

On motion of Councilman Waldron voted the report be accepted.

The following report from the same committee was read.

of the city of Rochester

Report on claim of J. R. Stobbs

The Special Com on Legal affairs to whom was referred the claim of John R. Stobbs for injuries alleged to have been received to his team on the 21st day of July 18[illegible] on the highway leading from Rochester to Mendelson [illegible] having investigated his claim would recommend the payment of twenty five dollars in full settlement of the same should he accept such sum in full satisfaction

G. A. Stoyt
Geo. W. Cochrane
C. H. Barker
J. Thomas Dodge
Com on Legal affairs

On motion of councilman Josselyn voted the report be accepted.

The Ordinance for the establishment and maintenance of a Free Public Library was on motion of councilman Barker recommitted for amendment.

Petition of A. D. Whitehouse

The petition of A. D. Whitehouse [illegible] presented at the last meeting and referred to the committee on revision of ordinances was on motion of Councilman Barker referred to the Com on Fire Dept.

Referred

The committee on Shade Trees Parks and Commons reported not advisable to remove the tree near the [illegible] store removed and on motion of councilman Dodge voted

Councilman Barker presented the following.

Resolution in regard to Railroad crossings.

Resolution in regard to R R crossings

Resolved by the city council of the city of Rochester.

That the committee on Legal affairs together with the City Solicitor constitute a special committee to confer with the officials of the Railways passing through the city of Rochester in regard to providing suitable protection for the public at the various Railroad crossings within the city limits and to draft and submit to the city council ordinances for the regulation of the running of trains over said crossings, and the providing of suitable gates or flagmen at the same.

On motion of councilman Waldron voted the resolution be adopted.

Councilman Stone presented the following resolution.

Connecting water pipes between [illegible] and [illegible]

Resolved that the committee on Water-works be instructed to make the necessary connection between Central Avenue and [illegible] streets. On motion of councilman Rollins voted the resolution pass.

Committee to confer with [illegible]

Moved by councilman Josselyn that the mayor and committee on Roads Bridges and Drains be authorized to confer with Ezekiel [illegible] in regard which said Wentworth is about to erect, and the motion prevailed.

Communication from the chief engineer of the Fire Dept in relation to fire escape on Hayes block.

On motion of Councilman Dodge voted that Capt Hayes be requested again to erect a fire escape on his block and to take legal steps to compel him to do so unless he complies with the request. — Fire esc. on Hayes block

On motion of Councilman Dodge voted the committee on Shade Trees Parks and Commons investigate the trees on the public streets, and direct the street commissioner to [illegible] such as may be necessary. — Com. on S. T. P. & C. Shade trees

On motion of Councilman Josselyn voted that when we adjourn we adjourn to next Saturday night at 7-30.

Councilman Barker presented the following

Resolution for paying Charles L. Hodgdon for damages on Highway. — Resolution to pay Hodgdon's claim

Resolved by the City Council of the City of Rochester

That the sum of two hundred ninety five and [illegible] dollars be paid to Chas L. Hodgdon in full settlement of his claim against the city for damage on the highway. On motion of [illegible] be suspended and the resolution pass.

On motion of Councilman Dodge voted the adjournment [illegible].

A true record
attest Chas W Brown
City Clerk.

City of Rochester
April 29 1[illegible]

Adjourned meeting of the city council met according to adjournment. Roll of council called to which the following answered,

Ward two Hanson and Rollins
Ward three Warren and Hayes
Ward four Josselyn
Ward five Madden and Hanson
Ward [illegible] Barker Woodward and Stevens

Record of last meeting read and approved.

Petition of Geo. P. Wiley for leave to temporarily obstruct the sidewalk at the corner of Main and [illegible] streets, read and on motion of Councilman Rollins voted the petition be granted.

The Committee on Highway

of S. B. Martin.

To the Hon. Mayor and Council of the City of Rochester. — Report on petition of S. B. Martin.

Your com[illegible] on the petition of S. B. Martin to place [illegible] sign in [illegible] it is unfavorable.

James B. Stevens
Joseph [illegible]

On motion of Councilman Woodward voted the report be accepted.

The Mayor stated arrangements had been made with [illegible] Wentworth as to the widening of Market St.

[illegible] motion voted the matter be passed for the present.

Further time was granted the Committee for the consideration of the petition of [illegible] Whitehouse [illegible]

Councilman [illegible] presented the following resolution.

Resolved that the chief Engineer of the Fire Department be instructed to report to this council what parties have been [illegible] to provide fire escapes to their buildings and who have complied.

On motion of Councilman [illegible] voted the resolution pass.

Bill of [illegible]

[illegible] for services on [illegible] committee on claims and accounts.

The amended Ordinance for the establishment of a Free Public Library read and referred to Committee on bills in their second reading with instructions to report at this meeting. The Committee reported the bill in proper form, and on motion of Councilman Barker voted the rules be suspended and the resolution pass to be engrossed. Recess of ten minutes declared after which a petition [illegible] by [illegible] and others for the widening of Market street [illegible]. On motion of Councilman Stevens voted that the usual reference to a Committee be waived and a hearing on the petition be ordered Tuesday evening May 16 at 7.30 P.M. at the Council rooms.

On motion of Councilman [illegible] voted that when we adjourn we adjourn to meet Wednesday May 3 at [illegible] [illegible] on motion voted to adjourn.

Attest

[illegible]

City Clerk

City of Rochester
May 2-1893

Council called to order by the Mayor. The roll call showed the following councilmen present;
Ward 1 Allen
Ward two Hoorn
Ward three Flagg
Ward four Bickford Josselyn and Duval
Ward five Dodge and Stover
Ward six Barker and Stevens.
and the following members joined the council later. Wallace of ward two
Hayes of ward three and Woodward of ward six.

Record of last meeting read and approved.

Petition of Chas. H. Keates and others, for the confinement and safe keeping of Charles H. Hayes. who is believed to be insane. Petition for Confinement of C. H. Hayes

The committee on highways made the following report on the petition to widen Factory Court

To the Hon Mayor and Council of the City of Rochester N. H. Report on petition to widen Factory Court

Your committee on the petition to widen and straighten Factory Court would recommend that you give them a hearing

On motion of councilman Dodge voted that the report be accepted and adopted.

Also from the same committee, the following report was read.

To the mayor and council of the city of Rochester N. H.

Your committee on the petition for a street at East Rochester would recommend that you give them a hearing

James B Stevens
Geo H Bickford

Rochester N. H. May 2-1893.

On motion of councilman Josselyn voted to lay on the table.

The committee on fire department made the following report.

The committee to whom was referred the petition of the members of the S. D. Whitehouse Hose Co at Gonic report that it is inexpedient to take action on said petition

C. Josselyn } Committee
C. D. Barker }

On motion of councilman Dodge voted that the report of the committee be accepted

The city treasurer's report for April was read and ordered to be placed on file

City marshal's report for April read and ordered to be placed on and councilman Barker made an explanation in relation to the same.

On motion of councilman Josselyn voted the committee on claims and accounts be authorized to approve the same. Assessor Bill for Team

On motion of councilman Stone voted the petition in relation to Chas. H. Hayes be referred to committee on legal affairs. Petition for compensation of Chas. H. Hayes referred to committee on legal affairs

On the matter of amending the ordinance regulating the salary of the city physician. Moved by councilman Dodge that the salary of the city physician remain as it is. The motion did not prevail. Moved by councilman Josselyn that the ordinance be so amended that the fees of the city physician be two hundred dollars including all medicines. The mayor declared the motion carried. The yeas and nays being demanded the roll was called 5 voting yea and 8 nay as follows.

Yea councilmen Allen Josselyn Duval Stone and Barker.

Nay. councilmen Willard Stone Hagg Hayes Bickford Dodge Woodward and Stevens, and the motion did not prevail.

On motion of councilman Josselyn voted to proceed to the hearing on the road petitions. On motion of councilman Dr. Spaulding voted a recess to look over

After the recess the council called to order and on motion of councilman Barker voted the hearings on the petitions for the streets from Pine and Summer streets be continued to Friday May 5th. Hearing on said petitions continued

Petition of Christy Pelchat who was injured while at work for the city laying water pipe for compensation for loss of time and medical attendance was on motion voted to be referred to the committee on legal affairs. Petition of Christy Pelchat

The resignation of Dr. L. Stokes as City Physician was read and on motion of councilman Dodge voted it be accepted. Resignation of Dr. L. Stokes

On motion of councilman Stevens voted to proceed to elect a city physician. The mayor appointed councilmen Josselyn and Woodward as tellers. Election of City Physician

Whole number of ballots cast 12
Chas. Hayes had 1
J. L. Stokes " 1
W. B. Downs " 11

and W. B. Downs was elected.

On motion of councilman Josselyn voted the committee on Roads Bridges and Sewers look into the matter of overhead signs, and take such steps in relation thereto as thought advisable. Overhead Signs

On motion of councilman Josselyn voted to adjourn to Friday May 5 at 7.30

City of Rochester

May 5–18[illegible]

City council met this evening at the hour of adjournment. The mayor in the chair.

The following councilmen responded to the roll call. Willard and Rollins of ward two. Stages of ward three. Josselyn of ward four. Harmon Dodge and Stone of ward five. Barker Woodward and Stevens of ward six.

Record of last meeting read and approved.

Petition of J. H. Dawson for leave to erect a steam shingle and jobbing mill on Harrison Avenue presented and on motion of councilman Doty voted the petition be granted.

Petition of J. H. Dawson to erect a steam mill

The Committee on Legal affairs made the following report.

Report on case of Chas. H. Hayes

To the Mayor and Council of the City of Rochester,

The committee on Legal affairs to whom was referred the petition of Charles H. Keates and others asking that steps be taken towards the confinement and safe keeping of Charles H. Hayes as a dangerously insane person having in mind certain proceedings in the Probate Court for [illegible] proceedings are continued subject to renewal on request of the former petitioners. Your committee report that in their opinion this petition addressed to the City Council should have been presented to the Probate Court which has already exercised jurisdiction in the matter of Mr. Hayes mental condition.

C. H. Hoyt
J. Thane Dodge
C. S. Barker
G. E. Cochrane
Com. on Legal affairs

On motion of councilman Josselyn voted the report be accepted.

The committee on the revision of ordinances presented the amendments that had been proposed from time to time.

On motion of councilman Dodge voted that the Rules be suspended and the ordinances as amended be accepted and adopted.

The following paper from the Chief Engineer of the Fire Department presented at the request of the council.

To the Honorable Mayor and City council of the City of Rochester

Gentlemen,

The board of Engineers have notified the enclosed list of people to place fire escapes on their buildings.

Chas Mansion agent of Rochester Mfg Co
S Meader . Gone
I Salinger C H & C Wallace
F C Whitney agent McDuffee Block
Willard Springfield agent George Block
Henry Kimball Supt of Schools
Capt A M Hayes. John Burleigh
Cocheco Plain Mfg Co
Houghton Stebbins & Warren
A S Parshley agent Odd Fellows Building Ass

They have all complied with the request with the exception of S S Sharp who gave his order some time ago and as I have been told is nearly completed.
C H & C Wallace these will be ready the first of next week. A S Parshley was not notified until last week. Capt A M Hayes I have notified a second time according to instructions from this Honorable body

M. C. Sanborn
Chief Engineer

On motion voted the communication be accepted and placed on file. *Road hearing continued*

On motion of Councilman Woodward voted the hearing on the road petition of A R Reed be continued

On motion of councilman Stevens voted the hearing on the petition of D W Hanson & others for a street from

On motion of councilman Woodward voted that the City Civil Engineer prepare a plan of the public highway running from Willow Brook to the Stone bridge on Market Street the same to be prepared as soon as possible *Market St to be surveyed*

Councilman Dodge presented the following.

Resolution in regard to printing the City ordinances

Resolved by the City Council of the City of Rochester That in addition to the printing of the City Reports already ordered there be printed and bound one hundred copies of the revised ordinances of the City of Rochester. *Ordinances to be printed*

On motion of councilman Barker voted the resolution pass.

Councilman Stevens made a statement in relation to land damages to Mrs Mason occasioned by the widening of Winter St. *Land damages to Mrs Mason*

On motion of councilman Woodward voted that the mayor appoint a committee of two to confer with Mrs Mason and report to the council.

The Mayor appointed councilman Stevens and Woodward as that committee. *Committee to confer appointed*

On motion of councilman

adjourn to meet one week from next Tuesday May 16 at 7-30 p m.

On motion voted to adjourn

attest Chas W Brown
City Clerk

City of Rochester

May 16 1893

The city council met this evening as per adjournment with the mayor in the chair The following councilmen were present Rollins of ward two.
Warren and Hayes of ward three.
Josselyn and Duval of ward four
Walden and Stowe of ward five
Barker Woodward and Stevens of ward six.

Record of last meeting read and approved.

Communication from [illegible], asking for an extension of time in which to erect fire escapes in Odd Fellows Block which was granted — Communication [illegible]

Petition of R. H. Edgerly & others asking the council to take some steps in relation to the blocking of streets by the railroad trains On motion voted to refer to the committee already appointed to confer with the railroad officials — Petition in regard to R.R. Crossings

Petition of Sylvester [illegible] and others of East Rochester to remove the band stand located at the junction of Main Street and Rochester Avenue On motion of Barker voted — Petition in relation to Band Stand

parties present were P. H. Hartigan and | Hearing
Ezekiel Wentworth with his counsel John Kivel Esq. | Wentworth
Moved by councilman Stevens that | Market St.

Market Street be widened and straightened by relocating the Northeasterly side line of said street as follows Viz: Beginning at the westerly corner of Orange Block thence running in a straight line North westerly across Pickering Street land of Ezekiel Wentworth Patrick H. Hartigan and Charles W. Pickford to the corner of the [illegible] as it now stands at the intersection of Union Street with said Market Street including the land between said line and Market Street and that damages be awarded said land owners. The above motion was seconded by councilman Woodward
After the examination of witnesses the question was called and the motion was carried.

On motion of councilman Barker voted that when we adjourn we adjourn to one week from to night May 23. at 7-30 p. m.

On motion of councilman Barker voted the hearing on the above petition be continued to one week from to night.

Moved by councilman Barker | Hearing on
that a hearing be granted on the petition of P. H. | petition to
Hartigan and others for the widening of Pickering | widen Pickering
Street on the first day of June next at two o'clock p. m. | Court
and the motion was declared not carried
The yeas and nays being demanded resulted [illegible]

[illegible] Woodward Stone [illegible]
[illegible] Hollins [illegible] Woodward [illegible] Stevens.
and the motion was carried.

Moved by councilman [illegible] that the petition for a street from [illegible] to [illegible] street be dismissed. The motion did not prevail.

On motion of councilman Barker voted the hearing on the petition for a street | Hearing on
from Portland St. to Broadway street be continued | Broadway St.
to June first and that the city engineer prepare | continued
and present a plan of the proposed street at that time.

On motion of councilman [illegible] voted that a notice be served on the parties commencing to build a Wakefield street on land formerly owned by Pearl [illegible] a survey [illegible] be made by the engineer | Claim of
Claim of Sarah A. Howe for | Sarah A. Howe
damages caused by the emptying of main street sewer into her field near the Common. Referred to committee on Legal affairs.

Bond of Treasurer presented and on motion voted the bond be placed on | Resolution
file for the present. | to purchase
Councilman Stone | land at
presented the following resolution for purchasing | Reservoir
land adjoining the Reservoir of the City Water Works.

Resolved by the City Council [illegible]

of two hundred and seventy five dollars is hereby appropriated from the unexpended balance in the City treasury on account of the extension of the City Water works for the purchase of land adjoining the Reservoir from William Howard.

On motion of councilman Barker voted that the rules be suspended and the resolution pass.

The following communication from Simpson Post. G. A. R.

Head Quarters Simpson Post No. 22 G. A. R.
Rochester May 8 1892

To the Hon Mayor Common Council and City Clerk of the City of Rochester.

Simpson Post request the honor of your presence ride in the procession on memorial day May 30 — (Simpson Post Invitation)

Very Respectfully
Edwin [illegible]
Commander

On motion of councilman Woodward voted the invitation be accepted.

Voted to take up unfinished business again.

On motion of Councilman Barker voted that the city engineer present the plan of River Street as proposed by the petition to widen. (Plan of River Street to be prepared)

On motion voted to [illegible]

City of Rochester
May 23 1892

Council met this evening as per adjournment with the Mayor in the chair.

The following councilmen were present
Ward one Tibbetts and Richards
Ward two Willand [illegible] and Collins
Ward three Warren and Hayes
Ward Four Jasselyn and Duval
Ward Five Waldron and Home
Ward Six Barker Woodward and Stevens

Record of last meeting read and approved.

Petition of James F. Seabrook and others for a street from Green street to Main St East Rochester referred to committee on Roads Bridges and Drains. (Petition for street at E. Rochester)

The committee on legal affairs made the following report (Report on claim of [illegible])

The committee on legal affairs to whom was referred the communication of [illegible] asking the consideration of the council for injuries sustained on the 24th day of April last, by reason of the caving in of the earth at the ditch in [illegible] Court where he was employed by the city, having considered of such injuries incurred an expense of ten dollars for medical attendance and being in needy circumstances has been unable to prosecute any labor since said date. would recommend the payment to him of forty dollars for loss of time past and prospective and the additional sum of ten dollars for medical attendance provided he release the City from any and all real or supposed claims he may have against it by reason of his said injuries.

Rochester N.H. May 20, 1895 [illegible] } Committee
C. S. [illegible] } legal affairs.
George S. Cochrane }

On motion of Councilman Warren voted the report be accepted and adopted.

On motion of Councilman Baker voted the claim of Mrs Mason for land damages incurred from the widening of [illegible] street be referred to the Committee on Roads Bridges and Drains for further investigation. — *Claim of Mrs. Mason referred to Com. on Roads, Bridges & Drains.*

The council then proceeded to the election of trustee of the Free Public Library.

Councilmen Richards and [illegible] appointed tellers. — *Election of trustees, library.*

Trustee for Ward One.

Whole number of ballots cast 14

J. H. Whittier had 14 and was elected.

Trustee for ward [illegible]

W. W. Allen had 14

and was elected

Trustee for ward 3

Whole number of ballots	14
C. S. Smith had	1
J. H. Richardson	6
C. S. Whitehouse	7

and there was no choice.

2nd ballot

Whole number of ballots	14
J. H. Richardson had	6
C. S. Whitehouse	8

and C. S. Whitehouse was elected

Trustee for ward 4

Whole number of votes	14
John Young had	14

and was elected.

Trustee for ward 5

Whole number of ballots	12
James [illegible] had	12

and was elected.

Trustee for ward 6

Whole number of ballots	14
Henry Kimball had	1
C. M. Brown had	5
J. C. McDuffee	8

and J. C. McDuffee was elected.

The [illegible] lay on the table and on motion of

and placed on file.

Petition of Sylvester Seebuck and others for the removal of Band Stand taken from the table. On motion of Councilman Woodward voted the councilmen from ward one be authorized to dispose of the band stand, the proceeds to be paid into the City treasury.

Band Stand

The following lay out and widening of Market Street was read.

Lay out and widening of Market St

Upon the foregoing petition we appointed a hearing and gave notice thereof as aforesaid and on the 16th day of May 1891 at seven and one half o'clock in the afternoon at the Council Room in the City of Rochester the time and place appointed. Osborn M. Ramsey and Eden M. Corson and Ezekiel Wentworth appeared as parties and said hearing was adjourned to the 20th day of May 1891 at seven and one half o'clock in the afternoon at the Council Room in said City and having heard all parties interested who attended and desired to be heard and all evidence offered by them, and examined them and their witnesses under oath and made a personal examination of said proposed widening and straightening we are of the opinion that for the accommodation and benefit of the public there is occasion to widen and straighten said highway (Market Street) and made therefore

By extending the Northeasterly side line of said Market Street as follows viz: Beginning at the westerly corner of George Block thence running in a straight line Northwesterly across Rectory Court land of Ezekiel Wentworth, Patrick H. Hartigan and Charles W. Bickford to the corner of the fence as it now stands at the intersection of Union Street with said Market Street including the land between said line and Market Street.

and we award damages to the respective owners of land over which said highway is widened and straightened to be paid by said City as follows,

To Ezekiel Wentworth Four Hundred and Eighteen dollars

To Patrick H. Hartigan Two Hundred and twenty eight dollars,

To Charles W. Bickford One Hundred and ninety six dollars.

Rochester N. H. May 20, 1891

O. H. Hayes Mayor

Joseph Warren, Edmund Josselyn, John W. Tibbetts, Charles E. Woodward, A. W. Rollins, Simon L. Hoar, Chas. W. Willand, Dudley L. Varden, James B. Stevens, Charles W. Horn, Frank B. Hayes, Ernest Duval, H. L. Richards, Chas. S. Barker — Councilmen of City of Rochester.

On motion of Councilman Barker voted that the hearing lay out and widening of Market Street be placed on file and the same to be recorded by the City Clerk.

voted that when we adjourn we adjourn to June 1st at two o'clock in the afternoon

Councilman [illegible] presented the following resolution

Resolved that the committee on Shade Trees Parks and Commons attend to the Commons and use that diligence and care to preserve the same for the purposes intended — *Resolution in regard to Commons*

On motion of councilman Josselyn voted the resolution be adopted.

The city engineer made a report in relation to the lot on Wakefield street owned by Kingston that the fence on said lot was some ten feet on the highway.

A Communication from the Superintendent of the water works in relation to a broken hydrant at [illegible] — *Hydrant to be repaired*

On motion of councilman Warren voted that the supt of the water works notify Mr Watson (who broke the hydrant) to have it repaired

On motion of councilman Josselyn voted the Electric light company be instructed to remove the electric light poles from [illegible] Square — *Poles to be removed*

Councilman Warren presented the following resolution.

Resolved by the mayor and City council of the city of Rochester — *Resolution to settle contract*

That the sum of three [illegible] in the treasury not otherwise appropriated for the purpose of carrying out the contract entered into by the water committee of the town of Rochester and John [illegible] and Samuel D. [illegible] and the mayor is hereby authorized to take a deed of a tract of land fifty feet wide running from Chestnut street to [illegible] street for the purposes of a street and in full satisfaction for all damage in laying the water pipe across said land

On motion of councilman [illegible] voted to refer to the committee on bills in their second reading until the next meeting.

The following resolution presented by councilman [illegible]

Resolution for paying the sum awarded to Christie [illegible]

Resolved by the city council of the city of Rochester.

That the sum of fifty dollars be paid to Christie [illegible] in accordance with the report of the committee on legal affairs adopted by the city council of the city of Rochester May 23 1898.

On motion of councilman Josselyn voted the rules be suspended and the resolution pass

Thomas [illegible] claimed damage caused by water flooding his cellar owing to the insufficiency of culverts referred to [illegible]

for quieting deputations of the Board of Health presented and on motion of councilman [illegible] voted that the committee on Claims and Accounts be authorized to approve the same.

Communication from Dominicus Strudthaus Charles L. C. Hanaw in relation to the sewering of Hanaw street presented and ordered to be placed on file

Communication of Hanaw to be filed

On motion of councilman Richards voted to adjourn to the time specified

Attest

Chas W. Brown

City Clerk

City of Rochester

June 1. 1813

The council met at time of adjournment. The mayor in the chair

The following councilmen responded to the roll call

Allen of ward one

Mills[illegible] and Horn of ward two.

Hayes of ward three

Bickford [illegible] and Daval of ward four

Waldron Dodge[illegible] Horne of ward five

Barker Woodward and Stevens of ward six

Records of previous meeting read and approved

The petition of P. H. Hartigan and others for the widening of Pattay Court was taken up and considered. The interested parties present were Hartigan Bradford and Wentworth after the consideration of the petition a recess of five minutes was declared to view the premises, after which the council called to order and on motion of councilman Horn voted that the petition be dismissed

Consideration of petition widening Pattay Court

Petition dismissed

Petition for a street from Portland to Leonard street called up and on motion of councilman Barker voted the petition be dismissed, then on motion of the same councilman voted the petition for a..

Petition for street Leonard to Portland dismissed

dismissed. and on motion of the same councilman voted that the petition for the widening of River Street be dismissed. [illegible] Chestnut Dismissed

Petition of Kiesel Brick Co for a highway to their factory beyond Orchard street presented and on motion of councilman Barker voted to be placed on file. Kiesel St. [illegible] dismissed

On motion of councilman Josselyn voted that the resolution in the hands of the committee on bills in their second reading be taken from the committee and acted upon. Petition of Kiesel Brick Co

On motion of councilman Barker voted that the council do not pass the resolution. Resolution in relation to street [illegible] Chestnut not passed.

The mayor nominated as an additional Special Police Samuel P. Corson and on motion of councilman Woodward voted that the nomination be confirmed. Special Police appointed

Charles Pearl presented a claim for damages sustained from an alleged defect in the highway. Claim of Chas Pearl

On motion of councilman Dodge voted the claim be dismissed and placed on file. dismissed

Councilman Barker presented the following resolution for paying G. W. Bickford P. H. Hartigan and Ezekiel Wentworth the sums awarded them for widening and straightening Market street. Resolution to pay for widening of Market Street.

the city of Rochester.

That the sum of eight hundred and forty two dollars be appropriated from any unexpended balance remaining in the city treasury for the purpose of paying the sums awarded to the above named as follows: to G. W. Bickford 196 dollars, to P. H. Hartigan 228 dollars and to Ezekiel Wentworth 418 dollars.

On motion of councilman Dodge voted that the rules be suspended and the resolution pass.

On motion of councilman Barker voted that when we adjourn we adjourn to June 20 at 1 30 p.m.

On motion of councilman Woodward voted that a committee be appointed to confer with the cemetery association in relation to the purchase of one of their hearses for the use of the city. Committee appointed to confer about hearse

The mayor appointed as that committee councilmen Woodward Josselyn and Willand.

Voted to adjourn to the time specified.

Attest
Chas. N. Brown
City Clerk

June 20. 1893

Council met according to adjournment with the Mayor in the chair

The following responded to the roll call.

Ward three Noyes

Ward Four Bickford & Josselyn

Ward Five Waldron and Stowe

Ward Six Barker Woodward and Stevens

No quorum being present the mayor adjourned the council to June 27 at 7 30 p.m.

Attest Chas. W. Brown

City Clerk

[illegible]

[illegible] city council met as per adjournment with the Mayor in the chair

The following councilmen answered to roll call

Ward One Tebbets and [illegible]

Ward two Willard [illegible] [illegible]

Ward three Warren and Noyes

Ward four Josselyn

Ward five Dodge

Ward six Barker Woodward and Stevens

Records of last meeting were read and approved

Petition of Terence [illegible] for permit to move a building was on motion of Councilman Dodge voted to be granted.

Petition of [illegible] for permit to move a building [illegible] to [illegible] Street presented [illegible] on motion of Councilman Dodge voted the request be granted.

Petition of Chas. W. [illegible] and others for an electric light at the foot of King street presented and referred to committee on Street lights.

The following communication from Joseph [illegible] by his attorneys Worcester Gregory and Snow was read:

To the City Council of the

[illegible] to [illegible] to move building

Permit to [illegible] to move building

Petition of [illegible] for electric light

Communication from Joseph [illegible]

Joseph Bruno that the Three Thousand Dollars deposited by him as security in the matter of constructing sewer for said City may be paid back to him.

June 20 1894 Joseph [illegible] by
[illegible] Worcester [illegible] his Attys.

On motion of Councilman Richards voted to refer to Committee on Sewerage for investigation.

City Engineer [illegible] reported that [illegible] had put a fire escape on his block but it did not meet the approval of the board of engineers. — *Fire escape [illegible]*

On motion of Councilman Richards voted to refer to Committee on Fire Department.

Report of the City Marshal for May was read and on motion of Councilman Dodge voted the report be accepted and placed on file. Report of the [illegible] for May [illegible] and on motion of same Councilman voted it be accepted and placed on file. Communication from S. D. [illegible] requesting the removal of the water pipe from his land near [illegible] Spring [illegible] was on motion of Councilman Barker voted to be referred to Committee on Water Works. Communication from Board of — *Notice for removal of pipe from land of S. D. [illegible]*

presented and placed on file.

The [illegible] in behalf of the Committee to confer with the [illegible] in relation to crossings made a verbal report of the result of the conference.

On motion of Councilman [illegible] voted that the railroad company be [illegible] requested to put up gates at the Main Street crossing as soon as possible. — *Gates at Main St crossing*

Councilman Dodge [illegible] the following resolution for repairing the clock in the Methodist Church belfry.

Resolved by the City Council of the City of Rochester. — *Resolution to repair town clock*

That the Committee on public buildings are hereby instructed to have the clock in the belfry of the Methodist Church cleaned and repaired at the expense of the City of Rochester.

On motion of Councilman Dodge voted the resolution pass.

Councilman [illegible] presented the following. — *Resolution to pay for [illegible]*

Resolution to pay for [illegible] floors of Stock and [illegible] House and providing stable room for the city horses.

Resolved by the City Council of the City of Rochester that a sum not exceeding three hundred dollars be and the same hereby is appropriated from any not otherwise appropriated for the purpose of [illegible] the floors of the [illegible] and [illegible] House and providing stable room for the City horses.

On motion of Councilman Barker voted the rules be suspended and the resolution pass.

Councilman [illegible] presented the following Resolution for appropriating money for the establishment and maintenance of a Free Public Library by the City of Rochester. — *Resolution appropriating for Public Library*

Resolved by the City Council of the City of Rochester.

That the sum of two thousand dollars is hereby appropriated from any unexpended balance remaining in the City treasury for establishment and maintenance of a Free Public Library by the City of Rochester.

On motion of Councilman Dodge voted the rules be suspended and the resolution pass.

Councilman [illegible] presented the following Resolution for repairing the Engine House at East Rochester. — *Resolution Repair Engine House East Rochester*

Resolved by the City Council of the City of Rochester,

Sec 1. That the sum of thirty dollars is hereby appropriated from the annual appropriation of repairing the Engine House at East Rochester by building a hose tower on the same.

Sec 2. That the above sum be expended under the direction of the [illegible] fire department.

On motion of Councilman Richards voted that the rules be suspended and the resolution pass.

Councilman [illegible] then introduced the following Resolution for preserving the Public lands owned by the City and lying to the west of Gold Spring Park as a public Park. — *Resolution for preserving Public lands near Gold Spring Park*

Resolved by the City Council of the City of Rochester.

That the Committee on Shade trees Parks and Commons investigate and report to the City Council on the advisability of reserving as a public park all the lands owned by the City of Rochester lying west of the Gold [illegible] Park being the same through which the [illegible] brook runs.

On motion of Councilman Dodge voted the resolution pass.

Councilman [illegible] presented the following Resolution providing [illegible] a vacation for members of the police force. — *Resolution [illegible] Police*

Resolved by the City Council of the City of Rochester. That the City Marshal assistant Marshal and night watchmen [illegible]

[illegible] with pay. The time of said vacation to be determined by the Mayor and City Marshal. Rochester [illegible]

On motion of Councilman [illegible] voted the resolution be referred to a committee of three appointed by the Mayor.

On motion of Councilman Dodge voted that when we adjourn we adjourn to three weeks from next Tuesday, July 15th at 7.30 p.m.

On motion of Councilman [illegible] voted that the grade of sidewalks be established [illegible] and that estimates be made of cost of brick sidewalk on the south side of Liberty Street and the westerly side of [illegible] Street from the brick sidewalk to the stone bridge and for concrete sidewalk without [illegible] on the westerly side of [illegible] Street from the Baptist Church to where the concrete is now laid.

Grade of Sidewalks to be established on [illegible] Liberty [illegible] Estimates to be made Sidewalks

Councilman [illegible] offered the following Resolution for appointing a special committee on sidewalks.

Resolution to appoint Committee on Sidewalks

Resolved by the City Council of the City of Rochester.

That a special committee consisting of the Mayor and two members of the City Council appointed by the Mayor constitute a committee on sidewalks for [illegible] [illegible]

On motion of Councilman [illegible] voted [illegible]

The Mayor appointed as committee on [illegible] [illegible] and Richards and [illegible] Sidewalks with the Mayor [illegible] and Stevens.

Committee on Sidewalks Appointed

On motion of Councilman Dodge voted that the [illegible] by [illegible] investigate the [illegible] of the [illegible] streets.

Committee appointed to investigate

On motion of Councilman Dodge voted to adjourn to the time specified.

Adjourned [illegible]

[illegible]

[illegible]
City Clerk

City of Rochester

July 18. 1893

Council called to order by the mayor when on the calling of the roll the following named responded

Ward One Chas W. Allen

Ward two Willand and Rollins

Ward three, Bragg

Ward four. Josselyn

Ward five Stone

Ward six, Woodward

No quorum being present the mayor adjourned the council to Friday July 21st at 7.30 p.m.

Attest

Chas W. Brown

City Clerk

City of Rochester

July 21 - 1893

The city council met as per adjournment the mayor in the chair

Roll of council called to which the following responded

Abbott and Richards of ward one

Stone and Rollins of ward two.

Bragg of ward three

Josselyn ^Bickford^ of ward four

Waldron and Dodge of ward five

Woodward and Stevens of ward six.

Warren of ward three and Stone of ward five joined the council before the transaction of business.

Record of previous meeting read and approved

The committee on Highways reported on the petition of Jesse F. Richards and others for a street from Union Street to Weare street and recommended that a hearing be granted which on motion of councilman Richards was granted

Hearing recommended for street at Rochester

The committee on Water

Chas. W. Stone } Committee
Joseph Warren } on
John W. Tibbetts } Water Works

On motion of councilman Stevens voted the report be accepted.

The special committee on vacation of police reported as follows

To his Honor the Mayor and City Council. Report on Police Vacation

The committee to whom the resolution providing a vacation for members of the police force was referred would recommend that the resolution pass as presented.

C. C. Woodward }
A. L. Richards } Committee
Edward Josselyn }

On motion of councilman Tibbetts voted the report be accepted and the resolution pass.

The committee on sidewalks made a verbal report of estimated cost of sidewalks for Charles Liberty and Market streets.

Resignation of Charles S. Bugged as member of school board read and on motion of councilman Dodge voted the resignation be accepted and we proceed to the Resignation of C. S. Bugged member of School Board

Whole number of ballots 13 Election of
S. D. Wentworth had 1 Member of
Chas. L. Ward had 1 School Board
Dudley B. Waldron " 11

and Dudley B. Waldron was declared elected

Report of treasurer for six months ending July 1st read and on motion of councilman Dodge voted it be accepted and placed on file Report of Treasurer to July 1st

Report of the City Marshal for June read and on motion of Josselyn voted to accept and place on file Report of City Marshal for June

Claim of Smith Clark by his attorneys Worcester Gafney & Snow presented and on motion of councilman Josselyn voted to refer to committee on Highways. Claim of Smith Clark

Bill of C. S. Hubbard presented and referred to committee on legal affairs C. S. Hubbard bill referred

Councilman Stone presented the following resolution.

Resolved by the City Council of the City of Rochester

That the appropriation made for laying water mains on Wakefield St. be transferred to Park St. on motion Resolution for Water Pipe on Park St

Resolved by the City Council of the City of Rochester. That the sum of three hundred dollars be appropriated from any unexpended funds in City Treasury for purchase of Parker & Lowe lot as recommended by committee on Water Works, and the mayor is [illegible] authorized to take deed of same.

Resolution to purchase lots of Parker-Lowe

On motion of councilman Warren voted the rules be suspended and the resolution pass.

On motion of councilman Josselyn voted that permission be granted the Boston and Maine railroad to erect a signal station on Summer street.

Permit granted B. & M. signal station on Summer St.

On motion of councilman Dodge voted that the committee on Finance be instructed to invest the surplus money belonging to the water works as in their judgment shall be for the best interest of the city.

Water works surplus to be invested

On motion of councilman Dodge voted that when we adjourn we adjourn to two weeks from tonight August 4th.

On motion of councilman Rollins voted to adjourn to the time specified.

Attest

Chas. W. Brown

City Clerk

City of Rochester

August 4 – 18[illegible]

Council called to order by the mayor.

The following named councilmen responded to the roll call

Allen of ward one.

Stone & Rollins of ward two

Warren of ward three

Josselyn of ward four

Barker and Woodward of ward six.

No quorum being present the mayor adjourned the council to Friday August 11 –

Attest

Chas. W. Brown

City Clerk

City of Rochester

August 11 · 1893

The city council met to night with the mayor in the chair.

The following named councilmen responded to the roll call.

Ward two Horn and Rollins

Ward three Hagg and Hayes

Ward four Bickford and Josselyn

Ward five Waldron and Dodge.

Ward six Parker Woodward and Stevens.

Record of previous meeting read and approved.

Petition to extend water pipes on Charles St

Petition of Harry Hayes and others for extension of water pipe on Charles street read and on motion of councilman Dodge voted to refer to committee on Water Works.

Petition to erect Hay Scale at Woodsbury

Petition of Chas P. [illegible] and others for permission to erect Hay Scales near the Highway at Woodsbury corner read. Moved by councilman Bickford that the petition be granted. Councilman Woodward offered an committee on Sewerage.

Lease of land near H. & L. House

Councilman [illegible] of the committee on Fire Department made a verbal report in relation to the leasing of land for entrance to the Stable at the Hook and Ladder House.

On motion of councilman Woodward voted that the lease be confirmed.

The committee on Legal affairs made the following report.

Report on claim of Jessie M. Smith

To the Mayor and Council of the city of Rochester.

The claim of Jessie M. Smith against said city for injuries alleged to have been received by reason of a defective sidewalk on Charles Street on the 18th day of September 1892 having been considered by your committee they would recommend the payment of Seventy five dollars to said claimant in full settlement thereof provided the receipt for such payment be signed by Marshall F. Smith father of said Jessie M. Smith.

O. A. Hayes } [illegible]

and the Honorable Council of the City of Rochester

The action of Lillie B. Brown [illegible] of Barrington against the City of Rochester is now pending in the Supreme Court and is ordered for trial at the coming September term. It is brought to enforce a claim for injuries alleged to have been received April 20 1892 on the highway leading from [illegible] Village to Rochester Neck, by reason of certain defect as claimed by the plaintiff. Notice of this claim was duly served on the City but was for so large a sum your committee deemed it best to report adversely, and the report was accepted. At the present time and before the City has incurred any expense in the matter, a settlement can be effected by payment of one hundred and twenty five dollars. If contested in court it will be necessary to employ medical experts both before and at the hearing of the case. Your committee believe the payment of $125 to the claimant will be in the line of economy as such sum is less than the expense incident to the trial of said action. They therefore recommend the payment of $125 in full settlement of the claim.

Report on claim of Lillie B. Brown

C. A. Hoyt
C. S. Barker
George E. Cochrane
Thomas Dodge

Com. on Legal Affairs.

On motion of Councilman Stevens

The Mayor nominated as Special Police Almon R. Reed, William A. Grandson and Amos B. Young.

Special Police Appointed

On motion of Councilman Barker the nominations were confirmed.

Report of the City Marshal for July read and on motion of Councilman Dodge voted it be accepted and placed on file.

Report of Marshal for July

Report of the City Treasurer for July read and on motion of Councilman Dodge voted it be accepted and placed on file.

Report of Treasurer for July

Resolution granting two weeks vacation to the driver of the city team presented and on motion of Councilman Stevens voted it be dismissed.

Bill of [illegible] for printing presented and on motion of Barker voted to be paid.

Bill to be paid

The following Resolution for removing obstructions from Central Square and adjacent lands of the City presented.

Resolution to remove obstructions from the Square

Resolved by the City Council of the City of Rochester

That the Mayor of the City of Rochester is hereby directed to cause the removal of all obstructions from Central Square and the lands adjacent thereto owned by the City of Rochester.

Moved by Councilman

the motion was declared carried Councilman Dodge called for the Yeas and Nays which resulted as follows. Yeas Councilmen Horn Rollins Hayes Barker Woodward and Stevens 6 Nays Councilmen Blagg Bickford Josselyn Woodward Dodge 5 and the resolution passed.

On motion of Councilman Barker voted that the committee on Public buildings be instructed to report at the next meeting on the advisability of leasing the old town hall to Sturtevant Guards. Leasing [illegible] Town Hall [illegible]

Moved by Councilman Barker that rule 11 be suspended and that Councilman Daveis place on Committee on Claims and Accounts be declared vacant after some discussion the motion was withdrawn.

On motion of Councilman Barker that when we adjourn we adjourn to [illegible] September 5.
On motion of Councilman Brown voted to adjourn to the time specified

Attest

Chas. W. Brown
City Clerk

City of [illegible]

September 5 [illegible]

The city council met this evening as per adjournment. The mayor in the chair.
Roll called to which the following responded
Ward one Libbetts and Allen
Ward two Willard Horn and Rollins.
Ward three Blagg and Hayes.
Ward four Josselyn
Ward five Dodge
Ward Six Barker Woodward and Stevens.

Record of last meeting read and approved.

Petition of C. H. Bickford and others for the extension of the water pipes through Chamberlain St. presented
Petition for water pipes on Chamberlain St

On motion of councilman Dodge voted to refer to committee on Water Works.

Petition of A. C. Rockwood for permit to maintain a Lunch Wagon on some central place was on motion of councilman Dodge granted.
Petition for lunch wagon

On the petition of Harry Hayes and others the committee on Water Works made the following report.
Report on petition of H. Hayes & others

The within petition has been investigated and we would recommend the petition be [illegible]

On motion of councilman Dodge voted the report be accepted and adopted and the petition granted.

The committee on street lights made the following report on the petition of [illegible] Bailey and others. Report of [illegible]

To the Honorable Mayor and city council of the city of Rochester

The committee to whom was referred the petition for an electric light at the foot of King St signed by Chas H Bailey and others, having considered the same would recommend that the petition be granted.

J Thomas Dodge
C. S. Barker
Frank X Hayes.

On motion of councilman Robins voted that the report be accepted and adopted.

The committee on public buildings made the following report

To his Honor the mayor and city council of the city of Rochester.

The committee to whom was referred the matter of leasing the "old town hall" to Sturtevant Guards, having given the subject due consideration would recommend that it be leased to the Sturtevant Guards Town Hall [illegible]

[illegible]
Charles H [illegible] } Public Buildings

On motion of councilman Barker voted the report be accepted and the committee be authorized to execute a lease agreeably to the report of the committee.

The committee on legal affairs made the following report. Report of Comm. on legal affairs

To the mayor and council of the city of Rochester [illegible]

The committee on legal affairs would recommend the payment of one hundred and fifty dollars to King & Goddard in full settlement of suit now pending in the Supreme court in which suit they are plaintiffs and the city of Rochester is defendant

C A Hoyt
Geo C Cochrane
J Thomas Dodge
C. S. Barker

On motion of councilman [illegible] voted the report be accepted and claim settled.

The following report from the same committee.

To the mayor and council of the city of Rochester. Report of

The committee to whom was [illegible] referred the claim of the Hanson [illegible] estate [illegible] [illegible] said city as presented by [illegible]

considered the claim would recommend the payment of fifty dollars in settlement of said claim
Rochester N. H. Sept 9 - 1893

O. H. Hoyt
J. Thomas Dodge } Com
C. S. Parker

On motion of councilman Warren voted the report be accepted and damages settled as reported by the committee

Communication presented from Ammanuel Hanson relative to Hanson street and ordered to be placed on file — *Communication D. Hanson*

The mayor appointed Frank S. Edgerly, Frank Armstrong and John Bradford as special police and on motion of councilman Stevens voted the nominations be confirmed. — *Special police appointed*

Daniel P. Jenness appointed weigher of hay straw and coal and on motion of councilman Parker voted to be confirmed — *Appointment of D. P. Jenness*

Pay bills for Barrington and Shepard presented and on motion of councilman Dodge voted they be paid

City Marshals report for August read and on motion of councilman Dodge voted the report be accepted and placed on file

Report of treasurer presented and on motion of councilman

on file

Councilman Parker presented the following Resolution for paying award of damages to Lillie M. Brown — *Resolution to pay Lillie M. Brown*

Resolved by the city council of the City of Rochester.

That the sum of one hundred and twenty five dollars is hereby appropriated from the unexpended balance of the fund appropriated for miscellaneous expenses for the payment of the sum awarded to Lillie M. Brown for injuries received on a public highway in said city.

On motion of councilman Woodward voted the rules be suspended and the resolution pass.

By the same councilman the following. Resolution for paying award of damages to Jesse M. Smith for injuries received on Charles street.

Resolved by the city council of the city of Rochester. — *Resolution to pay Jesse M. Smith*

That the sum of seventy five dollars is hereby appropriated from the unexpended balance of the fund appropriated for miscellaneous expenses for the payment of the sum awarded to Jesse M. Smith for injuries received on Charles street.

On motion of councilman Woodward voted the rules be suspended and the resolution pass.

the following resolution to place electric lights in Engine House on Hanson Street.

Be it resolved by the city council of the city of Rochester.

That a sum not to exceed twenty dollars be appropriated from any unexpended money remaining in city treasury for the purpose of placing electric lights in Engine House on Hanson Street.

On motion of councilman Warren voted to refer to the committee on Street lights.

On motion of councilman Dodge voted that when we adjourn we adjourn to two weeks from tonight September 21

Councilman Parker introduced the following resolution for paying damages to Hale estate

Resolution to pay damages Hale estate

Resolved by the city council of the city of Rochester.

That the sum of $50. is hereby appropriated from the unexpended balance of the fund appropriated for miscellaneous expenses for the payment of above sum to C. R. Gafney [illegible] agent of the Hale estate for damages to said estate by the maintaining of a drain across the same.

The following resolution to settle claim of King and Goddard.

Resolution to pay King & Goddard

Resolved by the city council of the city of Rochester that the sum of one hundred and fifty dollars is hereby appropriated from the funds of the water works to settle the claim of King and Goddard against the city of Rochester.

On motion of councilman Warren voted the rules be suspended and the resolution pass.

On motion of councilman Warren voted, the matter of locating the night lunch wagon be left with the mayor.

On motion of councilman Dodge voted to adjourn to the time specified.

Attest

Chas. W. Brown

City Clerk

City of Rochester
September [illegible] 18[illegible]

City council called to order by the mayor [illegible] roll called. The following councilmen were present.
Ward two Willand? Rollins
Ward three Hayes.
Ward four Bickford and [illegible]
Ward six Barker Woodward and Stevens.
No quorum being present the mayor adjourned the council to October 6 at [illegible]
Attest Chas W [illegible]
City Clerk

City of Rochester
October 6 18[illegible]

Council met as per adjournment with the mayor in the chair [illegible] following named councilmen [illegible] their names as called
Ward one Allen
Ward two Hanson and Rollins
Ward three Warren and Hayes
Ward four Bickford and [illegible]
Ward five Waldron
Ward six Barker and Stevens.
Woodward of ward six joined the council after roll call.

On motion of Councilman Barker voted that the reading of the records of previous meeting be postponed to the next meeting.

Recess of [illegible] minutes declared after which council called to order when a communication was read from Dominicus Hanson in relation to [illegible] street. On motion of Councilman Stevens voted to place on file

Request of Worcester [illegible] [illegible] attorneys for State heirs to have the sewer running through the State field discontinued referred to committee on Sewerage

Petition of [illegible] Perry for permit to erect a sign on his barbers pole. On motion of Councilman [illegible] voted to refer to

Communication [illegible] Hanson

Request [illegible] [illegible] State field

Petition of [illegible] Perry to [illegible]

The mayor appointed Rodney C. Sears weigher of hay straw and coal and on motion of Councilman Fitzgerald voted the nomination be confirmed.

Report of the city marshal for September read and on motion of Joselyn voted to accept and place on file

Report of city treasurer read and ordered to be placed on file.

Council[illegible] introduced the following Resolution of appropriation for extension of water works on Broad St.

Resolved by the city council of the city of Rochester.

That the sum of seven hundred dollars and fifty dollars is hereby appropriated from the sum already appropriated to the construction account for the extension of water pipes on Broad Street.

On motion of councilman Parker voted the rules be suspended and the resolution pass.

Councilman Parker introduced the following resolution appropriating money for the fire department.

Resolved by the city council of the city of Rochester. That the sum of two hundred and fifty dollars is hereby appropriated from any unexpended balance remaining in the [illegible] the fire department

On motion of councilman Hayes voted the rules be suspended and the resolution pass.

An ordinance amendment to chapter XXIII of the General ordinances relating to the salary of the Police Judge. [illegible] and referred to the committee on Bills [illegible] second reading. The committee on street lights then made the following report.

Report of committee on electric lights on placing lights in the engine house on [illegible] street;

The committee on electric lights to whom was referred the petition for placing electric lights in the engine house [illegible] Hanson street, report that they have examined the [illegible] and recommend that two lights be placed in the building.

C. [illegible] Chairman
Frank P. Moyer } Electric Lights

On motion of councilman Warren voted the report be accepted and adopted.

Recess of ten minutes declared

After the council was again called to order [illegible] motion of councilman Joselyn voted to adjourn [illegible] to four o'clock P.M. [illegible] Oct [illegible]

attest
Chas W. Brown
City Clerk

City of Rochester

October 7 1893

The city council met agreeably to adjournment. the mayor in the chair. Roll of council called to which the following responded.

Allen of Ward one

Brown and Rollins of ward two

Warren and Hayes of ward three.

Bickford of ward four

Madison and Dodge of ward five

Barker Woodward and Stevens of ward six.

Record of last meeting read and approved. Petition of Chas W Bailey and others for a street from King to Main street a street presented. On motion of councilman Warren from King voted a recess for forty five minutes to look over to main the proposed route. after which council called to order. Mr Hall council for Chas H Berry said the line as laid out the center of the street being the line was satisfactory and would accept two hundred dollars award. Mr Pierce council for Mrs Mary A Sanborn said Mrs Sanborn would give the land so long as a public street was maintained.

On motion of councilman Warren voted that a hearing be granted the petitioners two weeks from next Tuesday Oct 24 at 7-30 p.m. On motion of councilman Barker voted to adjourn to October 24 —

www.ingramcontent.com/pod-product-compliance
Lightning Source LLC
Chambersburg PA
CBHW030318270326
41926CB00010B/1422

* 9 7 8 3 7 4 3 4 5 4 6 6 8 *